OXFORD HANDBOOK OF

Legal
Correspondence

Rupert Haigh

OXFORD
UNIVERSITY PRESS

OXFORD

UNIVERSITY PRESS

Great Clarendon Street, Oxford OX2 6DP

Oxford University Press is a department of the University of Oxford.
It furthers the University's objective of excellence in research, scholarship,
and education by publishing worldwide in

Oxford New York

Auckland Bangkok Buenos Aires Cape Town Chennai
Dar es Salaam Delhi Hong Kong Istanbul Karachi Kolkata
Kuala Lumpur Madrid Melbourne Mexico City Mumbai
Nairobi São Paulo Shanghai Taipei Tokyo Toronto

OXFORD and OXFORD ENGLISH are registered trade marks of
Oxford University Press in the UK and in certain other countries

ISBN-13: 978 019 4571937
ISBN-10: 0 19 4571939

Printed in China

ACKNOWLEDGEMENTS

The author and publisher are grateful to the following for help and
assistance with this book: Sally Blackmore, Michael Furmston,
Bill MacKeith, Jonathan Pool, James Rogers, Chris Rycroft, Renata Vystrcilová

Darbys Solicitors
52 New Inn Hall Street
Oxford OX1 2QD

D C Kaye & Co. Solicitors
Old Bank Chambers
2 Wycombe Road
Prestwood
Great Missenden
Bucks HP16 0PW

Contents

Words are the tools of the lawyer's trade. The ability to write effectively is a fundamental skill of the practising lawyer. It is exercised every day by every lawyer when writing letters for a variety of purposes, for example, negotiating the favourable outcome of a client's case, corresponding with a client, routine correspondence with institutions, or instructing other professionals in relation to a client's case.

The *Oxford Handbook of Legal Correspondence* is designed to give a sound working knowledge of:
— The particular skills required for effective legal writing.
— The purposes for which correspondence is used in important areas of legal practice.
— The kinds of language which can be used to achieve those purposes.

The book is intended for non-native speakers of English who are lawyers, legal assistants and legal secretaries, law students, students of legal English, and English language teachers. It is designed to demonstrate how to write more concisely without loss of meaning, how to write more persuasively without loss of clarity, and how to adapt the tone of each letter to the required purpose.

The first unit of the book deals with the main kinds of correspondence – letters, faxes, and email, the characteristics of each, and in what circumstances they should be used. Unit 2 deals with legal language, types of letter to different addressees, and questions of style, presentation, and vocabulary. Unit 3 and each of the following units deals with a different area of legal practice, and follows a regular pattern.

1 A short introduction to the area of legal practice with which the unit is concerned.

2 An analysis of the role of the lawyer in relation to that area of law.

3 Example letters, together with an analysis of the purpose of each type of correspondence, the different types of language that can be used to achieve that purpose, and questions and comments designed to test and enlarge understanding of the letter and the language used in it.

4 Points to remember: a brief review of the key points covered in the unit.

Unit 12 provides examples of internal correspondence typical of a law firm: memoranda, and various kinds of file notes – attendance note, telephone attendance note, and research note. Unit 13 provides examples of correspondence about applying for a job in a law firm, including the application letter, curriculum vitae (cv), and accepting the offer of a job.

The example letters reflect daily legal practice, so that readers will acquire an insight into the conventions and language used in legal practice in English-speaking countries, together with an understanding of the sometimes obscure terminology used in legal transactions. As well as being aimed at students and practitioners of the law, the book has been designed to give English language teachers, who may not themselves be familiar with the law and legal practice, a good grounding in the subject.

In addition to responding to the short questions following the example letters, students may choose to work in groups to conduct role plays based on the transaction to which a letter relates, for example, conducting a lawyer-client interview or telephone conversation, or a negotiation between the parties to a transaction.

The brief 'Points to remember' review at the end of each unit can also be used later as revision material. So, too, can the Glossary of legal terminology at the end of the book.

Students may use the book either in conjunction with a taught course or as a tool for self-study. By working through the units they will acquire a good understanding of important areas of legal practice, the terminology used in those areas, and the types of correspondence used for different purposes in each area of practice.

Throughout the text, legal terms are generally explained when they first occur. Legal terms that appear in SMALL CAPITALS when they first occur in a unit are explained in the Glossary at the back of the book. Any additional legal or technical terms introduced in the sample letters are explained in the Glossary.

The law stated in this book is English law. All cases mentioned were heard by English courts, and the statutes referred to are those in force in the UK.

The legal profession

In England and Wales, the legal profession is split into two distinct branches: solicitors and barristers. Solicitors work in law firms (also known as practices), and as legal advisers in commercial organizations. They carry out all types of legal work, but have limited RIGHTS OF AUDIENCE: they are only able to act as court advocates in certain courts, dealing generally with more minor cases. However, solicitors may increase their rights of audience by qualifying as a solicitor-advocate. To become a solicitor-advocate, a solicitor must pass rigorous advocacy examinations. If successful, the solicitor will have similar rights of audience to those of barristers. The work of solicitors in England and Wales is regulated by the Law Society.

Barristers are professional court advocates and have rights of audience in all the courts. They may work in law firms or as legal advisers in commercial companies, but more often work in *chambers*, which group barristers acting as independent court advocates. The work of barristers in England and Wales is regulated by the Bar Council.

The terms solicitor and barrister are employed in some countries that were once British colonies, such as Australia and New Zealand. The separate Scottish legal profession is divided into solicitors and advocates. In the US and in many other countries, the usual term for a qualified lawyer is attorney-at-law or simply attorney. In this book the word most often used is lawyer, but readers should bear in mind that, in the contexts represented by the sample correspondence, in England and Wales the term solicitor is often likely to be used.

In this book the terms *solicitor* and *lawyer* are generally used interchangeably.

The Civil Procedure Rules

The Civil Procedure Rules (CPR) were introduced in 1998 in England and Wales with the overriding objective of 'enabling the court to deal with cases justly'. They apply to most proceedings in the County Court, High Court, and the Civil Division of the Court of Appeal.

The CPR include the concept of case management whereby the courts are encouraged, among other objectives, to take a much more active role, to encourage the parties to cooperate with each other in the conduct of proceedings, to be more proactive in identifying the issues in dispute, to exercise firmer control over the progress of the case (fixing timetables, etc.), and to encourage the use of alternative dispute resolution (ADR) techniques where appropriate. Various cost benefits and penalties apply, depending on the efforts of each party to reach settlement before a case goes to court. The CPR have also altered the vocabulary used in civil litigation, with the aim of making it easier for laypersons to understand. For example, the word 'plaintiff' has been replaced by 'claimant', and the phrase 'particulars of claim' by 'statement of case'. However, the old terms are still used by some older lawyers and in some legal textbooks.

The advent of the CPR has introduced many changes to the way in which cases are initiated and progressed. For example, the court forms previously in use have been almost entirely superseded, and various protocols relevant to different types of case have been brought in. The CPR website at http://www.dca.gov.uk/civil/procrules_fin/ is a good starting-point for those interested in accessing further information on this subject.

1

Letters

LAYOUT 1

The letter opposite is from a private individual in Finland to a law firm in the UK. It shows the basic features of a simple legal letter.

Sender's address

In correspondence that does not have a letterhead ▶ **see page 9**, the sender's address is placed in the top right-hand corner of the page. Note that commas (,) do not appear after the separate lines of the address: it is not usual to put punctuation in addresses these days.

The *blocked style* is the most widely used, i.e. each line starts directly below the one above.

In contrast with practice in some countries, in the UK it is not usual to write the sender's name before his or her address. The sender's name should, however, appear in type beneath the complimentary close ▶ **see page 9**.

Date

The date is written directly below the sender's address, separated by a line space. In correspondence with a letterhead, it is usually written on the right-hand side of the page.

In British English, it is usual to write the day of the month first, then the month, then the year. The day should be written as a numeral, the month as a word, and the year as a numeral. No punctuation should be used between different parts of the date. For example, *3 November 2004*.

In American English, it is usual to write the month first, then the day of the month, then the year. The month should be written as a word, the day as a numeral with the abbreviation *-th*, *-st*, *-nd* as appropriate, and the year as a numeral. It is usual to place a comma after the day. For example, *November 3rd, 2004*.

Because of the differences between British and American conventions, the date should not be written in figures. To do so might be confusing. For example, *11.03.07* would mean *11 March 2007* in British English but *November 3rd, 2007* in American English.

Inside address

The inside address, the address of the person to whom correspondence is sent, is written below the sender's address and on the left-hand side of the page, and positioned so that it is visible in the envelope window.

Surname known

If you know the name of the person you are writing to, write it as the first line of the address. Include either the person's initial/s or his / her first given name, e.g. *Mr J. E. Smith* or *Mr John Smith*, NOT *Mr Smith*.

Courtesy titles used in addresses are:
— *Mr* (pronounced /ˈmɪstə/) is the usual courtesy title for a man. (The unabbreviated form *Mister* should not be used.)
— *Ms* (pronounced /mɪz/ or /məs/, no unabbreviated form) is used for both married and unmarried women. It is often used whether or not you know if the woman is married and it is certainly advisable to use this form of address when you are unsure, or do not know which title she prefers.
— *Mrs* (pronounced /ˈmɪsɪz/) may be used for a married woman. (The unabbreviated form is the archaic and never used *Mistress*.) The variants *Missus* and *Missis* occur in humorous or informal writing; they should *not* be used in legal or business contexts.)
— *Miss* (pronounced /mɪz/, not an abbreviation) may be used for an unmarried woman.
— *Messrs* (pronounced /ˈmesəz/, an abbreviation for the French *Messieurs*, which is never used in English legal or business contexts) is used occasionally for two or more men, e.g. *Messrs B. Johns and R. M. Hardwick*. More commonly it forms part of the name of a firm (often a partnership rather than a company), e.g. *Messrs Hardwick, Castle, and Clarke*. It is somewhat old-fashioned.

1 Sender's address

2 Date

3 Inside address

4 Attention line

5 Salutation

6 Subject title

7 Body of letter

8 Complimentary close

9 Signature

1 Jukka Virtanen
Korvatie 11A
00100 Helsinki
Finland

2 7 March 20—

3 Messrs Turner, Jones, Smith & Co.
Worcester House
7 Old Hall Street
Oxford
OX1 7PB
UK

4 **For the attention of the Residential Property Department**

5 Dear Sirs

6 **Purchase of The Croft, Whittlington**

7 Your firm has been recommended to me by one of your long-standing clients, Mr Simon Jones. Briefly, I have agreed to purchase the above property and wish to instruct a competent firm of solicitors to handle the conveyancing. I should be grateful if you would kindly send me a copy of your standard terms and conditions by return of post.

8 I look forward to hearing from you.

Yours faithfully

9 *Jukka Virtanen*
(Mr) Jukka Virtanen

Other courtesy titles include academic or medical titles, e.g. *Doctor* (*Dr*), *Professor* (*Prof.*); military titles, e.g. *Captain* (*Capt.*), *Major* (*Maj.*), *Colonel* (*Col.*), *General* (*Gen.*); and aristocratic titles, e.g. *Sir*, *Dame*, *Lord*, *Lady*. *Sir* usually means that the addressee is a knight, and is always followed by a first name, e.g. *Sir John Brown*, never *Sir J. Brown* or *Sir Brown*. It should not be confused with the salutation *Dear Sir* ▶**see page 11**.

Esq., the abbreviation for *Esquire*, is seldom used now. It can only be used instead of *Mr*, and is placed after the name. Do not use *Esq.* and *Mr* at the same time, e.g. *Bruce Hill Esq.*, NOT *Mr Bruce Hill Esq.*

All these courtesy titles, except *Esq.* are also used in salutations.

Note that a full stop is often used at the end of the abbreviation if it takes the form of the first few letters of the word, e.g. *Prof.* (*Prof*essor) but it is not necessary if it takes the form of the first and last letter of the word, e.g. *Dr* (*D*octo*r*). However, some people prefer to write *Dr.*, *Mr.*, *Mrs.*, etc. with a full stop. The key point is that whatever you choose to do, you should be consistent throughout your correspondence.

Job title known

If you do not know the name of the person you are writing to, but know their job title, you can use that in the inside address. Titles used in law firms and firms with legal departments are:
— Associate / Associate Lawyer
— Attorney
— Chief Legal Counsel
— Director
— Director of Legal Affairs
— Legal Adviser
— Legal Assistant
— Legal Counsel
— Legal Executive
— Legal Officer
— Managing Partner
— Paralegal
— Partner
— Personnel Manager
— Secretary
— Senior Attorney
— Senior Partner
— Solicitor

Department known

Alternatively, you can address your letter to a particular department of the firm. All but the smallest law firms, in addition to having some of the departments common to general commercial firms (e.g. *The Accounts Department*, *The Human Resources Department*), organize their legal practices into departments which cover different areas of law. Some law firms cover most major areas of legal practice, but others specialize only in certain areas of the law and will accordingly have departments that specialize in narrow sub-branches of these areas.

Names of departments found in medium-sized general legal practices include:
— Commercial Litigation Department
— Commercial Property Department
— Company and Commercial Department
— Criminal Law Department
— Employment Law Department
— Family Law Department
— Immigration Department
— Personal Injury Department
— Probate, Tax, and Wills Department
— Residential Property Department

Firm known

Finally, if you know nothing about the firm and do not know which person or department your letter should go to, you can simply address the letter to the firm itself, e.g. *Messrs Turner, Jones, Smith & Co.*

FAO

FAO (for the attention of) is an abbreviation commonly used at the start of the address (outside or inside) to ensure that a letter reaches a named individual in an organization ▶**see letter on page 102**.

Order of inside address

After the name of the person and / or firm receiving the letter, the recommended order and style of addresses in the UK is as follows:
— Name (if any) of house or building
— Number of building and name of street, road, avenue, etc.
— Name of town or city
— Postcode
— County (where appropriate)

— Name of country (if the letter is going abroad)

Worcester House
7 Old Hall Street
Oxford
OX1 7PB
UK

In other European countries, the number of the building may be placed after the name of the street, and the postcode in front of the town. For example:

Korvatie 11A
00100 Helsinki
Finland

It is simplest to follow the above order and style, though variations are possible. For example, the name of the county may be omitted, especially if the city is a large one; the postcode may be written on the same line as the town; the name of the town, as well as the country, may be in capital letters. As a general rule, the name of the county is only needed if the postcode is not included in the address.

Attention line

An alternative to including the recipient's name or job title in the address is to use an *attention line* ▶ **see letter on page 9**.

Salutation

Dear Sir opens a letter written to a man whose name you do not know.

Dear Sirs is used to address a firm where at least one of the members of the firm is male. When writing to American firms, *Dear Sir or Madam* is preferred, since it does not assume that the person who opens the letter will be a man.

Dear Mesdames is used to address a firm (rare!) where all the members are female.

Dear Madam is used to address a woman, whether single or married, whose name you do not know.

Dear Sir or Madam (or *Dear Sir / Madam*) is used to address a person when you do not know their name or sex.

When you know the name of the person you are writing to, but do not know them well, the salutation takes the form of *Dear* followed by a courtesy title and the person's surname. Initials or first names are not used with courtesy titles, e.g. *Dear Mr Smith*, NOT *Dear Mr J. Smith* or *Dear Mr John Smith*. Persons whom you know well can be addressed using just their first name, e.g. *Dear John*. However, although these used to be firm rules in the UK and the reader would be well advised to follow them, practice is changing. Do not be surprised if the other party uses your first name; once the other party has so addressed you, it is usually safe to do the same.

A comma after the salutation is optional, i.e. *Dear Mr Smith*, or *Dear Mr Smith*

Subject title

In most legal communication, it is customary to include a *subject title*, which should comprise a brief description of the matter you are writing about. This saves the trouble of introducing the subject in the first paragraph, it immediately draws attention to the topic of the letter, and allows the writer to refer to it throughout. The nature of the subject title varies according to the type of legal business being handled. The variation often depends on whether the type of legal business is NON-CONTENTIOUS (i.e. not involving court proceedings) or CONTENTIOUS (involving court proceedings).

For example, in a property sale (non-contentious) it is usual to put the address of the property:

Sale of 25 Hamley Drive, Groundwich

When the letter concerns litigation (is contentious), and the case has actually begun in court, the subject title may contain the standard case notation:

Bromley v. Arthurs

1

In correspondence between law firms, both of which are acting for a different client, whether on contentious or non-contentious business, a customary addition to the subject title is to identify the clients, e.g.:

Your client: John Smith
My client: Mary Pearce
Sale of 25 Hamley Drive, Groundwich

It is possible, but not necessary, to begin the subject title with *Re* (*with regard to*), e.g. *Re: Sale of 25 Hamley Drive, Groundwich*. When sending email messages this may even be confusing as *RE* is short for *reply*. In addition, it is worth noting that *Re.* is sometimes used as standard case notation in reports of certain types of legal cases.

Body of letter

The blocked style, with each line beginning directly below the one above, without indentation, is the one most often used for the body of the letter. The start of a new paragraph is indicated by a line space.

Complimentary close

If the letter begins *Dear Sir*, *Dear Sirs*, *Dear Madam*, *Dear Mesdames*, or *Dear Sir or Madam*, the complimentary close should be *Yours faithfully*. When writing to American firms, *Respectfully yours* (very formal) or *Yours truly* (less formal) should be used.

If the letter begins with a personal name, e.g. *Dear Mr Jones*, *Dear Mrs Brown*, or *Dear Ms Porter*, it should end with *Yours sincerely*. The American equivalent is *Sincerely yours*.

A letter to someone you know well may close with a number of different informal phrases. Examples include:

— *With best wishes*   — *Kind regards*
— *With best regards*   — *Regards*
— *Best wishes*   — *Best*
— *Best regards*

Avoid closing your letter with old-fashioned phrases, e.g. *We remain yours faithfully*.

Commas after the complimentary close are generally not used in legal letters. The complimentary close is usually placed on the left, aligned under the rest of the letter.

Signature

In many law firms, letters addressed to another law firm or an organization start *Dear Sirs* and are signed with the name of the firm; in the letter the writer refers to the firm as *we* ▶**see letter on page 31**.

Otherwise, and in correspondence with a client, always type your name and, if relevant, your job title below your handwritten signature. This is known as the *signature block*.

It is a matter of choice whether you sign with your initial / s, e.g. *D. Jenkins*, or your full given name, e.g. *Duncan Jenkins*, and whether you include your courtesy title in your

TITLE	STATUS	COMPLIMENTARY CLOSE
Mr	married or unmarried male	*Yours sincerely*
Mrs	married female	*Yours sincerely*
Miss	unmarried female	*Yours sincerely*
Ms	married or unmarried female	*Yours sincerely*
Sir	male – name not known	*Yours faithfully*
Madam	female – name not known	*Yours faithfully*
Dr / Professor / General	may be a male or female	*Yours sincerely*

signature block. But if you include neither your given name nor your title, your correspondent may not be able to identify your sex and may give you the wrong title when he or she replies.

LAYOUT 2

Opposite is the law firm's reply to the letter from the prospective client in Finland. It shows some more features of a typical legal letter.

Letterhead

The printed letterhead of a firm gives a great deal of information about it.

Type of firm
Most traditional law firms are in fact partnerships. This means that the profits of the firm are shared among its partners in accordance with the terms of their partnership agreement. The partners have joint and several liability in law, which means that if the partnership incurs debts both all the partners together and each individual partner can be sued for repayment of the debts.

The names of the partners are often included in the letterhead, either at the bottom or in a column on either side of the text.

Address
In addition to the address of the office from which the letter is being sent, the letterhead may also give the address of the head office and any branches or other offices the law firm maintains.

Telephone and fax numbers will also be included. The majority of law firms nowadays also use email and maintain a website, in which case these will also be included.

References

References are often quoted to indicate what the letter refers to (*Your ref.*) and the correspondence to refer to when replying (*Our ref.*). The majority of law firms use references to identify 1) the writer of the letter,

2) the client about whom they are writing, and 3) the number of the case. Firms usually adopt a relatively simple system for identifying client and case in the reference. For example, in the reference *RJ/SMIT.10–3*:

RJ identifies the lawyer handling the case – perhaps Richard Jones, for example

SMIT means clients whose surnames begin with SMIT (e.g. Smith)

10 identifies a particular client named Smith

3 identifies the third matter that the firm has handled for this client

Per pro

The abbreviation *p.p.* sometimes appears in signature blocks. It means *per pro*, i.e. *for and on behalf of*, and is used when someone – often an assistant or secretary – signs a letter on behalf of a colleague.

Enclosures

If there are any documents enclosed with a letter, although these may be mentioned in the body of the letter, it is also common to write *Enc.* or *Encl.* below the signature block. If there are a number of documents, these may be listed, e.g.:

> *Enc.*
> *1 Draft contract*
> *2 Licensing agreement*
> *3 Power of attorney*

Private and confidential

This phrase may be written at the head of a letter and, more important, on the envelope – often in the top left-hand corner, in cases where the letter is intended to be read only by the addressee. There are many variations of this phrase, e.g. *Confidential*, *Strictly confidential*, *To be opened by the addressee only* – but there is little difference in meaning between these phrases.

In practice, all lawyers and their staff are under a professional duty of strict

① Letterhead

② References

③ Per pro

④ Enclosure

---

① TURNER JONES SMITH & CO.

7 Old Hall Street
Oxford
OX1 7PB
telephone: +44 (0) 1865 37522
fax: +44 (0) 1865 37523
email: info@tjs&co.com

Your reference
② *Our reference*   GL/VIR.1–1
Date   12 March 20—

Mr J. Virtanen
Korvatie 11A
00100 Helsinki
Finland

Dear Mr Virtanen

Purchase of The Croft, Whittlington

Thank you for your enquiry. I confirm that this firm would be glad to act on your behalf in relation to this transaction. This matter has been passed to me to deal with, as a Senior Assistant Solicitor in this firm's Residential Property department.

I enclose a copy of our standard client care letter in duplicate. This sets out our terms and conditions. Please read these through, and, if they are acceptable to you, kindly sign and return the duplicate copy.

I look forward to hearing from you.

Yours sincerely

Louise Duncan

③ **p.p. Geoffrey Lamb**
Senior Assistant Solicitor

④ Enc.
Client care letter

CONFIDENTIALITY in relation to their client's affairs. Most law firms have in-house procedures that govern how incoming post is dealt with. Frequently, all incoming post is sorted by a member of staff (or, in a larger firm, a small team of staff) according to established rules. Typically, these may be as follows:

— All envelopes addressed simply to the firm as a whole are opened, and the contents are transferred to individual recipients, either a) on the basis of the reference quoted in the letter, or b) where there is no reference, as in a new enquiry, according to the type of legal matter indicated by the contents.

— All envelopes addressed to individuals are transferred to individual recipients unopened.

Therefore, in most cases writing *Private and confidential* on the envelope simply acts as an extra safeguard of confidentiality.

Copies

When copies are sent to people other than the named recipient, *c.c.* (*carbon copy*) is added at the end of the letter, before the name of the recipient / s of the copies, e.g.:

c.c. Messrs Turner, Jones, Smith & Co

Sometimes you will not want the named recipients to know that other people have received copies. In this case, *b.c.c.* (*blind carbon copy*), and the name / s of the recipient / s, are added on the copies themselves, although not, of course, on the top copy. These abbreviations are also used in emails and faxes, and mean exactly the same thing.

The reference to 'carbon copies' is strictly anachronistic, and relates to the time when official correspondence was produced on typewriters in three copies, each of a different colour. This method of producing correspondence disappeared when wordprocessing techniques became standard, but the convention of referring to carbon copies remains in use as described above.

ADDRESSING ENVELOPES

Envelope addresses are written in a similar way to inside addresses. But in the case of letters within or for the UK, the name of the town and the country may be written in capital letters, and the postcode may be written on a line by itself.

Ms R. Bannister
33 Church Road
BOURNEMOUTH BH1 7QD
Dorset

Messrs Sandford, Gleadon & Co
3-5 Hinchley Avenue
LONDON
W1N 6UZ

CLIENT CARE LETTER

A client care letter, or terms and conditions letter, is sent to all new clients. It sets out the terms and conditions on which the solicitor will work for the client. In effect, it forms the contract between the solicitor and the client according to which the solicitor provides professional services and the client pays for them.

The terms and conditions letter has three main purposes:

1 It deals with issues relating to the management and conduct of the client's case.

2 It sets out the solicitor's terms of business.

3 It raises certain regulatory matters which the solicitor is obliged to advise the client about.

Generally, these are legal requirements which govern the way in which solicitors may carry out work for clients.

The client care letter is sometimes referred to as a 'retainer letter'. When it is signed by the client it becomes the contract for services supplied by the law firm (i.e. the services for which the firm is *retained* by the client).

1

Letters, faxes, and emails

Client care (terms and conditions) letter

This is a fairly comprehensive terms and conditions letter sent by a partner in a medium-sized provincial law firm.

1

Example letter

Gumber & Partners Solicitors

1 Amberton Road, Leicester LE2 9TV
Telephone +44 (0) 116 892445, Fax +44 (0) 116 892446
Email: enq@g&p.co.uk

YOUR REF
OUR REF JTF/DAN.2–1

Mrs E. Dancey   3 August 20—
1B The Brambles
Leicester
LE1 8RC

Dear Mrs Dancey

Thank you for instructing Gumber & Partners to act on your behalf. I set out below the terms and conditions on which your case will be conducted.

Management of matter

I am a partner in this firm and will have overall responsibility for your case. Work will be delegated to other staff as and when appropriate.

If you have any queries at any stage, they should be raised initially with me. If I am unable to resolve the matter to your satisfaction, please contact our client care partner, Ms Felicity Matterson. The matter will then be investigated under our client complaints handling procedure with a view to resolving any differences. The result of any investigation will be notified to you as soon as possible. If we cannot resolve the matter to your satisfaction, the Law Society provides a complaints and redress system.

Terms of business

Basis of charging

This firm's general practice is to charge on a time basis.
My charging rate is £195 per hour.
Other applicable current hourly rates are:
● Partners / associates: £155–£195
● Solicitors / consultants: £125–£165
● Legal executives: £110–£140
● Administrators / case workers: £75–£140
● Trainee solicitors: £90
● Secretaries: £50

1

1 Under what circumstances can the firm bill at a higher rate than their usual charging rates?

2 When can payments on account be requested?

3 Can the firm cease to act for a client if bills remain unpaid after 30 days?

4 Can the firm provide financial services to clients?

5 How long after the matter is completed will Gumber & Partners keep the client's documents and files?

- All routine letters and telephone calls are deemed to be six-minute time units for the purposes of charging.

Our charges are reviewed annually and we will advise you of any increase or variation made. We are obliged to add to our charges VAT, currently at the rate of 17.5%.

It may be necessary from time to time to pay other expenses. These may include court and search fees, payments to counsel, valuations, travel expenses, and bank transfer fees. Some, but not all, of these costs attract VAT.

In the event that we are obliged to carry out urgent or particularly complex work on your behalf, or if we are required to carry out work after 8 p.m. or overnight or at weekends, a mark-up of 50% will be added to our charges.

Payments on account

This firm reserves the right to request payment on account where a matter is long-running or where significant costs will be incurred. All payments made on account will be placed in a client account in your name. Further payments may be requested as the matter progresses.

Billing periods

We send out bills at six-monthly intervals or when unbilled fees, disbursements, and expenses excluding VAT exceed £2,500, whichever is the sooner. However, we reserve the right to bill at two-monthly intervals if costs rise very quickly.

Terms of settlement

All our bills must be settled within 30 days, unless agreed otherwise.

We add interest to unpaid bills at the rate of 8% per annum, commencing from the expiration of the 30-day payment period.

The firm reserves the right to cease to act, and, where appropriate, to withdraw from the court record if:
1 invoices are not settled within 30 days and the firm believes that the level of invoices delivered and unpaid is unacceptable, or
2 payment on account has been requested and you do not within 14 days send the funds requested.

2

6 If the client fails to sign and return this letter, does this mean that the client is not bound by Gumber & Partners' terms of business?

Regulatory matters

Money laundering

The firm is obliged to obtain satisfactory evidence of the identity of its clients. If we are not familiar with you, we may ask you to produce evidence of your identity (e.g. passport or driving licence). We must cease to act where such evidence has been requested and is not produced within 14 days.

Data protection

The Data Controller for the purposes of the Data Protection Act 1998 is David Berkeley and any information provided by you to us will be used solely for the purposes of carrying out instructions received from you.

However, from time to time it may be necessary to release information on a strictly confidential basis to other advisers, for example, counsel or accountants.

Financial services

We are not authorized to provide financial services under the Financial Services and Markets Act 2000 but are able in certain circumstances to offer to clients a limited range of investment services by virtue of our membership of the Law Society. We are able to provide these services where they form an incidental part of professional services we have been engaged to provide.

Standard of work

We shall provide a friendly and efficient service. We are audited by external auditors from time to time, including the Legal Services Commission and the International Organization for Standardization. During the course of audits, your files may be checked but the information in them will remain confidential.

Emails

If you contact us by email or print an email address on any letters we receive from you, we shall assume that you have no objection to its use. We assume that we have the right to communicate in the course of business using un-encrypted email.

We cannot accept responsibility for intercepted emails or viruses.

We will assume safe arrival of emails 24 hours after they are sent.

3

Storage of papers

Unless we receive written instructions to the contrary, we shall keep your papers for at least seven years, after which they will be destroyed.

Any deeds, documents, or wills deposited in safe custody will not be destroyed.

No charge will be made for retrieval of files, although we may charge for producing particular documents to you.

On conclusion of a matter, we reserve the right to publicize the fact that we have acted for you.

Other matters

For insurance and safety reasons, we will only accept cash payments below the sum of £250. We reserve the absolute right to refuse to issue cheques or other forms of payment to third parties.

If the need arises for us to refer matters pursuant to the Proceeds of Crime Act 2002, you will by agreeing to these terms waive your right to legal professional privilege.

Governing law

The terms of this letter are governed by the laws of England and you irrevocably agree that the English courts shall have exclusive jurisdiction to settle any dispute which may arise out of or in connection with this letter.

Agreement

If you agree with the terms set out above, please sign and return one copy of this letter.

If you continue to instruct me before signing this letter, I shall deem you to have agreed the terms and conditions set out in this letter.

Yours sincerely

Jane Fletcher

Jane Fletcher (Mrs)
Partner

Your signature

I confirm my agreement to the terms of business set out in this letter.

Authorized signatory _____

Date _____

4

Faxes

The word *fax* comes from *facsimile*, meaning *exact copy or reproduction*. Like *email*, the word *fax* can be used as a noun, e.g. *I sent a fax*, or as a verb, e.g. *We will fax the document to you when we receive it.*

Despite the increasing use of email, the fax machine remains in frequent and constant use in the legal profession. This is because it has significant advantages over both conventional correspondence and email. The traditional advantage of using fax is that it is much quicker than conventional correspondence. This advantage has been partly eroded by the arrival of email, but the fax machine remains useful in circumstances where it is not possible to use email instead. In legal work, these circumstances may be summarized as follows:

1 For sending copies of original documents which only exist in a paper version. It is of course possible to scan these and send them as email attachments, but this can be time-consuming. Note, however, that faxes are only copies of documents and will not be acceptable where it is necessary to produce the original document itself. For example, an original BILL OF LADING gives TITLE to goods (i.e. you would own the goods if you had the bill in your possession) and would not be valid if it were a faxed copy.

2 For sending documents which have either been signed or need to be signed and returned urgently by the recipient. This situation often arises in legal work, particularly in court proceedings in which it is essential to produce original signed paper documents to the court. In most cases, signed faxes are acceptable as evidence in court proceedings, whereas emails containing the same information generally are not.

3 For sending documents containing diagrams or drawings.

4 For sending handwritten documents. This circumstance does not often arise in legal work. An exception might be where handwritten annotations are made to a word-processed document. If it becomes necessary to send a handwritten fax message, use a dark colour ink and make your writing large and clear.

5 For sending a document when speed is important and the recipient does not have email.

6 For sending a document more securely than can be done by email.

7 For sending a document when it is useful to be able in future to prove that it has been sent and that it has been received by the addressee's machine.

Different fax machines offer a wide range of facilities, including repeat dialling if the receiver's fax machine is engaged; a transmission report which gives details of the time, date, sender, receiver, number of pages, duration, and result; a verification mark at the foot of the page to confirm the fax was sent; and a number memory for frequently used numbers. Check the manual of your fax machine to find out what functions it can perform.

Preparing fax for transmission

Check that you have the correct fax number. Check that the paper on which your message is printed or written is suitable. If it is too big, too small, or in poor condition, photocopy the message on paper that can be accepted by the fax machine. Before using the machine, check that you know how to dial, send, cancel, and clear a paper jam.

When you send a fax it is a good idea to use a fax transmission cover form. This will help to ensure that the fax reaches its intended recipient safely. Most firms use their own headed fax transmission form, but you can easily create one for yourself, e.g.:

THE RADCLIFFE PARTNERSHIP
Radcliffe House
3 Orchard Close
Doncaster DN1 7GK

FAX MESSAGE
To:
From:
Fax no.:
Subject:
Date:
Page / s (including this):

Confidentiality notices

Because legal communications are usually highly confidential, extreme care must always be taken to ensure that 1) faxes are sent to the correct number, and 2) they are marked for the correct recipient. However, occasionally mistakes are made. Consequently, most faxes – and emails - sent by law firms include a CONFIDENTIALITY NOTICE. The purpose of the confidentiality notice is:

— To alert the recipient to the fact that the contents of the communication are confidential.
— To make it clear that unauthorized recipients may not disclose the information contained in the communication.
— To request that if the fax is received in error the sender should be notified.

Here is an example of a confidentiality notice:

CONFIDENTIALITY
The information contained in this facsimile is confidential. It may also be legally privileged. It is intended only for the named recipient(s) and access to it by any other person is unauthorized. If you are not a named recipient, you must not disclose, copy, circulate, or in any other way use or rely on the information contained in this facsimile. Such unauthorized use may be unlawful. If you have received this message in error, please notify the sender immediately.

Style

Generally faxes are similar to letters in style, level of formality, and the use of conventions; but a fax may be shorter and the language more direct, like an email, as there is a time element in the cost of sending them. However, basic standards of professional courtesy and factual and legal accuracy should be adhered to at all times – bear in mind the possibility that your fax may one day form part of evidence in a court of law ▶ **see Unit 2**.

In practice, many faxes sent by law firms simply consist of ordinary letters which are faxed with a transmission cover form on the top. In this way the transmission cover form acts as a covering letter. In such cases, the text on the cover form will simply refer the recipient to the enclosed letter (*'see enclosed'* or *'Please refer to the enclosed letter'*). For very short correspondence, the whole of the communication may be contained in the transmission cover form.

1

Fax as covering letter

In this fax the short message on the transmission cover form refers to the pages of the completed fixtures and fittings form that follow.

THE RADCLIFFE PARTNERSHIP

Radcliffe House
3 Orchard Close
Doncaster DN1 7GK
Telephone: 01302 77552
Fax: 01302 77553
Email: enq@radcliffeptnr.co.uk

Fax message

To:	Jane Sanders
From:	Michael Burton
Fax no.:	01865 789231
Subject:	17 Lander's Green, Doncaster
Date:	14 January 20—
Page / s:	16

Please find herewith the fixtures and fittings form completed by our clients in respect of this property.

Yours faithfully

M. Burton

Michael Burton
The Radcliffe Partnership

The information contained in this facsimile is confidential. It may also be legally privileged. It is intended only for the named recipient(s) and access to it by any other person is unauthorized. If you are not a named recipient, you must not disclose, copy, circulate, or in any other way use or rely on the information contained in this facsimile. Such unauthorized use may be unlawful. If you have received this message in error, please notify the sender immediately.

Emails

Email (short for *electronic mail*) is a means of sending messages (emails) between computers. To send and receive email you need access to the Internet. An Internet Service Provider (ISP) will provide you with connection software, which is often free. This will give you Internet access, storage for incoming mail, and the capability to read your messages. Finally, you need email software, generally already installed in modern computers, so that you can write, send, receive, and read messages.

Advantages

There are numerous advantages to email. It is personal and easy to use. It can be used both within and between companies, and is an effective way to communicate quickly and easily with people all over the world. It can be used from a hotel or Internet café when you are travelling abroad. It is especially useful for short messages and for everyday correspondence, e.g. setting up a meeting, passing on information, and making or replying to a request.

You can pick up your email messages, even when you are travelling, via a laptop or palmtop. With compatible systems, you can access text and graphic documents, and spreadsheets. And whatever you send or receive can be quickly and easily filed.

Disadvantages

The disadvantages of email include technical problems which may result in the unexpected non-delivery of messages, or attachments arriving in unreadable form. Also, the ease with which messages can be sent results in large amounts of 'junk' emails and unnecessary communication which wastes time.

Virus emails are an even bigger problem: these can disable your computer or cause it to send out emails randomly to persons whose email addresses are stored in your computer. This problem can be tackled by installing and maintaining effective virus protection software on your computer. Another practical measure that should be taken is to avoid opening any emails that look suspicious in any way – e.g. those which are from an unknown sender, have an unconventional subject line, or a short generic message.

As with faxes, a major drawback is the lack of privacy and security. Digital signing and encryption (coding data, so that it can only be read by authorized users), which both work along similar lines, can make email more secure. However, do not use email to communicate confidential information; do not send anything by email that you would not wish a judge to read.

In the legal sphere, one of the main disadvantages of email is that it cannot be used to send documents which have to be signed in order to be effective, e.g. in a court of law. As noted above, a faxed document with a signature on it is usually valid in a court of law, while an email generally is not. It is also difficult to prove that an email was sent when you say it was.

When other forms of correspondence are preferable

There are several areas of legal communication where more traditional forms of correspondence are still the most suitable. These include:

1 To communicate information or send documentation which is confidential.

2 To send documents or communications which require a signature.

3 For personal or sensitive communications. Email has a slightly perfunctory, impersonal feel to it. Therefore, it is not suitable for any communication where a personal touch is required, e.g. messages of congratulation, condolence, and complaint (or a response to a complaint).

Typical email message

1

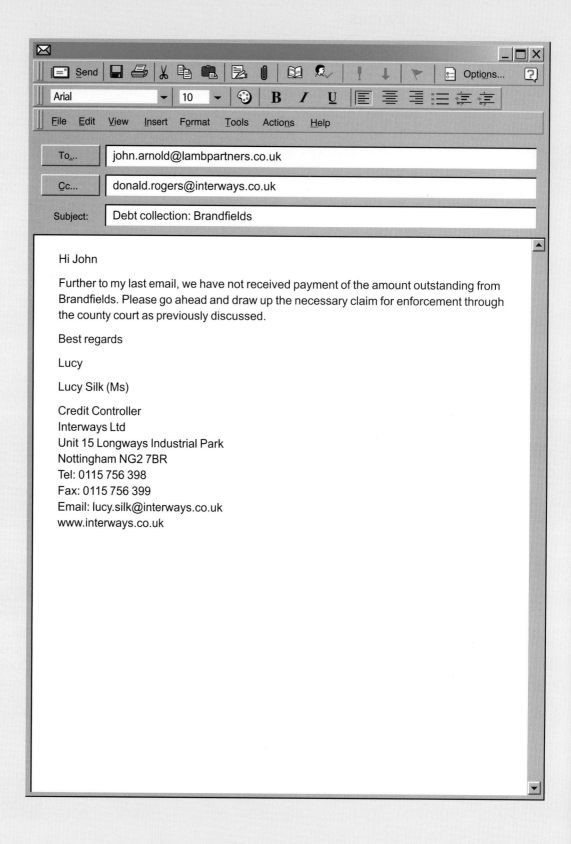

To... john.arnold@lambpartners.co.uk

Cc... donald.rogers@interways.co.uk

Subject: Debt collection: Brandfields

Hi John

Further to my last email, we have not received payment of the amount outstanding from Brandfields. Please go ahead and draw up the necessary claim for enforcement through the county court as previously discussed.

Best regards

Lucy

Lucy Silk (Ms)

Credit Controller
Interways Ltd
Unit 15 Longways Industrial Park
Nottingham NG2 7BR
Tel: 0115 756 398
Fax: 0115 756 399
Email: lucy.silk@interways.co.uk
www.interways.co.uk

4 For job applications. In general, most firms still expect your application to consist of a completed paper form or curriculum vitae together with a covering letter. However, this should be checked on a case-by-case basis, as some firms nowadays are becoming more open to emailed applications.

Email addresses

Typical email addresses look like this:

jdodgson@interways.co.uk

lars.johansson@moberg.dk

enquiries@lambpartners.co.uk

As a rough rule, there are two kinds of email address:
— One which identifies a particular person. In this case, the first part of the email address is usually either the first name or the initials of the person you are contacting, followed by their surname. The second part, which appears immediately after the @ (at) is the name of the ISP or organization, or the abbreviation of it.
— One which identifies a function in an organization. This is typical of larger organizations which are arranged into departments. In this case, the first part of the address identifies a function rather than a person, e.g. enquiries, sales, office. An email sent to such an address will usually then be allocated to a particular person to deal with according to the nature of the email sent.

The last part of the email address includes the domain name suffixes referring to the type of organization, e.g. '.co' for company, '.ac' (academic) for a university, and to the country from which the message was sent, e.g. '.es' for Spain, '.uk' for the United Kingdom.

Other examples of domain name suffixes referring to types of organization include:

.biz   *business*
.gov   *government office*
.org   *non-profit-making organization (e.g. a charity)*
.pro   *profession (e.g. medicine, law)*

Note that the names of countries in their main languages often differ significantly from their names in English, and this is sometimes reflected in their domain name suffixes, e.g.:

.de   *Deutschland (Germany)*
.za   *Zuid Afrika (South Africa)*

LAYOUT

Header information

The header gives essential information about the message. It typically includes the following:

c.c.

This stands for carbon copies, which means much the same as it does on a letter. Here you insert the email addresses of anyone you want to send copies of the message to.

b.c.c.

This stands for blind carbon copies which, as in a letter, you should use if you do not want the main recipient to know who has received copies.

Subject line

The subject line in an email operates as in a letter or fax. It should consist of a brief description of the matter you are writing about. In emails, the subject line is in fact more important than in a letter or fax. There are two reasons for this:
— When checking emails received on a computer, one may only see the subject line instead of the whole email. Therefore, the subject line must contain such words as will alert the reader to the matter on which you have written to him or her.
— Because most people receive many emails a day in the course of their professional life, there is a tendency to delete any emails which look as if they are suspicious, junk, viruses, or unsolicited and unwanted communications. Therefore, a properly worded subject line may save an important email from being deleted in error.

Attachments

Icons of any attachments will appear here.

NOTE The amount of header information, and the order in which it appears, will vary according to the software being used, so do not worry if the messages you send and receive do not look exactly like the one in the example.

Message text

The presentation of the text in an email is often less formal than in a letter. In this first example, the communication is clearly intended for another member of staff within the same firm. Therefore, the informal tone is appropriate. Informal, however, does not mean unprofessional. Do not allow the apparent informality of email to lure you into breaches of confidentiality or into writing communications which would be professionally embarrassing if disclosed to persons other than the intended recipient.

In legal work, as a general rule, all communications with persons outside the firm should be no less formal than in a letter or fax. Always remember that any such communications may potentially form part of evidence presented to a court of law one day.

Signature

This is like the signature block in a letter, although it usually includes more details, e.g. the sender's company or private address, and telephone and fax numbers. You can program your email software to add your signature automatically to the end of outgoing messages.

Confidentiality notices

As with faxes, emails sent by law firms invariably contain confidentiality notices, which are designed to provide for the possibility that an email may accidentally be sent to someone other than the intended recipient. As with faxes, the purpose of the confidentiality notice is:

— To alert the recipient to the fact that the contents of the communication are confidential.
— To make it clear that unauthorized recipients may not disclose the information contained in the communication.
— To request that if the fax is received in error the sender should be notified.

Here is an example of a confidentiality notice:

The information contained in this email and in any attachments hereto is confidential. It may also be legally privileged. It is intended only for the named recipient(s) and access to it by any other person is unauthorized. If you are not a named recipient, you must not disclose, copy, circulate, or in any other way use or rely on the information contained in this email or in any attachments hereto. Such unauthorized use may be unlawful. If you have received this email in error, please notify the sender immediately.

Style

Email is a relatively recent development, and because it is perceived as a quick and informal means of communication, people are often unclear about the style and conventions they should use in business situations.

In legal work, while email correspondence may tend towards informality, it should follow the same general principles as any other form of business correspondence ▶ see Unit 2.

Here are some basic tips about style in emails:

— In general, email messages follow the style and conventions used in letters or faxes. For example, you can use salutations such as *Dear Mr Archer* or *Dear Gerald*, and complimentary closes such as *Yours sincerely*. However, if you know the recipient well, or if you are exchanging a series of messages with one person, you may dispense with the salutation and complimentary close altogether.

— Make a clear mental division between personal messages and messages written in the course of legal work. In a message written in the course of legal work, the same rules of writing apply as for a letter: write clearly, concisely, pay attention to the accuracy of factual information and legal advice given, and observe high standards of professional courtesy; consider audience, purpose, clarity, consistency, and tone.

— Use correct grammar, spelling, capitalization, and punctuation, as you would in any other form of correspondence.

— Do not write words in capital letters in an email message. This can be seen as the equivalent of shouting and therefore have a negative effect. If you want to stress a word, put asterisks on each side of it, e.g. *urgent*.

— Keep your email messages short and to the point. People often receive a lot of emails at work, so conciseness is especially important.

— In general, limit yourself to one topic per message. This helps to keep the message brief and makes it easier for the recipient to answer, file, and retrieve it later.

— Check your email message for mistakes before you send it, just as you would check a letter or a fax message.

Email abbreviations

TLAs (three-letter acronyms)

In order to keep email messages short, people sometimes use abbreviations for common expressions, just as they do in text messaging. These are known as TLAs (three-letter acronyms), although some of them are more than three letters long. Here is a list of some of the most commonly used TLAs:

AFAIK	*as far as I know*
BFN	*bye for now*
BTW	*by the way*
COB	*close of business*
FYI	*for your information*
IOW	*in other words*
NRN	*no reply necessary*
OTOH	*on the other hand*
POV	*point of view*
TBA	*to be announced / to be agreed*

TLAs are highly informal, and are therefore not suitable for the vast majority of email correspondence. They should never be used in letters or faxes.

Emoticons

Emoticons (a combination of the words emotion and icon), also known as smileys, are often used in informal email correspondence. They express emotions which may not be evident from the words alone, e.g.:

> :-) *a smile*
> :-(*a frown*
> ;-) *a wink*

Emoticons should never be used in emails sent in the course of legal work – using them will destroy your professional credibility.

Points to remember

Letters

Many of these points apply to faxes and emails as well.

1 The layout and presentation of your letter are important as they give the recipient the first impression of your company's efficiency.

2 Write both the sender's and the recipient's address in as much detail as possible and in the correct order.

3 Make sure you use the recipient's correct title in the address and salutation. If in doubt as to whether a woman is single or married, use *Ms*.

4 Write the date like this: *2 November 20—*.

5 Do not write the month of the date in figures.

6 Choose the correct salutation and complimentary close:

   Dear Sir / Madam with *Yours faithfully*
   Dear Mr / Ms Smith with *Yours sincerely*

7 Make sure your references are correct.

8 Make sure that you include an accurate subject line – one which will enable the recipient to identify at a glance the matter you are writing about.

9 Make sure your signature block tells your reader what he or she needs to know about you.

Faxes

1 Fax is an open system, so it should not be used for confidential correspondence.

2 Ensure that every fax you send includes an appropriately worded confidentiality notice.

3 Write clearly, using a dark colour when sending handwritten messages.

4 Remember that faxes are copies, and cannot be used when original documents are required.

5 Prepare your transmission carefully before you send it.

6 In general, the language of faxes is the same as that of letters, although faxes can be briefer and more direct, like email messages.

Emails

1 Email is very fast and effective, but should never be used for confidential correspondence.

2 Email addresses usually give the name of the person or department, then the @ (at) symbol, followed by the name of the company or institution, and finally the domain names, which indicate the type of organization and the country from which the message was sent.

3 Do not allow the apparent informality of email to lure you into breaches of confidentiality or into writing communications which would be professionally embarrassing if disclosed to persons other than the intended recipient.

4 Email is not suitable for sending and receiving documents which need to be sent or received in a signed form.

5 Ensure that every email you send includes an appropriately worded confidentiality notice.

6 It is better not to use special abbreviations, e.g. TLAs, in legal correspondence, as they are too informal. If you use them, do not confuse your recipient by using abbreviations he or she may not know or understand. Neither use abbreviations which have more than one meaning (e.g. TBA) in circumstances where there may be confusion about which is intended.

Content and style

2

LEGAL DOCUMENTS

It is important to remember that legal correspondence is only a small part of the writing done by lawyers. Most lawyers also spend a considerable amount of time creating legal documents, which may be intended for use either in court proceedings or in non-contentious business such as sales of land, goods, or services.

Typical documents prepared by lawyers for use in court include STATEMENTS OF CASE, WITNESS STATEMENTS, DIVORCE PETITIONS, petitions for BANKRUPTCY, and AFFIDAVITS.

Typical documents prepared by lawyers for non-contentious purposes include transfers of land (or land transfers), contracts for sale of goods, wills, DEEDS, ARTICLES OF ASSOCIATION for companies, LICENCES, and OPTIONS.

The style of writing used in legal documents differs from the style used in legal correspondence. This is because the purpose of legal documents is different.

Most legal documents used in court proceedings either act as evidence in support or defence of some claim, or make allegations and arguments in support or defence of a claim. Most legal documents used in non-contentious business record an agreement between parties. Such documents are intended primarily to regulate all aspects of the agreement reached between the parties. They lay down the obligations each party must carry out and specify the consequences of failure. They are intended to be legally effective in court. Consequently, the language used in legal documents displays certain typical features which often make them difficult to read. These include:
— *Use of terms of art.* These are words which have a precise and defined legal meaning. They may not be familiar to the layperson, but cannot be replaced by other words. Examples of terms of art include *lien* (the right of one person to retain possession of goods owned by another person until the possessor's claims against the owner have been satisfied), and *indemnity* (an agreement by one person to pay to another sums that are owed, or may become owed, to him or her by a third person).
— *Use of defined terms.* Many legal documents contain a definitions section in which the parties agree that certain words used repetitively throughout the document shall have an agreed meaning. For example, the parties may agree that the words 'completion date' shall mean 12 May 2006, or that the words 'the Company' shall mean a company called Greystokes Ltd.
— *Use of obscure legal terminology.* This can be confusing to the layperson, either simply because the language is unfamiliar, or because the words used have a different meaning in ordinary English. For example, in legal English the word *construction* is often used to mean *interpretation*, *furnish* is used to mean *provide*, and *consideration* refers to the price agreed between the parties to a contract.
— *Use of doublets and triplets.* These are series of words used in place of one word for reasons of legal tradition. Examples include *null and void*, *all and sundry*, and *give, devise, and bequeath*.
— Repeated use of the words *shall* and *must* to express obligations, and *may* to express discretions (where the parties are entitled to do something but are not obliged to do it).
— *Lack of punctuation.* Many legal documents, e.g. leases, contain little punctuation; even full stops are often omitted.

LEGAL CORRESPONDENCE

The writing used in legal correspondence usually has a different purpose. It is generally intended to provide information and advice, to put forward proposals, and to provide instructions to third parties.

The main aims of legal correspondence in all cases are clarity and accuracy. However, the style of correspondence will differ slightly according to whom the correspondence is being written for.

Letter to another lawyer

This letter relates to a claim for compensation made in a personal injury case.

TURNER JONES SMITH & CO.

7 Old Hall Street
Oxford
OX1 7PB
telephone: +44 (0) 1865 37522
fax: +44 (0) 1865 37523
email: info@tjs&co.com

Your reference	HB/BAN.7–2
Our reference	LD/VIR.1–1
Date	12 March 20—

Messrs Pearson and Wain
16 Friars Avenue
Reading
RG1 7FG

Dear Sirs

Our client: Gail Angus
Your client: Banner Insurance Ltd

Thank you for your letter of 5 March. We are pleased to note that liability is no longer in dispute.

We enclose by way of service the following documents:

1 Copy of medical report prepared by Dr L. Hobson.
2 Copies of our client's payslips for the six months preceding our client's accident.

Kindly acknowledge receipt.

You will note that Dr Hobson's opinion is that our client will be able to return to full-time employment within about four months. Therefore, in addition to general damages, our client will be seeking compensation for loss of wages calculated from the date of the accident to a date four months hence.

There are further expenses which our client has incurred as a direct result of the accident. These include medical, care, and travel expenses. We will revert to you shortly with the schedule of special damages.

Yours faithfully

Turner, Jones, Smith & Co.

Turner, Jones, Smith & Co.

Enc. 1 Medical report   2 Copies of payslips

When writing to another lawyer, the writer can assume that legal jargon and terms of art will be understood and do not need to be explained. When writing to clients and other third parties, this assumption cannot be made; care should be taken to explain legal technicalities in terms that a layperson can understand.

Letters to other lawyers

These letters may cover a whole range of different matters, according to the type of legal business that is being handled. Typically, letters between lawyers are formal in tone, observe certain standards of professional courtesy, are carefully worded, and are written in order to move the client's case forward. They may, for example, put forward offers or counter-offers, propose timetables for the completion of certain steps, make allegations, refute allegations, put forward legal analysis, serve documents upon the other party, and request or provide information.

In the example letter on the previous page, Gail Angus has been in an accident which was caused by someone insured by Banner Insurance. Some special vocabulary is used in this letter. The reference to LIABILITY being no longer in dispute means that Banner Insurance accept that the person they insured was at fault in causing the accident, and that therefore they must pay compensation to Gail Angus. Therefore, her solicitors are writing to Banner Insurance to provide evidence supporting the compensation sought. They *serve* the documents (in this case they enclose the documents by way of SERVICE) upon Banner Insurance, which means that they are sent formally in accordance with court directions.

Ms Angus can obtain compensation for the pain and suffering caused by the accident. These are the GENERAL DAMAGES. She can also obtain compensation for particular sums of money lost or expended as a result of the accident, such as wages. These are the

SPECIAL DAMAGES. The *schedule of special damages* is a formal document which sets out the exact sums claimed as special damages.

Letters to clients

The main purposes of the correspondence written by the lawyer to the client are to provide legal advice, request information, provide information, request further instructions from the client, advise as to the progress of the case, and provide documents that the client needs.

The language used in this letter is adapted to the needs of the client. Laura Davies avoids using legal vocabulary that the client may not understand. Where it is necessary to use legal vocabulary (the schedule of special damages), she takes the trouble to explain what it means.

Letters to third parties

Lawyers need to write to a wide range of third parties. For example, in contentious cases, lawyers need to correspond with the court, with barristers briefed to represent the client in court, and possibly with witnesses who will give evidence in court. They may also need to write letters to instruct experts and professional advisers to prepare reports on behalf of clients. For example, in personal injury cases, it is customary for one or more medical reports to be prepared detailing the client's injuries and prognosis. (If there is an exchange of letters in which one or both parties are seeking a settlement through negotiation, a letter may be headed 'WITHOUT PREJUDICE' ▶**see page 176**.) In non-contentious cases, lawyers need to correspond with various agencies such as Companies House or the Land Registry, and also with professional advisers (e.g. with accountants on a company share sale).

It will be noted that the language contained in this letter is more formal than in the letter to Ms Angus, but steers clear of obscure legal terminology.

Letter to a client

In this letter a solicitor brings a client up to date on their case for damages for loss of wages and other expenses arising from an injury.

TURNER JONES SMITH & CO.

7 Old Hall Street
Oxford
OX1 7PB
telephone: +44 (0) 1865 37522
fax: +44 (0) 1865 37523
email: info@tjs&co.com

Your reference
Our reference   LD/VIR.1–1
Date   17 March 20—

Ms G. Angus
71 Parker Road
Oxford
OX2 6FT

Dear Ms Angus

Your accident

I am pleased to be able to report that after receiving the statements of Brian Jennings and Clare Newman who, as you will remember, saw your accident occur, Banner Insurance have indicated that they will not fight your claim. Therefore, what we need to do now is finalize the sum claimed from Banner Insurance and agree this with them.

I have now received the medical report requested from Dr Hobson, a copy of which I enclose for your reference. You will see that Dr Hobson believes that you will be able to return to full-time work within four months. Therefore, you will be able to claim compensation for loss of wages from the date of the accident to a date four months hence. You will also be able to claim compensation for other expenses incurred as a result of the accident. I have the details of these expenses on file and will shortly put together a schedule of special damages. This is a document showing all the expenses which you have incurred as a result of the accident, which we will claim from Banner Insurance. Once it is ready, I will forward a copy to you for discussion.

I will be in touch again shortly. In the meantime, do not hesitate to contact me or my assistant, Jane Seaforth, if you have any queries.

Yours sincerely

Laura Davies

Laura Davies (Ms)
Partner

Enc. Medical report

Letter to a third party

In this letter a solicitor writes to the doctor of a client seeking a medical report for use in pursuing a claim for damages arising from the client's injury.

TURNER
JONES
SMITH
& CO.

7 Old Hall Street
Oxford
OX1 7PB
telephone: +44 (0) 1865 37522
fax: +44 (0) 1865 37523
email: info@tjs&co.com

Your reference
Our reference   LD/VIR.1–1
Date   20 February 20—

Dr L Hobson
The Denton Practice
136 Ifford Road
Oxford
OX2 1DR

Dear Madam

Ms Gail Angus

We act for Ms Angus in relation to an industrial accident she suffered on 22 August last year. We understand that you are Ms Angus's general practitioner.

Ms Angus is pursuing a claim for compensation in relation to her accident, and it will be necessary to have a medical report from you in order to assist her in this claim. We enclose our client's signed form of authorization together with her statement relating to the accident, and should be grateful if you would prepare a short report dealing with the following issues:

1 The nature and extent of the injuries suffered by Ms Angus.
2 Whether these are consistent with the account of events contained in the enclosed statement.
3 The likely prognosis: please indicate whether you expect Ms Angus to make a full recovery, whether she will be able to return to full-time work, and, if so, when.

We look forward to hearing from you. If you require any further information or assistance, please do not hesitate to contact our partner, Laura Davies, or her assistant, Ms Jane Seaforth.

Yours faithfully

Turner, Jones, Smith & Co.

Turner, Jones, Smith & Co.

Enc.
1 Signed form of authorization
2 Statement of Gail Angus

PLANNING YOUR LETTER

Clarity of expression comes from clarity of thought. Start by considering the overall purpose of your letter. Think about what you are going to say and how you are going to say it. Ask yourself these questions:

— What am I trying to say?
— Who am I trying to say it to?
— What do they need to know?
— What sort of tone should I adopt?
— What words will express what I am trying to say?
— How will I structure what I am going to say?
— How can I divide my writing into manageable sections?
— Could I make it shorter?

Paragraphs

Your letter should be divided into manageable sections using paragraphs. Paragraphs should not be defined by length. They are best treated as units of thought. In other words, each paragraph should deal with a single thought or topic. Begin a new paragraph when shifting to a new thought or topic.

Paragraphs should start with the main idea, and then deal with subordinate matters. The writing should move logically from one idea to the next. It should not dance about randomly between different ideas.

The paragraphs in legal letters are sometimes numbered, to break up the text and make individual paragraphs in the letter easier to refer to. Numbered paragraphs are more suitable in some types of legal correspondence than in others. They are particularly suitable in longer letters, for example, when 1) outlining steps to be taken, or 2) enumerating different parts of a legal argument. They are less suitable when the letter is short and / or its content is largely descriptive or non-technical.

One-sentence paragraphs should not be used too often, but can be useful in certain circumstances.

Pay attention to the way the paragraphs look on the page. Text evenly divided into manageably sized paragraphs, with occasional shorter ones, looks inviting to the reader. Huge, unbroken sections of text are very off-putting to the reader and should be avoided. So, too, should untidy sequences of very short paragraphs.

First paragraph

The opening sentence or paragraph is important as it sets the tone of the letter and creates a first impression.

If you are replying to a previous letter, start by thanking your correspondent for their letter:

Thank you for your letter of 5 May 2006.

If you are writing to someone for the first time, use the first paragraph to introduce yourself, the subject of the letter, and why you are writing:

We act on behalf of Smith Holdings Ltd and write concerning the lease on 22 Fairfields Avenue, Farnley Trading Estate.

Middle paragraphs

The main part of your letter will concern the points that need to be made, answers you wish to give, or questions you want to ask. The exact nature of these will depend very much on the type of letter being written.

Final paragraph

At the end of your letter, if it is to a client or to a third party, you should indicate that you may be contacted if your correspondent requires further information or assistance. If appropriate, you might also indicate another person in your office who may be contacted if you are absent. For example:

Please do not hesitate to contact me, or my assistant, John Bowles, if you require any further information.

However, it is not usual to do this in a letter to another lawyer acting for another party in a case.

2

CLARITY

Once you have planned the basic structure of your letter, and know roughly what kinds of paragraphs you are going to need, clarity can be achieved by paying attention to the smaller units of writing that you will be creating – that is, the sentences and words.

Sentences

Keep sentences as short as possible. This does not necessarily mean that all sentences should be short (which might create a displeasing, staccato effect) but that all unnecessary words should be removed.

Try to have only one main idea per sentence. Where you want to add more than one piece of additional information about a subject introduced in a sentence, consider starting a new sentence. Also consider the sequence in which information is presented in a sentence. In general:

1 Start with the most important piece of information, then deal with lesser matters. This may mean that you will need to use more than one sentence in order to establish a natural priority of information. For example:

The company specializes in pharmaceutical products. Its headquarters are in Oxford, and it made a record profit last year.

instead of:

The company, the headquarters of which are in Oxford, specializes in pharmaceutical products and made a record profit last year.

2 State the general rule before any exception to the rule, not the other way about. For example:

The goods must be delivered within 21 days of an order being received, unless more than 100 units are ordered.

instead of:

Unless more than 100 units are ordered, the goods must be delivered within 21 days of an order being received.

3 If you can cut words out without affecting the meaning of the sentence, do it. It will make your writing much more vigorous. In particular, pay attention to phrases which introduce new pieces of information or argument. These can often be reduced to single words. For example, *have a detrimental effect upon* can usually be reduced to *harm*, and *notwithstanding the fact that* can usually be reduced to *despite* or *although*.

Words

Use the words that convey your meaning
Use the words that convey your meaning, and nothing more.

Never use words simply because they look impressive and you want to try them out, or because you like the sound of them. There is a tendency in legal writing to use unnecessary, obscure words rather than their ordinary equivalents, perhaps out of a feeling that the obscure words are somehow more impressive. Never use a long word where a short one can be used. For example, avoid words like *notwithstanding* where simple words like *despite*, *still*, or *even if* can be used instead.

Never use a phrase where you can use one short word. There is a creeping tendency to include unnecessary phrases like *with regard to*, *with respect to*, *in reference to*, and so on, instead of *about*.

Use ordinary English words where possible
Do not use a foreign phrase or jargon if you can think of an ordinary English word which means the same thing. For example, do not write *modus operandi* when you can write *method*, nor *soi-disant* when you can write *so-called*.

In legal English, this is more difficult to achieve in practice than it is in ordinary English, because much of the terminology used (*inter alia*, *ab initio*, *force majeure*, *mutatis mutandis*) comes from French and Latin. These phrases often act as shorthand for a longer English phrase. For example, *inter alia* comes out in English as 'including but not limited to'.

Therefore, as a rule of thumb, the use of a foreign phrase is permissible 1) when it is in common use in legal writing, and 2) when it expresses a legal idea more succinctly than can be achieved in English. Your choice of vocabulary – between English or French and Latin – will also be influenced by who you are writing to.

Avoid legal jargon

Do not use legal jargon or terms of art in a letter to a client or other non-lawyer unless it is unavoidable. In such cases, consider whether you need to explain what the words you have used mean.

Grammar

Avoid negative structures

Avoid negative structures where possible. There is a tendency in much business and legal writing to try to soften the impact of what is being said by using *not un-* (or *not im-, il-, in-,* etc) formations such as:

not unreasonable
not impossible
not unjustifiable
not unthinkable
not negligible

Such structures make what you are saying less clear and definite. They become very hard to follow when more than one is used within a single sentence, e.g.:

It is not impossible that this matter will have a not inconsiderable bearing upon our decision.

Translated into ordinary English, this reads:

It is possible that this matter will have a considerable bearing upon our decision.

or:

This may considerably influence our decision.

Use active verbs

Use active verbs rather than nominalizations where possible: *consider* instead of *give consideration to*; *oppose* instead of *be in opposition to*; *contravene* instead of *be in contravention of*. In the longer phrases, known as nominalizations, a verb has become buried in a noun. Anglo-American lawyers particularly are addicted to them.

The use of nominalizations makes writing longer and less dynamic. For example:

We are in agreement that our firm will give consideration to the documents.

This sentence would be better expressed:

We agree that our firm will consider the documents.

However, there are certain occasions in legal writing when nominalizations are appropriate. For example, lawyers don't agree to *arbitrate* but to *go to arbitration*: arbitration is a defined legal process and should be referred to in its nominal form.

2

STYLE AND LANGUAGE (INCLUDING TONE)

Simplicity

A traditional problem of legal correspondence is its tendency to be pompous, obscure, and verbose. This problem is often worsened by a failure to simplify or explain complex legal jargon for the benefit of laypersons. Here is an example of such writing; the letter is likely both to antagonize and to mystify the recipient.

2

The above letter could be written in much simpler language, as here.

Dear Madam

We have been appointed to act on behalf of your spouse, Mr Gerald Taggart, in connection with your matrimonial situation. Our client has informed us that the matrimonial relationship has irretrievably broken down by reason of a new relationship which you have formed with one Arthur Longsdale. We understand that this is a matter that you would in no way seek to deny in any future divorce proceedings. This being so, we have advised our client that he would have grounds to present to the court a petition for divorce based on your adultery, and we are in receipt of his instructions to pursue the same.

We would respectfully advise you to seek independent legal advice from solicitors of your choice upon the contents of this letter, and we should be obliged to hear from the same at your earliest convenience.

Yours faithfully

Dear Madam

We have been consulted by your husband regarding your marriage. He has told us that you have now formed a new relationship with Arthur Longsdale, and that you would be prepared to admit to this. If so, this would mean that your husband would be entitled to commence divorce proceedings against you based on your adultery with Mr Longsdale.

Your husband has asked us to prepare a divorce petition based on your adultery and this will be sent to the court shortly.

We would recommend that you consult another firm of solicitors about the contents of this letter, and look forward to hearing either from them or from you shortly.

Yours faithfully

Courtesy

Your style should not, however, be so simple that it becomes rude or abrupt, or begins to sound naïve. Here is an example of a letter that is too short and simple.

This letter sounds unprofessional. It would be likely to give a poor impression of the credibility of the law firm that sent it.

Dear Sir

Our client: Grange Supplies Ltd

Outstanding invoice for supplies of office stationery

We saw Mr Grange of Grange Supplies today. He told us that they sent you a bill for £10,750 four months ago with a payment period of 28 days. You have not paid it yet despite being chased several times for it.

This is to give you a last chance to pay up. If you do not pay in full within the next 14 days, we will sue you. No more excuses will be accepted.

Yours, etc.

In this version of the letter, certain techniques are used to improve it and to achieve a more professional tone:
— More formal or sophisticated expressions are used: 'We are instructed by Grange Supplies Ltd' instead of 'We saw Mr Grange…'; 'we are instructed to commence proceedings' instead of 'we will sue you'.
— Sentences are joined together by relative pronouns ('which' in the first sentence) and conjunctions ('unless' in the second sentence).

Dear Sir

Our client: Grange Supplies Ltd

Outstanding invoice for supplies of office stationery

We are instructed by Grange Supplies Ltd to seek recovery of sums unpaid on an invoice dated —, a further copy of which we enclose for ease of reference.

We write to advise that we are instructed to commence proceedings to recover the debt unless payment in full is received by our client within the next 14 days.

Yours faithfully

Idioms and colloquial language

As the letter above shows, it is important to try to strike the right tone in your letter. The right tone is one of professional neutrality. On the one hand, you should avoid pompous, obscure language. On the other hand, you should avoid language which is too informal or colloquial.

At all times, and particularly when writing to parties on the other side of a case from your client, you should avoid any tinge of personal animosity. This is important because although lawyers often find themselves having to threaten people or organizations with legal action on behalf of clients, the lawyer must ensure that basic standards of professional courtesy are adhered to at all times.

2

When seeking the right tone, certain things should be avoided:

— *Contractions.* A contraction is when a word is shortened, using an apostrophe, e.g. *I can't* and *I won't*. This is too informal for most legal contexts.
— *Slang.* This should be avoided, 1) because using it is unprofessional, and 2) because it may not be understood. Always use the correct, formal term, e.g. not a *fake* (person) but a *charlatan*.
— *Colloquialisms, proverbs, common metaphors.* Again, these both are unprofessional and may be misunderstood. Always state precisely what you mean rather than resorting to such a phrase. For example, do not write *prices have gone through the roof* but *prices have increased rapidly*.
— *Throwaway informality.* It is important to retain a quality of professional gravity in the tone of your writing. Therefore do not write, *it's all sorted to go*, but *the matter has been satisfactorily resolved*.

Sexist language

It is inappropriate to use the personal pronouns *he* or *his* in a letter or document to refer to a person whose sex might be either male or female. One option is to use *he / she* and *his / her*. English also has a number of gender-neutral words such as *person*, and gender-neutral pronouns such as *anyone*, *everyone*, and *no one*. However, it does not have gender-neutral singular personal pronouns, except *one*, which is generally unsatisfactory for most purposes in legal correspondence.

A good compromise stragegy is to use the plural pronoun *they* and the possessive form *their*, in the sense of *he / she* and *his / her*. The *Oxford English Dictionary* (2001) sanctions this use of *their* to refer to 'belonging or associated with a person whose sex is not specified'.

Other methods that can be employed to avoid using *he* or *his* in such cases include:

— Deleting the pronoun reference altogether if possible. For example, in *the lawyer read the documents as soon as they were delivered to him*, delete *to him*.
— Changing the pronoun to an article like *a* or *the*. For example, *the lawyer advised the client on his case* can be changed to *the lawyer advised the client on the case*.
— Using *who*, especially when *he* follows *if*. For example, *if he does not prepare cases thoroughly a lawyer cannot be an effective court advocate* should read: *a lawyer who does not prepare cases thoroughly cannot be an effective court advocate*.
— Repeating the noun instead of using a pronoun. For example, *When considering the conduct of litigation, the lawyer should retain an objective view. In particular, the lawyer* [repeat noun, don't use *he*] *should...*

ACCURACY

Prepositions

Special care should be taken when using prepositions. Minor differences in preposition usage can have a big effect on the meaning of a sentence, e.g.:

*The goods shall be delivered **in** seven days*

means that the goods are likely to be delivered on the seventh day.

*The goods shall be delivered **within** seven days*

means that the goods shall be delivered no later than the seventh day.
Or:

*The goods shall be delivered **on** 7 June*

means that the goods will arrive on that date.

*The goods shall be delivered **by** 7 June*

means that the goods will arrive no later than that date.

Such apparently minor differences may be of critical importance when trying to reach agreement on legal issues.

Spelling

Lawyers are trained to pay attention to detail. Therefore, spelling mistakes in a letter are likely to be noticed and will create a very bad impression. Spelling, punctuation, and grammar should all be checked carefully. Many people rely on the spell-checker in their computer to ensure there are no spelling mistakes. However, spell-checkers often prescribe American spellings, while clients and other correspondents may prefer British spellings. In any case, certain kinds of mistakes will slip through such a check, e.g.:

— Where a word may be spelt correctly but is the wrong word: *I saw it their* (instead of *I saw it there*).
— Where a compound word is incorrectly split into two words, or two words are incorrectly combined to form a valid compound word: *the good will of the company* (instead of *the goodwill of the company*).

There is no substitute for carefully proofreading each letter that you have written.

Titles, names, and addresses

Use the correct title in the address and salutation. Spell your correspondent's name correctly (nothing creates a worse impression than a misspelt name) and write their address accurately.

If you do not know your correspondent, do not assume that they are one sex or the other, i.e. use *Dear Sir / Madam* rather than *Dear Sir* or *Dear Madam*. If you know a correspondent's name but not their sex, use *Mr / Ms*, e.g. *Dear Mr / Ms Bromley*.

Better still, before you write, telephone the organization at which that person works and find out from the receptionist the sex of the intended recipient.

References

When replying to a letter, fax, or email, quote all references accurately so that it is immediately clear to your reader what you are writing about.

Prices, measurements, etc.

Special care should be taken when quoting prices or giving specifications such as measurements or weights. Quoting these incorrectly can cause serious misunderstandings.

Enclosures and attachments

Always check that you have actually enclosed any documents that you have mentioned in your letter are enclosed, and that any documents you say in an email that you attach are indeed attached.

Check, too, that the documents you have enclosed or attached are the right documents. If, for example, the document you are supposed to be enclosing is invoice PNT/21, make sure you do not enclose invoice PNT/12. It is important to ensure that any documents enclosed or attached appear in the order in which you have listed them in your communication.

CONVENTIONS

Abbreviations

Abbreviations can be useful because they are quick to write and easy to read. But they are not worth using unless you are confident that the recipient of your letter will understand what they mean.

Differentiate between those abbreviations that are used internationally and those that are basically parochial. For example, the abbreviations CIF (or cif, Cost, Insurance, and Freight) and FOB (or fob, free on board) are INCOTERMS which are used in international trade. However, you cannot be sure that abbreviations like p & p (postage and packing) and SAE (or sae, stamped addressed envelope) will be understood internationally. Similarly, purely national organizations are unlikely to be familiar to correspondents in other countries.

2

Note that international organizations such as UN, NATO, or EU have a different acronym in other languages and therefore are better spelled out when first mentioned.

Abbreviations which are used as grammatical shorthand, such as *e.g.* and *i.e.*, are usually written in lower case letters with dots between the letters.

Statutes and people that are likely to be referred to a number of times within a letter or memo are often given abbreviations, e.g. Data Protection Act 1998 ('DPA').

In general, abbreviations that refer to an entity, such as *UK*, *USA*, *NATO,* should be capitalized without dots between the letters.

Numbers

When inserting numbers into legal letters and documents, the general rule is that numbers up to and including ten should be spelt and numbers 11 and above should be put in numerals. However, there are certain exceptions to this:

— If numbers recur through the text or are being used for calculations, then numerals, not words, should be used.
— If the number is approximate (e.g. *around six hundred years ago*) it should be spelt out.
— Very large numbers should generally be expressed without using rows of zeros where possible, e.g. *$3.5 million*, not *$3,500,000*.
— Percentages may be spelled out (twenty per cent) or written as numbers (20 per cent or 20%).
— Numbers that begin sentences should be spelled out.

In British and American usage, the decimal point in a number is represented by a dot (.). This differs from the continental European system, where a comma (,) is used to represent the decimal point. Therefore, a British or American writer would write one and three-tenths like this: *1.3*, while a French speaker would write *1,3*.

In British and American usage, commas are not used to indicate a decimal point. Instead, the comma is used to break up long numbers. For example, *10,000,000* is ten million.

If there is the possibility of confusion, write the number in both figures and words, e.g. *£100.05 (one hundred pounds and five pence)*. This is standard practice in formal legal documents.

When referring to sums of money, the following rules apply:
— When writing numerical sums, the currency sign goes before the sum without a space between the sign and the figure, e.g. *$100*.
— When spelling out numbers, the name of the currency is normally placed after the number, e.g. *one hundred pounds sterling*.

Certain abbreviations for common currencies may also be used, including *USD* for US dollars and *EUR* for euros.

Statutes and cases

If you need to refer to statutes or cases in your letter, certain conventions must be followed:
— Statutes should be written without a comma between the name of the statute and the year it was enacted, e.g. *the Treaty of Amsterdam 1999*.
— The word *the* should not form part of the name of a statute. Therefore, one should write *the Single European Act 1986*, not *The Single European Act 1986*.
— When referring to a section of a statute write *section* in full using a lower case *s* (unless starting a sentence), e.g. *section 2* or *s.2 of the Law of Property (Miscellaneous Provisions) Act 1989*.
— When referring to a particular sub-section of a statute do not use the word *sub-section*. For example, instead of writing *sub-section 1* in the following, write *section 722 (1) of the Companies Act 1985*.
— The names of cases should be written in italics and the word *versus* should appear as *v.*, e.g. *Donoghue v. Stevenson*.

Points to remember

1 When writing to clients, keep legal jargon to a minimum and explain any jargon that is unavoidable.

2 Clarity of expression comes from clarity of thought: plan what you are going to write before putting pen to paper.

3 Avoid where possible: negative structures, nominalizations, contractions, slang, pomposity.

4 Do not use sexist language.

5 Accuracy and correct spelling are important. Pay special attention to titles and names, and to references, prices, and numbers.

6 Remember to check enclosures and attachments.

7 Check through what you have written when you have finished. Make sure everything is as it should be.

2

Commercial property: granting a lease

3

REAL PROPERTY

In legal terms, the word property means anything that can be owned. A distinction can be made between real property and personal property:

— *Real property* includes land and all corporeal and incorporeal hereditaments. Corporeal hereditaments are tangible items of property such as buildings. Incorporeal hereditaments are intangible rights in land capable of being passed to an heir, e.g. easements and profits à prendre – see below.
— *Personal property* includes all other kinds of property, e.g. CHATTELS (physical items of personal property that can be moved, such as jewellery or furniture), and CHOSES IN ACTION (certain kinds of rights, for example, a debt is a right to sue and so a chose in action).

Real property can be divided into two kinds of *estates* (ways in which land can be owned): freehold and leasehold. Both can be inherited.

Freehold

Freehold is the most complete form of ownership in the common law system. It means that the owner has a legal estate in land which can be inherited by heirs, is held from the state (sometimes referred to as 'the Crown' in the UK), and can only be overridden by compulsory purchase by the Crown. (Compulsory purchase might occur, for example, when a motorway or other major project is going to be built and a property is situated on land over which the motorway will pass. In these circumstances, the state has the right to purchase the land, at the market price, and ultimately the owner cannot refuse to sell.)

Leasehold

Leasehold is an estate in which land is held under a LEASE, i.e. for a period of fixed minimum duration. Therefore, the person who holds the land under the lease must give it up to the freeholder once the lease has come to an end. Leases may be granted by the owner of the freehold of the land.

It is also possible for a person who holds a lease to grant a sub-lease, provided the sub-lease is of shorter duration. So, a person who holds a 30-year lease over a piece of land from the freeholder would be entitled to grant a sub-lease of less than 30 years to another party in respect of that piece of land. In this way, freehold and leasehold interests can exist simultaneously in relation to the same piece of land. The period of a leasehold ownership depends on the terms of the lease: it may vary from a very short period (e.g. six months) to a very long period (999 years is quite common). Upon termination of the lease, the interest in the land of the lessee (tenant) reverts to the owner of the freehold.

The main kinds of leasehold estate are as follows:

— *Tenancy for a term of years*: an estate of fixed term and certain duration determined by calendar reference. The period may be a stated number of days, weeks, months, or years.
— *Periodic tenancy*: a tenancy in which rent is payable at fixed intervals, usually weekly, monthly, quarterly, or yearly. The tenancy continues automatically from one period to another until terminated by NOTICE.

Co-ownership

Co-ownership occurs where two or more persons have simultaneous and concurrent rights, sharing the title, use, and enjoyment of the real property. There are two main forms of co-ownership: joint tenancy and tenancy in common.

Joint tenancy

Joint tenancy means ownership of land by two or more persons who have identical interests in the whole of the land. A joint tenancy can only arise when what is known as 'the four unities' are satisfied. These are:

3

1 *Possession:* each tenant must be entitled to possession at the same time, i.e. each has the right to occupy the property at the same time.

2 *Interest:* the estate or interest that each has in the land must be identical. It is not a joint tenancy if one party holds the freehold and another holds a lease.

3 *Title:* each tenant must have the same title to the land, i.e. their ownership must be traced from the same instrument (legal document granting ownership).

4 *Time:* each tenant's interest must vest and subsist for the same time. For example, if one party gained an interest over the land on 13 October 2002 and this was due to subsist until 12 October 2010, and the other party gained an interest in the land on 5 July 2003 and this was due to subsist until 16 May 2007, there would be no joint tenancy between them.

On the death of one of the tenants, his or her interest passes automatically to the surviving tenant(s). The last survivor becomes the sole and absolute owner. This is known as the 'right of survivorship'.

Tenancy in common

Tenancy in common means EQUITABLE OWNERSHIP, or ownership in equity, by two or more persons in equal or unequal undivided shares. Each co-owner may sell or dispose of his or her share by will and a share does not pass automatically by the right of survivorship on the death of a co-owner but forms part of that person's estate. In other words, one co-owner will not automatically inherit the share of another co-owner who has died. (For a description of the branch of law known as *equity*, ▶**see overleaf**.)

Severance

Severance legally ends a joint tenancy during the lifetime of one of the tenants. It can be done, for example, by mutual agreement of the joint tenants or by service of a written NOTICE OF SEVERANCE by one tenant upon the others. The consequence of severing a joint tenancy is to convert it into an equitable tenancy in common. This means that, instead of there being a joint tenancy under which the interest of one tenant passes to the surviving tenants on death, when the joint tenancy is severed each tenant owns an equal share in the property which can be passed by will or sold.

Interests in land other than estates

Other legal and equitable interests exist in land that are less than estates but are nonetheless valuable property interests. Common examples are:

— *Easements.* An easement is a right enjoyed by the owner of one piece of land (known as the dominant tenement) over an adjacent piece of land (known as the servient tenement). Easements survive changes of ownership of either piece of land and are therefore said to 'run with the land'. Examples of easements include rights of way across land, rights to lay pipes across land, rights to light. They should be distinguished from licences, which are not interests in land but merely rights granted to particular persons in respect of particular property for a particular time and can be revoked.

— *Profits à prendre.* A profit à prendre is the right to enter onto someone else's land to take the produce of the land, be it plants, minerals, wild animals and fish, or oil and gas. Profits à prendre may exist independently of other estates in land and there is no need for a dominant and a servient tenement.

— *Restrictive covenants.* A restrictive covenant is an agreement restricting the use of land that benefits one party (the covenantee) and burdens the other (the covenantor). It can require the holder of the burdened property to do something (e.g. a promise to maintain a boundary fence) or to refrain from doing something (e.g. not to use the property for commercial purposes). As with an easement, there must be a dominant and a servient tenement.

— *Mortgages.* A mortgage is an interest in property created as a form of security for a loan or payment of a debt and terminated on payment of the loan or debt. The borrower, who offers the security, is the mortgagor. The lender, who provides the money, is the mortgagee.

Equity

Equity is a specialized area of law. It does not mean natural justice, but was inspired by it. It is based on the ancient practice whereby if a litigant could not obtain satisfaction through the courts, he or she would apply to the king as 'the fountain of justice'.

Equity is a form of discretionary justice. It mainly applies to land law trusts and consists of a series of propositions – 'equity will not suffer a wrong to be without a remedy', 'equity follows the law', 'he who comes to equity will come with clean hands', 'equitable remedies are discretionary'. One can have, for example, an equitable lease permitting the occupation of a property upon the payment of rent to a landlord without having any written lease. The fact that there is no written lease does not affect one's rights in equity.

The role of the lawyer

The role of the lawyer in the granting of commercial leases varies according to whether he or she represents the *landlord* (the person or company granting a lease or tenancy) or the *tenant* (the person granted the lease).

Normally, the landlord prescribes the form of the lease. Therefore, the most important role of the landlord's lawyer is to draw up the lease. If the lawyer acts for the tenant, his / her role will be to review the lease, to ensure that its terms are not unduly prejudicial to the tenant's interests, and to advise the tenant as to any matters of importance contained in the drafting of the lease.

Once a draft lease has been produced, the role of both the landlord's and the tenant's lawyer is to advise their clients on the terms of the lease, to assist in negotiating and then drafting any alterations to the terms of the lease agreed between the parties, and to ensure that the lease is properly executed and completed.

The example correspondence

The letters set out in this unit trace the progress of the granting of a new lease by a client, who owns a number of commercial properties, to a new tenant.

3

Landlord instructing a solicitor to draw up a lease

In this letter, the client provides instructions to the solicitor to draw up a lease in respect of the property. Since the client and the solicitor have a long-standing professional relationship, the solicitor has a sound grasp of the client's business dealings and, in particular, the general terms on which the client grants leases to commercial tenants. Therefore, the client needs only to provide basic information to the solicitor. The lease proforma document to which Anna Bannister refers would include basic details necessary for drawing up the lease, including details of the tenant, property, rent, etc.

The Pemberton Estate

2 The Stables, Shadwell Court, Penzance TR18 6FT
telephone: +44 (0) 1736 56341, fax: +44 (0) 1736 56342
email: info@pembertonestate.org

YOUR REF. REP/PEM.1–12
OUR REF. AHB/LEA/SAE

10 October 20—

FAO Roger Ponsonby
Sandersons Solicitors
15 Tradescant Avenue
Penzance
TR18 7DP

Dear Roger

Lease of 2B Tanner's Yard

Further to our telephone conversation yesterday, please prepare a draft lease together with any necessary supporting documents in relation to the above property.

I enclose the lease proforma and plans. Please do not hesitate to contact me if you require any further information.

With best wishes

Anna Bannister

A. Bannister (Mrs)
Director

Enc.
1 Lease proforma
2 Plans

Sandersons Solicitors

15 Tradescant Avenue
Penzance
TR18 7DP
telephone: +44 (0) 1736 55897
fax: +44 (0) 1736 55898
email: info@sandersons.com

Your reference   AHB/LEA/SAE
Our reference   REP/PEM.1–12

24 October 20—

Mrs A. Bannister
The Pemberton Estate
2 The Stables
Shadwell Court
Penzance
TR18 6FT

Dear Anna

Lease of 2B Tanner's Yard

Thank you for your letter of 10 October 20—.

I have now prepared the draft lease, and this is enclosed. Please let me know if there are any amendments that need to be made prior to preparing the engrossment to be sent to the tenants.

Best wishes

Roger Ponsonby

Roger Ponsonby
Senior Partner

Enc. Draft lease

Sending a draft lease for approval

The solicitor draws up the draft lease and sends it to the client for approval. The reference to the ENGROSSMENT refers to the final version of the lease to be sent for signature by the parties.

Client confirming that the lease is approved

This very brief letter from the client to the solicitor confirms that the draft lease is approved. The phrase 'approved as drawn' means that no amendments are required to the original draft.

The Pemberton Estate

✳

2 The Stables, Shadwell Court, Penzance TR18 6FT
telephone: +44 (0) 1736 56341, fax: +44 (0) 1736 56342
email: info@pembertonestate.org

YOUR REF. REP/PEM.1–12
OUR REF. AHB/LEA/SAE
28 October 20—

FAO Roger Ponsonby
Sandersons Solicitors
15 Tradescant Avenue
Penzance
TR18 7DP

Dear Roger

Re: Lease of 2B Tanner's Yard

Thank you for your letter of 24 October. We confirm that the lease is approved as drawn – please send the draft to the tenant.

With best wishes

Anna Bannister

**A. Bannister (Mrs)
Director**

Sandersons Solicitors

Sending landlord's draft lease to tenant

The solicitor now sends the draft lease to the tenant for consideration.

15 Tradescant Avenue
Penzance
TR18 7DP
telephone: +44 (0) 1736 55897
fax: +44 (0) 1736 55898
email: info@sandersons.com

Your reference

Our reference   REP/PEM.1–12

28 October 20—

Mr H. Monk
Smith Audio Engineering Ltd
15 Redbridge Road
Penzance
TR18 2CZ

Dear Sir

Lease of 2B Tanner's Yard

We act for the Pemberton Estate regarding the letting of 2B Tanner's Yard.

We now enclose the draft lease and the plan for your approval. Provided you are happy with the lease as currently drawn, we will prepare fair copies to circulate to the parties for signature in order to be ready to complete once the refurbishment works are finished.

We look forward to hearing from you or from solicitors appointed to act on your behalf.

Yours faithfully

RogerPonsonby

**Roger Ponsonby
Senior Partner**

Enc.
1 Draft lease
2 Plan

1 When does the solicitor propose that completion takes place?

2 What does the solicitor ask the tenant to do?

3 Which words used in the letter have the same meaning as the following?
   a distribute
   b engrossed versions
   c repair and / or redecoration

Tenant's response concerning draft lease

In this letter, the tenant sets out various matters with which it cannot agree. It will therefore be necessary for there to be further negotiations about the precise terms of the lease, and for the plan of the plot to be clarified to all parties' satisfaction. Note the use of the phrase 'as per', meaning *in accordance with*.

Smith
Audio Engineering Ltd

15 Redbridge Road
Penzance
TR18 2CZ
telephone: +44 (0) 1736 58993
fax: +44 (0) 1736 58994
email: enq@smithaudio.co.uk

YOUR REF   REP/PEM.1–12
OUR REF   PEM/0123
11 November 20—

Mr R. Ponsonby
Sandersons Solicitors
15 Tradescant Avenue
Penzance, TR18 7DP

Dear Sir

Re: lease of 2B Tanner's Yard

Thank you for your letter of 28 October.

Unfortunately, we are unable to approve the draft lease in its current form, as we have discovered two matters which do not correspond with the agreement reached in our previous discussions with Pemberton Estate. These are as follows:

Clause 4 (Term of Lease) currently states, 'a term commencing on the date hereof and expiring on 31 March 2010.' This is incorrect: we agreed in discussions that the lease would expire two years later, on 31 March 2012.

Clause 5 (Annual Rent) currently states, 'a yearly rent of SEVEN THOUSAND POUNDS (£7,000.00).' Again, this is incorrect: we had agreed in discussions that the yearly rent would be £6,500 per annum.

These two matters are of course fundamental terms of the agreement. Therefore, unless clauses 4 and 5 are amended as outlined above, we regret that we will be unable to proceed to completion of the lease.

In addition, we would advise that the plan you have supplied is seriously defective in that the north boundary of the plot is incorrectly drawn. We have amended it by hand. Please redraw it as per our amendments.

Yours faithfully

Harold Monk

**Mr H. Monk
Managing Director**

Enc.
Amended plan

Questions

1 There are three words / phrases in the letter which all mean *per year*. Which are they?

2 When will the lease commence?

3 What importance does Smith Engineering attach to the amendment of clauses 4 and 5?

4 What is wrong with the plan?

Sandersons Solicitors

15 Tradescant Avenue
Penzance
TR18 7DP
telephone: +44 (0) 1736 55897
fax: +44 (0) 1736 55898
email: info@sandersons.com

Your reference   AHB/LEA/SAE
Our reference   REP/PEM.1–12

17 November 20—

Mrs A. Bannister
The Pemberton Estate
2 The Stables
Shadwell Court
Penzance
TR18 6FT

Dear Anna

Lease of 2B Tanner's Yard

I enclose a copy of a letter and reconstituted plan received from Mr Monk of Smith Audio Engineering, the contents of which are self-explanatory, and look forward to receiving your instructions.

Best wishes

Roger Ponsonby

Roger Ponsonby
Senior Partner

Solicitor seeking further instructions

In this letter, the solicitor seeks further instructions from the client. The phrase, 'the contents of which are self-explanatory' is a very handy one for lawyers to use when forwarding correspondence to their clients and requesting instructions on its contents.

Landlord instructing solicitor on amendments

The client provides instructions to the solicitor as to whether the changes to the lease proposed by the tenant are acceptable. It is clear from the content of this letter that to some extent the tenant's vigilance was justified.

The Pemberton Estate

2 The Stables, Shadwell Court, Penzance TR18 6FT
telephone: +44 (0) 1736 56341, fax: +44 (0) 1736 56342
email: info@pembertonestate.org

YOUR REF. REP/PEM.1–12
OUR REF. AHB/LEA/SAE
25 November 20—

FAO Roger Ponsonby
Sandersons Solicitors
15 Tradescant Avenue
Penzance
TR18 7DP

Dear Roger

Re: Lease of 2B Tanner's Yard

Thank you for your letter of 17 November.

I now enclose the reconstituted plan, and confirm that the mention of 2010 as opposed to 2012 as the date of expiration of the lease was a simple error.

As regards the rent, again there is a simple error here. However, we did not agree rent at £6,500 as claimed by Mr Monk. It is true that this figure was discussed at some point in our negotiations with him, but the ultimate agreement reached in fact was that the yearly rent would be £7,000 paid quarterly in advance, with a rent review to take place at two-yearly intervals commencing 31 March 2006.

With best wishes

Anna Bannister

A. Bannister (Mrs)
Director

Enc.
Reconstituted plan

1 How many times a year does Mrs Bannister suggest rent should be paid?

2 How many rent reviews will take place during the course of the lease?

3 What does Mrs Bannister say about the date of expiry of the lease?

Sandersons Solicitors

15 Tradescant Avenue
Penzance
TR18 7DP
telephone: +44 (0) 1736 55897
fax: +44 (0) 1736 55898
email: info@sandersons.com

Your reference   PEM/0123
Our reference   REP/PEM.1–12
2 December 20—

Mr H. Monk
Smith Audio Engineering Ltd
15 Redbridge Road
Penzance
TR18 2CZ

Dear Sir

Lease of 2B Tanner's Yard

Thank you for your letter of 11 November on which we have now had the opportunity of taking our client's instructions.

Our client confirms that the date of expiration of the lease should indeed be 31 March 2012 as opposed to 31 March 2010. We also enclose a copy of the reconstituted plan. Kindly confirm that this is accepted as drawn.

As regards the rent, our client does not accept that there was any agreement that the yearly rent should be £6,500. We are advised that the agreement reached orally was that the yearly rent would be £7,000 payable quarterly in advance, with a rent review to take place at two-yearly intervals commencing 31 March 2006.

Kindly confirm that this is accepted so that we can send you the amended lease for approval.

Yours faithfully

RogerPonsonby

Roger Ponsonby
Senior Partner

Enc.   Reconstituted plan

The purpose of this letter is to attempt to finalize negotiations between the parties. To this end, the solicitor adopts a slightly presumptive tone at times, designed to usher the tenant into agreement. For example, the phrase 'kindly confirm that this is accepted' is commonly used in such situations in preference to more open phrases such as 'please let us know whether you accept'.

Tenant accepting solicitor's proposals

In this letter the tenant confirms that the proposals set out in the solicitor's letter are accepted.

Smith

Audio Engineering Ltd

15 Redbridge Road
Penzance
TR18 2CZ
telephone: +44 (0) 1736 58993
fax: +44 (0) 1736 58994
email: enq@smithaudio.co.uk

YOUR REF REP/PEM.1–12
OUR REF PEM/0123
10 December 20—

Mr R Ponsonby
Sandersons Solicitors
15 Tradescant Avenue
Penzance
TR18 7DP

Dear Sir

Re: lease of 2B Tanner's Yard

Thank you for your letter of 2 December. We confirm that we accept the amended plan and approve the proposed alterations to the lease. We look forward to receiving the amended lease for execution.

Yours faithfully

Harold Monk

Mr H. Monk
Managing Director

Sandersons Solicitors

15 Tradescant Avenue
Penzance
TR18 7DP
telephone: +44 (0) 1736 55897
fax: +44 (0) 1736 55898
email: info@sandersons.com

Your reference   PEM/0123
Our reference   REP/PEM.1–12
14 December 20—

Mr H. Monk
Smith Audio Engineering Ltd
15 Redbridge Road
Penzance
TR18 2CZ

Dear Sir

Lease of 2B Tanner's Yard

Thank you for your letter of 2 December, the contents of which we are pleased to note.

We now enclose the amended engrossed lease for execution. Kindly return it to us when you have signed it and we will complete the lease when the premises are ready and the landlord has signed its part.

Yours faithfully

Roger Ponsonby

Roger Ponsonby
Senior Partner

Enc.
Engrossed lease

Solicitor forwarding final (engrossed) lease

In this letter the solicitor forwards the amended lease to the tenant for signature. In this letter, 'EXECUTION' means the signature of the contract.

Points to remember

1 When a lease is granted, freehold and leasehold interests may exist simultaneously in relation to the same piece of land. The person (or company) who owns the freehold is entitled to grant leases. This person is known as the *landlord* or *lessor*. The person who is granted the lease is known as the *tenant* or *lessee*.

2 The main role of the solicitor in granting commercial leases is to draft the lease itself, and then to negotiate any alterations that need to be made to it.

3 When drafting leases, attention to detail is of paramount importance. In particular, the lawyer should be careful to ensure that the manner in which the lease is to be terminated is precisely specified and workable in practice.

3

Company and commercial: company formation

4

4

BUSINESS FORMATS

Company and commercial law is a wide area of practice touching on all aspects of trade and commerce. This brief introduction deals solely with business formats, which include:

Sole proprietor

A sole proprietor is an individual who runs an unincorporated business – i.e. not a company (see below) – on his or her own. Generally, a sole proprietor of a commercial business is known as a SOLE TRADER, and a sole proprietor of a professional practice (such as a solicitor or an accountant) is known as a SOLE PRACTITIONER.

Partnership

A partnership is an association of two or more people (the partners) formed for the purpose of carrying on a business. Unlike an incorporated company, a partnership does not have LEGAL PERSONALITY of its own. This means that the partnership does not form a separate legal entitiy in its own right, as is the case, for example, with a company. The partners have JOINT AND SEVERAL LIABILITY, which means that in the event of a claim against the firm by a third party both the partnership as a whole and the individual partners can be sued.

Private limited company

A private limited company is one in which the liability of the members in respect of the company's debts is limited. In the most common scenario this means that it is limited by shares, in which case the liability of the members on a WINDING-UP – i.e. the company being liquidated by a court order – is limited to the amount unpaid on their shares. (This status is indicated by 'Ltd' after the company's name.)

Public limited company

A public limited company in England and Wales is one registered under the Companies Act 1980 as a public company. Its name must end with the initials 'PLC'. It must have an AUTHORIZED CAPITAL of at least £50,000 of which at least £12,500 must be paid up. This means that the par value of the shares to that value must have been paid in full.
The par – or nominal – value is the value given on the share certificate. It may be, for example, £1 or £2. This value, however, does not represent the true market value of the shares, which will vary according to how well the company is doing. A PLC may offer shares and securities to the public on the stock exchange. The regulation of such companies is stricter than that of private companies. Most public companies are converted from private companies under the re-registration procedure in the Companies Act 1985.

Definition of a company

A company is a body corporate. This means that it is regarded in law as being a LEGAL PERSON, distinct from its members.
The following consequences flow from this, so that the company:
— is able to own property.
— is liable for its own debts.
— can sue its DEBTORS.
— is liable to be sued by its CREDITORS.
— has 'perpetual succession': the company does not cease to exist just because a member (however many shares he or she may own) dies or otherwise ceases to be a member.

COMPANY FORMATION

The following are required to form a company:
— *A memorandum of association*. This document sets out details of the company's existence and contains basic information such as the company's name, the objects of the company, its address, and a statement of limited liability.

— *Articles of association*. This is a more substantive document which governs the running of the company and constitutes the contract between the company and its members. It deals with such matters as the voting rights of shareholders, the conduct of shareholders' and directors' meetings, the powers of management, and the appointment of directors.

Directors

By law, a limited public company must have a minimum of two directors, and a limited private company, one; there is no maximum. However, the members can fix different limits by ordinary resolution (see below). Directors are appointed to carry out the day-to-day management of the company. They owe FIDUCIARY duties to the company and a duty of care in negligence. Their formal responsibilities include:
— Presenting annually to members the accounts of the company and the directors' report.
— Keeping a register of directors, a register of directors' shareholdings, and a register of shares.
— Calling the Annual General Meeting.
— Sending all relevant documents to the Registrar of Companies. The Registrar of Companies is a governmental body based at Companies House in London, which has responsibility for controlling the formation and renewal of companies.
— Submitting a statement of affairs (which sets out the company's financial position) if the company is wound up.

Directors may be discharged from office on an ordinary resolution (see 'Meetings and resolutions', below) with special notice (28 days) at a general meeting.

The relevant documents must be sent to the Registrar of Companies together with the appropriate fee, and, provided the papers are in order, the Registrar will then issue a certificate of incorporation.

Shareholders

A shareholder is an owner of shares in a limited company. As such they are a member of the company and their name is entered in the register of members. The powers of a shareholder are not easy to define, but a majority shareholder may have extensive powers of control ultimately exercisable by removing or threatening to remove a director from office.

In terms of duties, a shareholder must not commit a 'fraud on the minority'. This might occur, for example, if a shareholder or shareholders caused the articles of association to be altered in such a way as to discriminate against some of the shareholders or prejudice their interests. In formal legal terms, the relationship between the member shareholders and the company is a contractual one. It is based on the memorandum and articles of association of the company. The rights of a shareholder of a company include:
— The right to a dividend once lawfully declared.
— The right to a share in surplus capital on a winding-up.
— The right to vote at meetings.
— The right to apply to the court in certain circumstances, for example where the company's affairs have been conducted in a way unfairly prejudicial to the members, or where the directors have breached their fiduciary duty.

Shares

A share in a company constitutes a CHOSE IN ACTION; in other words, a right that can be enforced by legal action. Shares are issued with a *par value* (also called nominal value). This provides a way of measuring one shareholder's interest against the interests of other shareholders.

As noted above (see 'Public limited company'), the true value of the shares will fluctuate according to the level of success that the company is enjoying. Shares are issued or allotted by directors to the extent of the

4

4

nominal capital of the company. The issuing of shares can only be carried out in a way authorized in the articles of association of the company or agreed at company general meetings.

In some cases, different classes of shares may be issued. For example, instead of ordinary shares a company might issue the following share types.

— *Preference shares*, which yield a fixed rate of interest rather than a variable dividend. In the event of liquidation they are paid off after debt capital but before ordinary share capital.

— *Cumulative preference shares* are a type of preference share. The company remains liable to pay dividends to holders of such shares if these are not paid in the current payment period (i.e. the dividends accumulate). Dividends on cumulative preferred shares are an obligation regardless of the earnings of the company.

— *Redeemable shares* are ordinary or preference shares that the issuing company has the right to redeem under terms specified on issue.

— A *golden share* is a class of share that entitles the holder to specified powers or rights generally exceeding those normally associated with the holder's ownership interest or representation.

— A *deferred ordinary share* is either 1) a type of ordinary share, formerly often issued to founder members of a company, in which dividends are only paid after all other types of ordinary share have been paid and often entitling their owner to a large share of the profit, or 2) a type of share on which little or no dividend is paid for a fixed number of years, after which it ranks with other ordinary shares for dividend.

— *Subscription shares* are the shares bought by the initial subscribers to a company.

— *Term shares* are shares that cannot be sold for a given period.

A transfer of shares may be made by means of a sale or a gift inter vivos (i.e. a gift made during an individual's lifetime, often for inheritance tax purposes). Directors have some rights to veto sales of shares in certain circumstances.

Once the share sale is agreed, the vendor must execute a stock transfer form and send it together with the SHARE CERTIFICATE to the purchaser, who must pay the STAMP DUTY.

Meetings and resolutions

The types of meeting at which all members of the company can attend include *extraordinary general meetings* and *annual general meetings*. The term *board meeting* simply refers to a private meeting of the directors of the company.

Business at *general meetings* is transacted by passing resolutions on the issues which need to be decided. There are various types of resolution, including ordinary, extraordinary, special, and elective. The type of resolution required depends upon the nature of the business being transacted.

An *ordinary resolution* is the most commonly used resolution. It requires a simple majority of votes cast to be in favour to be passed.

An *extraordinary resolution* and a *special resolution* both require a three-quarters majority. The notice periods in respect of these kinds of resolution vary from that required in respect of an ordinary resolution.

A special resolution is required in many circumstances, including resolutions to alter the articles or objects.

An extraordinary resolution is required in a small number of circumstances where it is considered that minority shareholders require protection but the matter is urgent. One example is where a resolution is passed to commence a voluntary winding-up as a result of the company's liabilities.

Notice of general meetings must be given to all the members. The length of notice period required will vary according to the nature of the meeting being called and the resolutions to be proposed at it. The notice must state the date, time, and place of the meeting, together with a description of the business to be transacted. This description must be sufficiently detailed for the members to be able to decide whether they wish to attend.

The role of the lawyer

As noted above, company and commercial law touches on many areas which often form complete areas of legal practice in themselves, for example, commercial property, employment law, litigation, intellectual property. Larger law firms generally have separate departments dealing with each of these areas. The role of the solicitor dealing with company and commercial law is to take a broad view of the client's business affairs and to identify the different kinds of legal issue that are likely to become relevant. Once identified, the detailed work required may be assigned to specialists.

In the area treated by this unit, the process of forming a company, the role of the solicitor may be broken down into three parts: advice, procedure, and drafting. The solicitor must:

— Advise the client as to 1) what business format will best suit the kind of business under discussion, and 2) any specific agreements, safeguards, and provisions that need to be put in place. For example, when a new company is formed it is often desirable to draw up a shareholders' agreement to protect the individual interests of the shareholders in the company.

— Carry out the procedural steps necessary to form and register the company. This involves drafting the memorandum, articles, and supporting paperwork, and submitting the application for registration. It is a fairly straightforward process, but requires attention to detail.

— Draft the specific agreements required in the circumstances of the particular type of business being incorporated. These may include shareholders' agreements, employment contracts, service agreements, or joint venture agreements.

The example correspondence

The letters that follow outline the steps taken by a solicitor on behalf of a client who wishes to form a limited company with a colleague. The company will be used to run a small gardening and landscaping business.

In the UK, the office of the Registrar of Companies is known as Companies House. It contains a register of all UK private and public companies, their directors, shareholders, and balance sheets. It is a legal requirement that companies provide all this information, which is then available for public inspection. A new company cannot validly exist until it has been registered at Companies House.

4

Summarizing the client's instructions

This is the first letter from the solicitor to the client following the initial client interview. In it the solicitor summarizes the instructions he / she has been given by the client, advises on relevant issues, and indicates the steps that need to be taken to process the matter.

4

Tavermouth & Co.
SOLICITORS

3 Sea Parade, Felixstowe, IP11 4AU
telephone: +44 (0) 1394 67445
fax: +44 (0) 1394 67446
email: info@tav&co.com

our ref MGH/GRE.1–1
your ref

June 20—

Mr B. Finchley
16 Anderton Crescent
Felixstowe IP11 2RM

Dear Brian

Greenfingers Ltd

Thank you for coming in to see me yesterday when you instructed me to assist in the formation of a limited company under the name Greenfingers.

I have now carried out a search at Companies House and confirm that the name Greenfingers is not currently registered. This means that you are free to use that name.

We discussed the particulars of the company, which will be as follows:
1 The objects of the company shall be the provision of gardening and landscaping services.
2 The authorized share capital will consist of 1,000 £1 shares.
3 Initially 100 shares will be issued: 51 to you and 49 to Graham Shorter.
4 You and Mr Shorter will be the company directors. You will need in due course to decide who is to act as company secretary.
5 The registered office will be 16 Anderton Crescent.

The next step is for me to draw up the memorandum and articles of association, then transfer the company to you, issue the shares, and appoint directors and a company secretary.

We also discussed the question of the shareholders' agreement. Briefly, this is an agreement between the shareholders (in this case, you and Mr Shorter) about how the company should be run. It is worth having, mainly because it can be used to protect your individual interests in the company in ways which cannot be achieved through the articles of association. We should consider this issue in more detail once the company is registered.

I enclose this firm's client care letter in duplicate. Kindly sign, date, and return the spare copy.

With best wishes

Mark Howells

Mark Howells
Partner

Enc. Client care letter in duplicate

1 What has the solicitor done to find out whether the name Greenfingers is currently registered?

2 What documents will the solicitor now draw up?

3 How much of the share capital will be issued to begin with?

4 Who will the shareholders be?

5 Why is a shareholders' agreement desirable?

Tavermouth & Co.
SOLICITORS

3 Sea Parade, Felixstowe, IP11 4AU
telephone: +44 (0) 1394 67445
fax: +44 (0) 1394 67446
email: info@tav&co.com

our ref   MGH/GRE.1–1
your ref

7 June 20—

Companies House
Crown Way
Maindy
Cardiff
CF1 3UZ

Dear Sirs

Greenfingers Ltd

We enclose the following:
1   Form 1 duly completed.
2   Form 12 duly completed.
3   Memorandum of association.
4   Articles of association duly subscribed and witnessed.
5   Cheque for £20 in respect of the registration fee made payable
    to Companies House.

Kindly register the incorporation of the company and send us the
Certificate of Incorporation.

Yours faithfully

Tavermouth & Co. Solicitors

Tavermouth & Co. Solicitors

**Letter from
solicitor to
Companies House**

The solicitor now
draws up the
memorandum and
articles of association
and completes the forms
necessary to finalize
the incorporation of the
company. Form 1 gives
details of the first
directors and secretary,
and details of the
registered office of the
company. Form 12 is a
declaration to the effect
that all statutory
requirements relevant
to registering the
company have been
complied with. To save
time, the company is
first registered by the
solicitors' firm, and
ownership is later
transferred to the
intended owners
▶ **See next letter**.

Solicitor to client on steps to be taken following company registration

In this letter, Mr Howells advises his client that the company has been registered, outlines the steps that still need to be taken, and summarizes the issues that should be dealt with in the shareholders' agreement.

4

Example letter

Tavermouth & Co.
SOLICITORS

3 Sea Parade, Felixstowe, IP11 4AU
telephone: +44 (0) 1394 67445
fax: +44 (0) 1394 67446
email: info@tav&co.com

our ref MGH/GRE.1–1
your ref

15 June 20—

Mr B. Finchley
16 Anderton Crescent
Felixstowe IP11 2RM

Dear Brian

Greenfingers Ltd

I am pleased to be able to confirm that the company has now been incorporated, and I enclose the certificate of incorporation. This should be kept in a safe place – it is in effect the company's birth certificate. If you lose it, a duplicate may be obtained from Companies House on payment of a fee.

Transfer of company

We now need to deal with the papers necessary to transfer the company to you. I enclose the forms that you will need to complete in order for you and Mr Shorter to be appointed as directors of the company. These are:

1 Form 88 (2): Return of Allotment of Shares
2 Form 287: Change of Address of Registered Office
3 Form 288a: Appointment of Director or Secretary

When returning the forms to me, please indicate who is going to act as company secretary. If you would prefer us to fill that role for the moment, that is no problem.

Shareholders' agreement

The main issues that need to be covered in the shareholders' agreement can be summarized as follows:
1 The right of each party to be appointed as director, and whether there are to be any further directors.

1

1 What does Mr Howells suggest regarding the possibility of one party carrying out work outside the business?

2 What does he suggest regarding the acquisition of major assets?

3 What words and phrases used in the letter mean the same as the following?
  a dismissal
  b constraint
  c stipulation
  d employees

2 A list of any matters that are not to be undertaken without mutual agreement, e.g. acquisitions or disposals of major assets, hiring and firing of expensive staff, or changing the nature of the business.

3 Any arrangements to be made concerning the financing of the business.

4 Provisions regarding the transfer of shares. In particular, we need to consider what would happen if one of you were to die while a shareholder.

5 Any restrictions to be imposed on either party if one or other of you ceases to work for the company.

6 Any restrictions to be imposed on either party while you are still working for the company. For example, you may wish there to be certain restrictions on either party carrying out work on his own account where that work ought to be undertaken through the company.

I suggest we have a meeting to go through these issues, and perhaps you would care to telephone my secretary to arrange a suitable appointment.

With best wishes

Mark Howells

Mark Howells
Partner

Enc.
1 Certificate of Incorporation
2 Form 88 (2): Return of Allotment of Shares
3 Form 287: Change of Address of Registered Office
4 Form 288a: Appointment of Director or Secretary

2

Company and commercial: company formation

**Sending in forms
with company
details to
Companies House**

4

Example letter

Tavermouth & Co.
SOLICITORS

3 Sea Parade, Felixstowe, IP11 4AU
telephone: +44 (0) 1394 67445
fax: +44 (0) 1394 67446
email: info@tav&co.com

our ref   MGH/GRE.1–1
your ref

20 June 20—

Companies House
Crown Way
Maindy
Cardiff
CF1 3UZ

Dear Sirs

Greenfingers Ltd

We enclose the following:

1   Two forms 288a (Appointment of Director or Secretary)
2   Two forms 288b (Resignation of Directors or Secretary)
3   Form 287 (Change of Address of Registered Office)
4   Two forms 88 (2) (Return of Allotment of shares)

Kindly update your records accordingly.

Yours faithfully

Tavermouth & Co. Solicitors

Tavermouth & Co. Solicitors

3 Sea Parade, Felixstowe, IP11 4AU
telephone: +44 (0) 1394 67445
fax: +44 (0) 1394 67446
email: info@tav&co.com

Tavermouth & Co.
SOLICITORS

our ref   MGH/GRE.1–1
your ref
22 June 20—

Mr B. Finchley
16 Anderton Crescent
Felixstowe IP11 2RM

Dear Brian

Greenfingers Ltd

Thank you for returning the forms duly completed. I confirm that the relevant paperwork has now been lodged with Companies House.

I now enclose the draft shareholders' agreement. The most important provisions are as follows:

Clause 2 contains a list of matters requiring the unanimous agreement of the shareholders. It covers sales of assets, changes to the nature of the business, contracts of employment, acquisitions, partnerships with other entities (e.g. joint ventures), and alterations to share capital.

Clause 4 obliges the parties to carry out all their work through the company and not to compete with the company under any circumstances.

Clause 5 contains restrictions on transferring shares to third parties without offering them to the other party first. Where there is disagreement about the sale price, this will be resolved on application to the company's auditors.

Clause 6 provides an option for one party to acquire the other's shares if the other dies. It provides the deceased party's estate with the right to purchase the shares. Disagreements on price are to be resolved as in clause 5.

Clause 8 sets out your rights to act as directors of the company. It provides that no further directors may be appointed without both of you agreeing.

Clause 10 contains a requirement that both of your signatures are required for cheques or authorization of other money transfers of a value over £1,000.

Perhaps you could let me know if the draft is acceptable to you. Please let me know if there are any matters on which you would like further advice.

With best wishes

Mark Howells

Mark Howells
Partner

Enc. Draft shareholders' agreement

To client regarding shareholders' agreement

In this letter the solicitor provides a commentary on the provisions of the shareholders' agreement which he has drafted. It is of paramount importance that the client fully understands the nature of the agreement, as it will have important consequences for the future running of the business and for the client's relationship with his / her business partner.

Questions

1 Are the shareholders allowed to sell their shares to outsiders?

2 Who can buy the shares if one of the shareholders dies?

3 What happens if one shareholder wants to buy shares from another and they are unable to agree on the price?

4 Can more directors be appointed in the future?

Advising client on finalization of incorporation

In this letter the solicitor confirms that all matters relating to the incorporation of the company have been completed. He summarizes the particulars of the company and provides advice about procedural requirements.

Tavermouth & Co.

SOLICITORS

3 Sea Parade, Felixstowe, IP11 4AU
telephone: +44 (0) 1394 67445
fax: +44 (0) 1394 67446
email: info@tav&co.com

our ref   MGH/GRE.1–1
your ref

2 July 20—

Mr B. Finchley
16 Anderton Crescent
Felixstowe IP11 2RM

Dear Brian

Greenfingers Ltd

I am pleased to confirm that all matters relating to the incorporation and transfer of Greenfingers Ltd have now been concluded in accordance with your instructions.

The particulars of the company can be summarized as follows:

1 Both you and Mr Shorter are directors of the company. You are also the company secretary.
2 The authorized share capital consists of 1,000 £1 shares.
3 100 ordinary £1 shares have been issued. You hold 51 £1 shares, and Mr Shorter holds 49 £1 shares.
4 The registered office is at 16 Anderton Crescent, Felixstowe.
5 The relevant registrations have been made at Companies House effecting these changes, and the statutory books have also been prepared.

Under the provisions of the Companies Act 1985 the statutory books must be kept at the registered office. Should I send them to you, or will you collect them from our office in person?

Please do not hesitate to contact me if you have any further queries.

With best wishes

Mark Howells

Mark Howells
Partner

1 What formal positions does Mr Finchley hold in the company?

2 Why must the statutory books be kept at the registered office?

3 Where are the statutory books now?

4 How much of the share capital remains unissued?

Points to remember

1 Company and commercial law involves many different areas of legal practice. The lawyer's role is often to identify the issues involved and to seek specialist advice where it is needed.

2 Company and commercial law involves a great deal of procedure and form-filling. This is not especially difficult but calls for close attention to detail.

3 The language of company and commercial law is also the language of business. The practitioner in this area needs to be familiar with business and commerce and the language of business and commerce. He or she needs to be able to adapt the language used to the needs of the client. However, this should not be taken too far. It is important to distinguish between business slang and appropriate legal terminology. A business executive might talk in terms of *bean counters* and *lunchtime engineering*, but a lawyer should stick to *accountants* and *bribery*.

The companion to the present volume – A. Ashley, *Oxford Handbook of Legal Correspondence*, Oxford University Press – may help readers gain familiarity with the language of business and commerce.

4

5

Employment: constructive dismissal

FRAMEWORK OF EMPLOYMENT LAW

Employment law governs the relations between the employer and the employee and the conditions under which work occurs. It is usual to distinguish between individual employment law, which is the law governing the relationship between employer and employee, and collective labour relations law, which is chiefly the law governing relationships between trade unions and employers. In this unit we deal only with the former.

In the UK and the US, labour relations are generally not as heavily regulated as in, for example, most continental European countries. Therefore, in those countries the relationship between the employer and the employee is governed largely by the terms of the employment contract which the parties have agreed.

However, the following principles are generally accepted in most spheres of employment:
— Discrimination is generally not permitted on the grounds of sex, race, disability, religious belief, sexual orientation, marital status, pregnancy, or membership of a trade union.
— All employees have certain STATUTORY RIGHTS, including entitlement to at least the national minimum wage (if applicable), equal opportunities, itemized pay statements, equal pay for like work, maternity rights and benefits, notice of termination of employment, a healthy and safe working environment, statutory sick pay, time off (vacation, public duties, maternity / paternity leave, trade union activities, etc.), protected rights on transfer of a business, and a written statement of terms and conditions of employment.

Employment contracts

Employment contracts may either be concluded for an indefinite period or on a fixed-term, short-term, or part-time basis. In most cases, employers that employ staff on fixed-term contracts are obliged to:

— Pay the same hourly and overtime rate as for permanent staff.
— Ensure that fixed-term employees are not treated less favourably than permanent staff with regard to sick or maternity pay, holiday and bonus entitlement, etc.
— Avoid discrimination over access to pension schemes.
— Avoid excluding fixed-term employees from training.
— Advise fixed-term employees of any available permanent positions within the business.

A typical employment contract will contain clauses dealing with the following:
— commencement and job title
— salary
— deductions
— hours of employment
— holiday
— sickness
— collective agreements
— pension
— termination
— confidentiality
— anti-competition
— disciplinary procedures
— notices
— staff handbook
— governing law
— data protection

Termination of employment contracts

Fixed-term contracts of employment expire without notice once the agreed period has finished. An employment contract for an indefinite period can be terminated by either party on giving the required period of notice. The notice period will usually be specified in the employment contract.

When redundancies are being considered, prior to giving notice to an employee the employer must consider whether the employee can be employed in another capacity in the organization, or whether he or she can be practically retrained to fill another position. In all cases the employee must be informed as soon as possible about the

5

impending redundancy and must be allowed to take time off to look for other employment.

An employee may be dismissed without notice if he or she is guilty of gross misconduct. What constitutes gross misconduct will vary from case to case, but typical examples include theft, damage to the employer's property, incapacity for work due to being under the influence of alcohol or illegal drugs, physical assault, and gross insubordination.

Wrongful dismissal

Wrongful dismissal refers to a situation where the employer has dismissed the employee in such a way as to breach the employment contract. It should be differentiated from unfair dismissal (see below).

Unfair dismissal

Unfair dismissal can be described as dismissal which is technically not in breach of the employment contract but which is illegal because it breaches the employee's statutory right not to be unfairly dismissed from work. Note that, generally speaking, unfair dismissal is regarded by employment tribunals as more serious than wrongful dismissal, and claimants are accordingly often awarded higher sums of money for unfair dismissal claims than for those in respect of wrongful dismissal. However, an employee must be employed for at least one year to qualify for the right to claim unfair dismissal, although rights do arise earlier where dismissal is for sex, race, or disability discrimination.

The role of the lawyer

In the field of employment law, the lawyer's role varies according to whether he or she is instructed by the employer or by the employee. The lawyer advises the employer on the relevant employment laws which govern what must be included in employment contracts, on the commencement and termination of employment contracts, and on the various duties laid on the employer during the currency of an employment contract (e.g. duties to consult with trade union representatives on changes in working practices, or employers' duties regarding safety in the work place). The lawyer may also assist an employer in drafting suitable employment contracts, and act for an employer in defending legal proceedings for unfair dismissal, discrimination, etc., and assisting in the negotiation of settlement of such disputes.

The lawyer can assist an employee by advising on the proposed terms of an employment contract, and in acting for an employee – including assisting in negotiating with the employer or, if necessary, taking proceedings before an employment tribunal – where the terms of an employment contract have been breached or where it appears that an employer has acted unlawfully in relation to an employee. Such cases may include, for example, when an employee has been dismissed unlawfully, or has been the victim of unlawful discrimination (e.g. on grounds of race, sex, or age), or where the employer has failed in their duty towards the employee – for example, in failing to provide a safe working environment or in failing to protect the employee against harassment in the workplace.

The example correspondence

The example letters that follow relate to a case of *constructive dismissal*. Constructive dismissal occurs when an employee leaves of their own accord, but because of the conduct of the employer. It occurs where in effect the employee has no choice but to resign. The employee must actually resign in order to be able to bring a claim for constructive dismissal. The circumstances in which an employee will be regarded as having been constructively dismissed vary from case to case. They may include, for example, situations in which an employee terminates a contract of employment because the employer has shown that they do not intend to be bound by some essential term of the contract. This may occur, for example, when an employer unilaterally varies the terms of an employment contract in such a way that the employee loses the position which he or she was hired to fill, and is demoted without good reason to a lesser position within the organization. Unscrupulous employers sometimes resort to such tactics because it is not possible simply to dismiss an employee from a position without good reason.

5

Solicitor seeking to avoid constructive dismissal of client

In this letter, the employee's solicitor states the nature of his client's grievance against his employer, that he was constructively dismissed, and outlines the client's legal remedies, with a view to encouraging Chem-Pro to reconsider their position.

Douglas Jarrold
Solicitors

1 Cannon Drive, Bournemouth, Dorset, BH1 9RU

telephone +44 (0) 1202 95673
fax +44 (0) 1202 95674
email enq@djarrold.co.uk

YOUR REF
OUR REF BHS/GRI.5–2
3 September 20—

STRICTLY PRIVATE & CONFIDENTIAL

Chem-Pro Group plc
1 Portsdown Drive
Salter Industrial Estate
Poole
Dorset
BH1 4AC

Dear Sirs

Our client: Ronald Griffiths

We are instructed by the above-named client in relation to his employment with your organization.

We are instructed that our client has been employed by your organization since 12 May 1999 as a Senior Sales Manager, and that he has recently been allocated, without consultation, to the position of Sales Representative, which effectively represents demotion within the organization.

We are instructed that our client was informed of the decision to move him to a new position during a meeting which took place on 28 August 20— with our client's supervisor Mr James Parker. Our client notes that there had been no previous criticism of his work – on the contrary, Mr Parker recently praised our client for the exceptional sales figures he had achieved during the second quarter of this year. Nor had any consultation taken place with our client prior to the company making its decision. We understand that a new position of Area Sales Manager has been created, for which our client, though eminently qualified to fill the position, was not invited to apply. We note that the position of Area Sales Manager has been awarded to an

1

1 How did Chem-Pro fill the position of Area Sales Manager?

2 What alternative position was Mr Griffiths offered?

3 What piece of evidence do Mr Griffiths' solicitors offer to show that Mr Griffiths' work was satisfactory?

4 What possible ways of settling the dispute do Mr Griffiths' solicitors mention?

5 Which words used in the letter are synonyms for the following?
   a transferred
   b role
   c given
   d suggestions

outside applicant and that there was no proper internal advertisement of the position. This of course amounts to discrimination.

In the light of the above, it is clear that our client's employment contract has been unilaterally varied in such a way that amounts to constructive dismissal. Our client would be fully entitled, therefore, to resign and bring a tribunal claim for constructive dismissal. We have advised him that he would stand excellent prospects of success before the Employment Tribunal.

Our client would, however, be prepared to attend a meeting with the Human Resources Department to explore alternative means by which this matter might be resolved. We look forward to hearing from you with your proposals in this regard.

Yours faithfully

Douglas Jarrold Solicitors

Douglas Jarrold Solicitors

c.c. Ronald Griffiths

2

Initial advice given by solicitor to employee

In this letter, the employee's solicitor summarizes advice given to the employee during an earlier meeting.

DOUGLAS JARROLD
Solicitors

1 Cannon Drive, Bournemouth, Dorset, BH1 9RU

telephone +44 (0) 1202 95673
fax +44 (0) 1202 95674
email enq@djarrold.co.uk

YOUR REF
OUR REF BHS/GRI.5–2

3 September 20—

Mr R. Griffiths
44 Tredwith Road
Bournemouth
Dorset
BH1 4AC

Dear Mr Griffiths

Your employment situation

I write further to our meeting on 1 September and now enclose a copy of the letter I have sent to Chem-Pro. I will contact you as soon as I receive a reply.

As previously discussed, my advice is that you have a valid claim for constructive dismissal in the light of Chem-Pro's conduct. In the event that it is not possible to negotiate this matter to a successful conclusion with Chem-Pro – i.e. leading to your reinstatement in a position that reflects your skills and experience – it would be open to you to bring proceedings before the Employment Tribunal with a view to securing compensation. My advice is that you would have excellent prospects of success with such a claim.

While writing, I enclose this firm's client care letter in duplicate. Please read this through carefully and then sign, date, and return the enclosed duplicate.

Yours sincerely

B. Smallwood

**Brian Smallwood
Partner**

c.c. Ronald Griffiths

Enc.
1 Copy of letter to Chem-Pro
2 Client care letter in duplicate

1 What advice does Brian Smallwood give to Mr Griffiths?

2 What does Brian Smallwood ask Mr Griffiths to do?

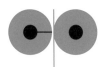

Chem-Pro Group PLC

1 Portsdown Drive • Salter Industrial Estate • Poole • Dorset • BH1 5 6KC

Telephone: +44 (0) 1202 94578 • Fax: +44 (0) 1202 94579 • Email: info@chem-pro.com

Your reference	BHS/GRI.5–2
Our reference	BRF/347Q

12 September 20—

Douglas Jarrold Solicitors
1 Cannon Drive
Bournemouth
Dorset
BH1 9RU

Dear Sirs

Re: Ronald Griffiths

Thank you for your letter of 3 September.

We cannot accept the interpretation you place upon the discussions held concerning Mr Griffiths' employment within this firm. It is clear that Mr Griffiths has simply misunderstood the position. The new position of Sales Representative which has been offered to him is not materially different from the position he has filled up to now. It is simply a proposal at this stage. In any case, if Mr Griffiths had a grievance regarding this matter, the proper procedure would have been for him to use our internal grievance procedure in the first instance.

As regards the new position of Area Sales Manager, at no stage did Mr Griffiths show any intention of applying for this position. Furthermore, this role required skills that he simply does not possess.

Yours faithfully

Barbara Furness

Ms B.R. Furness
Human Resources Co-ordinator

From employer's solicitor denying claims

In this letter, the employer forcefully denies the claims made by the employee's solicitor. The employer's aim is to use strenuous denial as a means of brushing aside these claims. By doing so, the employer is seeking to test the strength of the employee's will – if the employee persists with the claim, this is likely to force the employer to take a more conciliatory approach.

1 How do Chem-Pro justify moving Mr Griffiths to the post of Sales Representative?

2 What reasons do Chem-Pro give as to why Mr Griffiths would have been unable to fill the post of Area Sales Manager?

3 What do Chem-Pro suggest Mr Griffiths should have done?

Employee's solicitor seeking further instructions

The purpose of this letter is to seek instructions from the client on the claims made by the employer. The solicitor will wish particularly to clarify whether the client had any opportunity of applying for the position of Area Sales Manager, whether he was aware of this post requiring any special skills which he does not possess, and whether he was made aware of the internal grievance procedure which his employers state he should have used – all of these issues will have some bearing on the strength of the employee's possible claim.

5

Example letter

DOUGLAS JARROLD
Solicitors

1 Cannon Drive, Bournemouth, Dorset, BH1 9RU

telephone +44 (0) 1202 95673
fax +44 (0) 1202 95674
email enq@djarrold.co.uk

YOUR REF
OUR REF BHS/GRI.5–2
14 September 20—

Mr R. Griffiths
44 Tredwith Road
Bournemouth
Dorset
BH1 4AC

Dear Mr Griffiths

Your employment situation

I enclose a copy of a letter I have received from your employers. You will see that they strenuously deny the claims we have made – this is fairly standard tactics at this stage, and I remain confident that you have a valid claim to pursue.

However, I do need your instructions on the matters raised in the enclosed letter, in particular the following:

1 Did you have any opportunity of applying for the position of Area Sales Manager?
2 Were you aware of this post requiring any special skills which you do not possess?
3 Were you made aware of the firm's internal grievance procedure – and if so, at what stage?

I look forward to hearing from you.

Yours sincerely

B. Smallwood

Brian Smallwood
Partner

Douglas Jarrold
Solicitors

1 Cannon Drive, Bournemouth, Dorset, BH1 9RU

telephone +44 (0) 1202 95673
fax +44 (0) 1202 95674
email enq@djarrold.co.uk

YOUR REF   BRF/347Q

OUR REF   BHS/GRI.5–2

17 September 20—

Chem-Pro Group plc
1 Portsdown Drive
Salter Industrial Estate
Poole
Dorset, BH15 6KC

Dear Sirs

Our client: Ronald Griffiths

We thank you for your letter of 12 September, on which we have now had the opportunity of taking our client's instructions.

We are instructed that our client was not at any stage informed of the grievance procedure. Furthermore, our client's position clearly does not represent a 'misunderstanding' as you characterize it, but a serious and legitimate grievance.

You have failed to acknowledge that the position offered to our client is a demotion, as it undoubtedly is. Your contention that it is merely 'a proposal at this stage' is wholly untenable in the light of our client's instructions that the management team had already decided on the change before advising him of it: at his meeting with James Parker on 28 August, Mr Griffiths was explicitly told that his existing position would be lost and he would be assigned to a new position. He had no choice in the matter, and indeed was asked to sign off his new job description there and then at the meeting. In effect, he had to accept the new position or leave the company.

It is also quite absurd for you to allege that our client did not 'show any intention of' applying for the position of Area Sales Manager – this is hardly surprising given that he had no knowledge that such a post was going to be

1

Second letter from employee's solicitor to employer

In this letter the employee's solicitor responds to the letter sent by the employer, and states in full the employee's argument. The purpose of this letter is both to present the argument in full and at the same time to make it clear to the employer that the employee 'means business' – and that therefore it will not be possible simply to brush this claim aside. Consequently, the language used in the letter is assertive, bordering on aggressive, although of course just within the bounds of professional courtesy. To increase the pressure on the employer, the employee's solicitor sets a deadline within which the employer must provide constructive proposals, failing which EMPLOYMENT TRIBUNAL proceedings (i.e. a claim) will be issued.

Questions

1   What reason does the employee's solicitor give as to why Mr Griffiths did not apply for the post of Area Sales Manager?

2   Why does the employee's solicitor deny that moving Mr Griffiths to the post of Sales Representative is just 'a proposal at this stage'?

3   What does the employee's solicitor say are the legal consequences of forcing Mr Griffiths to accept the post of Sales Representative?

created until it had actually been filled by a candidate recruited from outside. Furthermore, it is clear that our client did indeed have the skills required for this position.

If our client has in fact been made redundant from the position of Senior Sales Manager, you have failed to acknowledge this. In the circumstances, the change of post forced upon our client must be treated as a fundamental breach of his employment contract, amounting to constructive dismissal.

In the circumstances, our client has no option but to resign and issue tribunal proceedings. We have instructions to issue proceedings if we do not receive from you concrete proposals for settlement of this matter within the course of the next 14 days.

Yours faithfully

Douglas Jarrold Solicitors

Douglas Jarrold Solicitors

c.c. Ronald Griffiths

2

5

Telephone attendance note

A note of a telephone consultation between the employee's solicitor and client. For a discussion of file notes including attendance notes,
▶ see pages 185–90

TELEPHONE ATTENDANCE NOTE

DATE: 22 September 20—
CLIENT: Ronald Griffiths
FILE: BHS/GRI.5–2
Re: **Employment claim**

BHS attending Mr Griffiths on the telephone. He reported that he had received a call from Barbara Furness, Head of Human Resources at Chem-Pro. Furness had acknowledged that 'some mistakes had been made' in the way this matter had been handled, and had suggested a meeting to try to reach settlement. This will take place tomorrow. Mr Griffiths will attend alone.

Engaged: 12 mins

Chem-Pro Group PLC

1 Portsdown Drive • Salter Industrial Estate • Poole • Dorset • BH15 6KC
Telephone: +44 (0) 1202 94578 • Fax: +44 (0) 1202 94579 • Email: info@chem-pro.com

Your reference	BHS/GRI.5–2
Our reference	BRF/347Q

27 September 20—

Douglas Jarrold Solicitors
1 Cannon Drive
Bournemouth
Dorset
BH1 9RU

Dear Sirs

Re: Ronald Griffiths

We write further in this matter.

As you may know, a meeting was held on 23 September between your client and myself. The outcome of this meeting is that this firm has agreed to acknowledge that your client was effectively made redundant by the changes to his job description. We are now in the process of negotiating Mr Griffiths' redundancy package, and trust that this concludes matters.

Yours faithfully

Barbara Furness

Ms B.R. Furness
Human Resources Co-ordinator

Employer acknowledges employee made redundant

In this letter, the employer explicitly acknowledges that Mr Griffiths was effectively made redundant by the changes to his job description – a positive result for Mr Griffiths and his lawyer.

Employment: constructive dismissal

5

Example letter

Points to remember

1 Employment law governs the relationship between the employer and employee and the conditions under which work occurs.

2 Constructive dismissal occurs when an employee terminates a contract of employment because the employer has shown that he or she does not intend to be bound by some essential term of the contract.

3 The role of the lawyer in this area of law varies according to whether he or she is acting for the employer or the employee. It may involve non-contentious work, such as drafting or reviewing employment contracts, or extend to litigation (for example, representing an employee or employer in relation to a case of unlawful dismissal).

5

Intellectual property:
Internet domain names

INTELLECTUAL PROPERTY

Intellectual property is the general name given to INTANGIBLE ASSETS which derive from creative effort. That is to say, property that does not have a physical existence. For example, while a book exists physically, the rights of the author in that book (copyright) do not. They are therefore said to be intangible.

Intellectual property includes patents, trademarks, industrial design, and confidential information, as well as copyright (property rights in literary, musical, artistic, photographic, and film works, and in maps and technical drawings). The different kinds of intellectual property are briefly described below.

Patents

A patent is the grant of an exclusive right to exploit an invention. In the UK patents are granted by the Patent Office. In order to be able to obtain a patent for an invention, the applicant must show that the invention to be patented is new, not obvious, and can be used for industrial purposes.

Patents may be acquired for processes as well as for machines and other devices. For example, the process by which Hovis bread is made has been patented. The application for a patent is often prepared by a PATENT AGENT. It is then submitted to the Patent Office, which makes the decision on whether to grant a patent. If the patent is granted, it remains legally valid for twenty years. This means that during that period the owner of the patent has a monopoly on the product or process patented.

The owner of the patent (the PATENTEE) may assign the patent to other people or companies, or grant licences to third parties to use it. If the patent is infringed by another party – for example, when the invention which has been patented is used without permission – the patentee is entitled to apply to the court for an INJUNCTION, DAMAGES, or an ACCOUNT OF PROFITS.

It is not possible to gain a patent for:
1) literary, dramatic, musical, or artistic work;
2) schemes, methods for performing a mental act, playing a game, or doing business;
3) computer programs; 4) inventions likely to encourage offensive, immoral, or antisocial behaviour; 5) biological processes for the production of animals or plants;
6) discoveries, scientific theories, or mathematical methods.

Trademarks

A trademark consists of a distinctive symbol (which may be three-dimensional) that identifies particular products of a trader to the general public. It may consist of a graphic device or words or a combination of the two. The Coca Cola lettering is an example of a trademark device. By registering a trademark in the UK, the registrant acquires the following rights: 1) the exclusive right to use that trademark for a period of ten years (the registration may be renewed when this period has ended); 2) the right to assign the trademark to third parties or, provided the Registrar's permission is obtained, allow others to use it; and 3) the right to sue anyone who uses the trademark without permission, or anyone who uses a mark which resembles the registered trademark to the extent that it is likely to be confused with it, for an injunction, damages, or account of profits.

A trademark may be lost if it loses its distinctiveness – i.e. if the product identity becomes generic.

The law on trademarks has similarities to that on PASSING OFF, which is available as a remedy if the trademark has not been registered . Passing off is open to more flexible remedy since matters other than the distinctiveness of the mark may be argued in court in respect of a passing off action. On the other hand, passing off depends on factors which may be vague and difficult to prove, whereas if a registered trademark exists it is a quick and easy process to produce evidence in support of this.

Registered designs

Registration of a design gives exclusive rights over the outward appearance of an article. 'Outward appearance' means its shape, configuration, pattern, or ornament. To be registered, a design must be 1) new, and 2) the design of an industrial product ('industrial' in this context means mass-produced). Designs which are primarily artistic rather than industrial in nature (e.g. sculptures) cannot be registered. A registered design must have 'eye appeal' – some aesthetic quality which may be judged by the eye. Eye appeal does not include features of shape dictated solely by the function of the object.

Registered designs are subject to STRICT LIABILITY in respect of infringement (but no damages may be claimed against an innocent infringer – i.e. someone who is not aware that he or she is infringing a registered design). Registration provides protection for five years. An extension can be applied for every five years up to twenty-five years.

Unregistered designs

Rights in a design arise automatically when an original design is recorded in a design document or an article has been made according to the design. A design includes any aspect of shape or configuration of the whole article or part of an article. The rights last fifteen years from the end of the year in which the design was created, or ten years from the end of the year in which the articles made to the design were sold, whichever is the less.

Such rights cannot include: 1) a method or principle of construction; 2) surface decoration (unregistered design rights are limited to three dimensions); 3) features of shape or configuration of an article which enable the article to be connected to or placed in, around, or against another article so that either article may perform its function ('must fit'); and 4) features of shape or configuration of an article which are dependent on the appearance of another article, of which the article is intended by the designer to form an integral part ('must match').

Confidential information

Breach of confidentiality is an equitable wrong (i.e. not necessarily dependent on any contract between the parties) and is based entirely upon case law. The 'test' for confidentiality was laid down in *Coco v A.N. Clark (Engineers) Ltd [1969] RPC 41*. The judge in that case said that in order for a court to find that a breach of confidentiality has taken place, the following elements must be present:

— The information must have the necessary quality of confidence about it. In other words, where it would be injurious to the owner and / or advantageous to a competitor if disseminated, and the owner of the information must believe it to be confidential / secret / not in the public domain.
— The information must have been given in circumstances which made it clear that there was an obligation of confidence.
— There must have been unauthorized use of that information to the detriment of the party communicating it.

Confidentiality can be protected by means of a CONFIDENTIALITY AGREEMENT. Legal remedies for breach of confidentiality include injunction, damages, account of profits, and delivery up or destruction of property.

Copyright

Copyright consists of the exclusive right to reproduce artistic, dramatic, literary, or musical works, which comes into existence at the time the work is produced. The right lasts for the author's lifetime plus seventy years from the end of the year in which the author died. Copyright can be assigned or transmitted on the death of the author (for example, in the author's will). Breach of copyright is sometimes known as PIRACY. The principal remedies for breach of copyright include injunction, damages, and account of profits.

In order to qualify for copyright protection, the work must be: 1) recorded, i.e. it must exist in a permanent form somewhere; 2) original, there is no need for it to be novel, but it must not be copied (e.g. translations of books into foreign languages have separate copyright); and 3) truly a 'work'. The meaning of this is that in order to gain copyright protection, the work cannot be something that is trivial. A shopping list, for example, is not copyrightable.

The author has moral rights in the work which consist of: 1) the right to be shown as the author of the work; 2) the right to object to 'derogatory treatment' of the work (this means that the author has the right to object if the work is treated in an insulting manner; for example, if an author has written a serious religious text which is then adapted into a frivolous theatrical performance); 3) the right to restrain false attribution of authorship of a work to a person who is not the author; and 4) the right to privacy. This might arise, for example, if photographs or films were commissioned for private and domestic use. In such cases, the photographs or films in question may not be issued to the public without the permission of the person who commissioned the photograph or film.

The role of the lawyer

Intellectual property may be the most valuable property that a company or an individual owns – it is often what gives them a competitive edge in the market. The lawyer's role is to help protect that intellectual property either by prevention or by cure.

As far as prevention is concerned, the lawyer can help ensure that employees and third parties are not able to make use of company intellectual property, by drawing up confidentiality agreements to be signed by employees, subcontractors, and other business partners, and by including appropriate secrecy clauses in employment and subcontractor contracts. The lawyer can also ensure that the company takes appropriate steps to apply for patents, and register trademarks and designs wherever this is viable, with a view to maximizing the protection afforded to the company.

As far as cure is concerned, the lawyer can assist a company or individual by actively defending a company's intellectual property rights after they have been infringed by a third party. In some cases, successful solutions can be achieved by correspondence and negotiation with the infringer (as in the correspondence below). In other cases, it may be necessary to initiate legal proceedings to obtain an injunction, damages, or an account of profits.

The example correspondence

The example letters below relate to Internet domain names. An established academic institution is in the process of registering trademarks to protect its name, and while doing so discovers that a company or private individual has already registered this name. The question that arises is whether the institution has rights over the name even though it is not registered.

The law on domain names can be divided into two areas. The first involves domain name piracy (often called 'cyber-squatting'). The second arises out of the 'first come, first served' principle. This principle is applied by the registries where one party has legitimately registered a domain name which is identical or similar to a registered trademark.

Cyber-squatters deliberately register domain names similar or identical to the trademark of another party with the intention of either selling / licensing them to the trademark owner or of using them for their own benefit by exploiting the goodwill of another company. The second category involves the registrant using a domain name identical or similar to a registered trademark of a third party.

The courts have held that in such cases of cyber-squatting, the ownership of the domain name in dispute will be transferred to the trademark owner. As to the second category, the general principle is that the domain name registrant has the right to the domain name unless such use constitutes trademark infringement.

6

Bell & Acton Solicitors

2 Randell Avenue
Oxford
OX2 2WQ
Telephone: +44 (0) 1865 46424
Fax: +44 (0) 1865 46425
Email: enq@b&a.co.uk

Tenbridge & Co. Solicitors
15 Henley Road
Oxford
OX4 2RT

Your reference
Our reference   SLW/LON.5–5
1 May 20—

Dear Sirs

London Institute

We refer to our telephone conversation this morning between our Sandra Wells and your Herman Volker.

As discussed, the difficulty about which the institute have consulted us concerns domain names. We understand that in the course of registering trademarks – e.g. 'London Institute' – our client discovered that a company has registered the domain name 'london-institute.com'. The issue that arises is whether the Institute has rights over this name by long-term use even though it has not registered it. Can the registration be challenged?

We look forward to hearing your preliminary thoughts as to what options our client has, the prospects of success, and the likely costs involved.

Yours faithfully

Bell & Acton Solicitors

Bell & Acton Solicitors

Solicitor seeking help from specialist firm

Solicitors Bell & Acton have decided that they lack the appropriate expertise in the specialized field of domain names to assist London Institute effectively. However, rather than sending an established client to another firm, the firm decides to instruct a specialist law firm to assist with the case as consultants. London Institute agrees to this course of action.

1   When did London Institute discover that the domain name 'london-institute.com' had been registered?

2   What possible arguments could London Institute use?

3   What information is requested from Tenbridge & Co?

Advising client of steps being taken

In this letter, the solicitor advises the client as to the steps being taken on the case and requests certain further information.

6

Bell & Acton Solicitors

2 Randell Avenue
Oxford
OX2 2WQ
Telephone: +44 (0) 1865 46424
Fax: +44 (0) 1865 46425
Email: enq@b&a.co.uk

FAO Michael Jarman
London Institute
College Road
Ealing
London
W5 7LH

Your reference
Our reference SLW/LON.5–5
1 May 20—

Dear Michael

Domain names

As previously discussed, this is a case that calls for in-depth knowledge of Internet law, which, as you will appreciate, is a relatively new and somewhat specialized field. It is therefore appropriate to seek advice from solicitors who specialize in this area, and to this end I have contacted a firm with whom we work regularly and asked them to outline your options. They will evaluate the institute's chances of success, the steps that should be taken, and the likely costs involved.

I will contact you again as soon as I have anything further to report. In the meantime, it would be helpful if you could let me know which trademarks have been registered thus far and in what jurisdictions.

With best wishes

Sandra Wells

Sandra Wells (Ms)
Partner

Advice letter from specialist firm

In this letter, Tenbridge & Co present their findings and advice on how to proceed.

Tenbridge & Co. Solicitors

15 Henley Road
Oxford
OX4 2RT

Telephone: +44 (0) 1865 42661
Fax: +44 (0) 1865 42662
Email: info@ten&co.com

Bell & Acton Solicitors   Our ref   HV/BEL.4–8
2 Randell Avenue   Your ref SLW/LON.5–5
Oxford   5 May 20—
OX2 2WQ

Dear Sirs

London Institute

Thank your for your letter of 1 May 20—. We have now established that the domain name 'london-institute.com' was registered by an individual called Roy Miller who has an email address at Bristol University.

We would suggest that it would be sensible to check what else Roy Miller has registered and whether he has been at any time the defendant in legal proceedings concerning domain names.

We could then consider in the first instance sending him a neutral email inviting him to discuss transfer of the domain name to London Institute. If this does not have the desired effect, we should write a letter before action. As regards the chances of success in any proceedings against Mr Miller, the general principle adopted by the courts is that the domain name registrant has the right to the domain name unless such use constitutes trademark infringement. Where the domain name is very close to the name of another institution – as it is in this case – the chances of success are high.

As to our fees, the cost of the initial action as outlined above will be £500 plus VAT. We enclose a copy of our standard terms and conditions in duplicate, and look forward to receiving your further instructions.

Yours faithfully

Tenbridge & Co. Solicitors

Tenbridge & Co. Solicitors

Enc. Terms and conditions in duplicate

1 Who has registered the domain name 'london-institute.com'?

2 What further inquiries do Tenbridge recommend making?

3 What will the action proposed by Tenbridge cost?

To client requesting further instructions

The solicitor relays the advice given by the specialist firm and asks for further instructions.

6

Bell
Acton
Solicitors
&

2 Randell Avenue
Oxford
OX2 2WQ
Telephone: +44 (0) 1865 46424
Fax: +44 (0) 1865 46425
Email: enq@b&a.co.uk

FAO Michael Jarman
London Institute
College Road
Ealing
London
W5 7LH

Your reference
Our reference   SLW/LON.5–5
7 May 20—

Dear Michael

Domain names

I write further to my letter of 1 May 20—, having now heard from the specialist firm which we have consulted on this matter.

It appears that the domain name 'london-institute.com' has been registered by an individual called Roy Miller who has an email address at Bristol University.

The advice I have received is that we should now check what else Roy Miller has registered and whether he has been at any time the defendant in legal proceedings concerning domain names.

Once this has been done, we could consider in the first instance sending him a neutral email inviting him to discuss transfer of the domain name to London Institute. If this does not have the desired effect, we should write a letter before action. As regards the chances of success in any proceedings against Mr Miller, the general principle adopted by the courts is that the domain name registrant has the right to the domain name unless such use constitutes trademark infringement. Where the domain name is very close to the name of another institution – as it is in this case – the chances of success are high.

The fees which our specialist advisers will charge for carrying out the work outlined above will be £500 plus VAT. Perhaps you could confirm whether the Institute is happy to proceed on these terms.

With best wishes

Sandra Wells

Sandra Wells (Ms)
Partner

Tenbridge & Co. Solicitors

15 Henley Road
Oxford
OX4 2RT

Telephone: +44 (0) 1865 42661
Fax: +44 (0) 1865 42662
Email: info@ten&co.com

Bell & Acton Solicitors
2 Randell Avenue
Oxford
OX2 2WQ

Our ref   HV/BEL.4–8
Your ref   SLW/LON.5–5

15 May 20—

Dear Sirs

London Institute

We have now carried out further searches and have established that
Mr Miller owns ten different combinations of 'london-institute.com'
preceded by the names of different towns in the UK. He is not involved in
any other domain name disputes.

On the basis of this rather small and select portfolio of domain names and
lack of involvement in other disputes, it is unlikely that Mr Miller is a
'cyber-squatter'. A cyber-squatter is someone who deliberately registers
domain names similar or identical to the trademark of another party with
the intention of either selling / licensing them to the trademark owner or of
using them for their own benefit by exploiting the goodwill of another
company.

In the event that Mr Miller is an innocent infringer, it may be that he
will be amenable to negotiation. We enclose a draft of a letter to him –
and we would be glad if you would let us know whether you are happy
for it to be sent out in its present form.

Yours faithfully

Tenbridge & Co. Solicitors

Tenbridge & Co. Solicitors

Enc.
Draft letter to prospective defendant

From specialist firm outlining further findings

Having received London Institute's confirmation that it is prepared to proceed on the terms outlined in Sandra Wells's letter, Bell & Acton instructs Tenbridge to carry out the work outlined in the correspondence above. Tenbridge now write outlining their further findings. The phrase 'exploiting the goodwill of another company' means to obtain financial advantage arising from the reputation of another company – for example, by posing as that company.

---

1   What facts have Tenbridge & Co. established?

2   Why do Tenbridge & Co. think that Mr Miller is not a cyber-squatter?

3   Why do they think Mr Miller might be prepared to negotiate?

4   What words used in the letter are synonyms for the following?
  a   controversy
  b   preliminary version
  c   intentionally
  d   profit from
  e   agreeable

Draft letter to owner of domain name

Here is the letter that Tenbridge & Co. propose to email to Mr Miller.

6

Tenbridge & Co. Solicitors

15 Henley Road
Oxford
OX4 2RT

Telephone: +44 (0)1865 42661
Fax: +44 (0)1865 42662
Email: info@ten&co.com

Our ref   HV/BEL.4–8
Your ref   SLW/LON.5–5
14 May 20—

Mr R. Miller
BY EMAIL

Dear Sir

London Institute

We act on behalf of the London Institute regarding protection and enforcement of its intellectual property rights in the UK. We are instructed to write to you regarding the registration of the domain name 'london-institute.com'.

As you may know, the London Institute is a world famous academic institution established in 1825. Its alumni include Sir Roger Peabody-Brown and Dame Elizabeth Robertson. Our client has therefore built up significant goodwill in its name, and this goodwill has developed into a proprietary right owned by our client. Your registration of the domain name 'london-institute.com' represents a clear infringement of that right, as a result of which our client would be fully entitled to bring legal proceedings against you.

The purpose of this letter is to find out whether you would be prepared to discuss the transfer of the domain name to our client. To this end, we look forward to hearing from you or from solicitors appointed to act on your behalf within the course of the next 14 days.

Yours faithfully

Tenbridge & Co. Solicitors

Tenbridge & Co. Solicitors

1 Match words or phrases used in the letter with the following definitions:
 a suit
 b ordered
 c former students
 d relating to ownership
 e the advantage arising from the reputation and trade connections of a business

2 What is the significance of mentioning the alumni of London Institute?

3 What do Tenbridge & Co. ask Mr Miller to do?

Bell & Acton Solicitors

2 Randell Avenue
Oxford
OX2 2WQ
Telephone: +44 (0) 1865 46424
Fax: +44 (0) 1865 46425
Email: enq@b&a.co.uk

FAO Michael Jarman
London Institute
College Road
Ealing
London
W5 7LH

Your reference
Our reference   SLW/LON.5–5
18 May 20—

To client forwarding draft letter

In this letter, Bell & Acton report to the client and forward the draft letter to the client for approval.

Intellectual property: Internet domain names

6

Example letter

Dear Michael

Domain names

I write further in this matter, having now received further information from our advisers.

It appears that Mr Miller owns ten different combinations of '-institute.com' preceded by the names of different towns in the UK. He is not involved in any other domain name disputes.

On the basis of this rather small and select portfolio of domain names and lack of involvement in other disputes, our advisers believe it unlikely that Mr Miller is a 'cyber-squatter'. A cyber-squatter is someone who deliberately registers domain names similar or identical to the trademark of another party with the intention of either selling / licensing them to the trademark owner or of using them for their own benefit by exploiting the goodwill of another company.

Due to this, it may be that he will be amenable to negotiation. Accordingly, I enclose a copy of the draft letter which it is suggested we send to Mr Miller. Perhaps you could let me know whether you are happy for it to be sent out.

With best wishes

Sandra Wells

Sandra Wells (Ms)
Partner

Enc.
Draft letter to prospective defendant

Specialist firm reporting response of prospective defendant

Having received London Institute's agreement to the draft letter being sent to Mr Miller, Tenbridge duly send the letter by email. Some days later, they receive a response which is duly reported to Bell & Acton.

Tenbridge & Co. Solicitors

15 Henley Road
Oxford
OX4 2RT

Telephone: +44 (0) 1865 42661
Fax: +44 (0) 1865 42662
Email: info@ten&co.com

Our ref   HV/BEL.4–8
Your ref   SLW/LON.5–5
           25 May 20—

Bell & Acton Solicitors
2 Randell Avenue
Oxford
OX2 2WQ

Dear Sirs

London Institute

We write further in this matter, and now enclose a copy of an email we have received from Mr Miller.

You will note that Miller indicates a basic willingness to transfer the domain name to your client provided 'appropriate compensation' – to use his phrase – can be agreed. He has disclosed his mobile number for the purpose of discussing the same, and invites calls after 11 a.m. on weekdays.

Since it is now simply a matter of agreeing a price, we imagine that you will now wish to deal with these negotiations yourselves, and accordingly enclose a note of this firm's charges. We thank you for your instructions; please do not hesitate to contact us if we can be of further assistance to you in relation to this or any other matter.

Yours faithfully

Tenbridge & Co. Solicitors

Tenbridge & Co. Solicitors

Enc.
1 Copy email
2 Invoice

1 What condition does Mr Miller set for the future transfer of the domain name?

2 How does Mr Miller want to be contacted?

3 Why do Tenbridge & Co. assume that Bell & Acton will wish to deal with the matter from now on?

Points to remember

1 Intellectual property law is a complex and fast-changing area. If a matter lies outside your expertise, engaging specialists on a consultancy basis is a good option.

2 Prevention is better than cure: the lawyer should ensure that the client makes full use of appropriate secrecy clauses in contracts, and registers all the rights which it is entitled to register.

3 Pay attention to new buzzwords and jargon used by the layperson (e.g. cyber-squatting). Differentiate them from formal terms (e.g. domain name piracy).

6

Breach of contract: possession proceedings

7

FORMATION AND USES OF CONTRACTS

Contracts have central importance in legal practice. They are the means by which all business deals are cemented between the parties. A contract is the agreement made between the parties. It specifies what the parties have agreed, the rights and duties of each party, and what will happen if things go wrong.

In Anglo-American legal systems, contracts may be made either in writing or orally. An oral contract is just as valid as a written one. However, in practice most important business contracts will be made in writing. In that way, the parties have clear written evidence of what they have agreed.

Most commercial contracts between companies relate to things that one company provides to the other for money. There are few limits to what may be bought or sold by means of a contract, but a contract to sell something which is illegal will be VOID (i.e. it cannot be enforced in law), as are gaming contracts (contracts for the purposes of gambling). The following are typical subjects of contracts:
— *Goods*: physical items such as machinery, food, books, computer software, furniture, vehicles.
— *Land*: rights over land are granted by contracts, typically leases.
— *Services*: intangible information-based products such as business consultancy, training, professional development, accountancy.
— *Rights*: many contracts between companies are about rights granted by one company to another. For example, franchising, licence agreements, distributorships. In such contracts, one company usually sells the other company a right to exploit its goods or services, and the reputation attached to those goods or services, for commercial gain.

STRUCTURE OF CONTRACTS

Most commercial contracts follow this structure:
— The *names and addresses* of the parties to the contract.
— *Recital*: this sets out the background to the contract. It usually explains why the parties have decided to form the contract and the purpose of the contract.
— *Definitions*: this sets out the meaning of certain terms used throughout the contract. For example, it might be agreed that a certain company will simply be referred to as 'the Company' throughout the contract. Or it might be agreed that the day on which the contract is to take effect is to be referred to in the contract as 'the Completion Date'.
— *Conditions precedent*: these are things which must be done before the contract can come into effect. For example, in a share sale a company might have to seek permission from the shareholders before the contract can go ahead.
— *Agreements*: the main terms of the contract which reflect the heart of the deal struck between the parties. They include such things as the amount and type of the items to be sold, the price at which they will be bought, billing, and the terms on which the sold items will be delivered.
— *Representations and warranties*: these include statements about the goods or services being sold which the parties are entitled to rely upon. The parties can claim DAMAGES (compensation) if a warranty is breached.
— *Boilerplate clauses*: these are clauses which are routinely inserted into many different kinds of contract. They relate to the way in which the contract works rather than the heart of the deal itself. They may include clauses dealing with SERVICE OF NOTICES (the means by which documents which relate to the contract must be sent) and ASSIGNMENT (whether and on what basis the parties can transfer the contract to other parties), together with many other types of clause.

7

— *Schedules*: If the contract contains certain very detailed agreements or information, the parties often prefer to put this in schedules which are contained at the end of the contract, instead of cluttering up the main part of the contract with a mass of detail. For example, if a contract must contain a very detailed price list for various kinds of goods sold under the contract, this is usually placed in a schedule.

— *Signature section*: the signature section usually appears at the end of the main part of the contract. The parties' names are usually printed together with the date of the contract, and the parties must then add their signatures to the contract. It is common practice for contracts to be produced in duplicate. This means that two copies of the contract are made – one for each party – and the parties each sign both copies of the contract.

— *Appendices*: these usually contain documents which are referred to in the contract. Unlike schedules, these may simply be put there because they are useful reference material for the parties. They don't necessarily need to be part of the substantive agreement between the parties. For example, in a contract for the sale of machine parts by one company to another, the appendices to the contract might contain detailed drawings or specifications for the machine parts.

PERFORMANCE OF CONTRACTS

The general rule is that a party must perform exactly what they undertook to do in the contract. Contracts may, however, be varied by mutual agreement. Alternatively, where a party agrees to a request of the other party to the contract not to insist on performance of part of the contract, that second party is said to have WAIVED his or her right to insist on performance in the manner originally agreed. The parties are then bound by the terms of the waiver and no consideration is necessary to support this. It is usual for the parties to agree that waivers should be in writing and appended to the original contract.

The terms of a contract may be divided into two categories: conditions and warranties.

— *Conditions* are *major terms*, those that are of the essence of the contract. Breach of a condition constitutes a fundamental breach of the contract and entitles the injured party to repudiate the contract.

— *Warranties* are *minor terms* of the contract, breach of which will entitle the innocent party to damages but not to repudiate the contract. Note, however, that in UK insurance law, a warranty has the same meaning as the definition of a condition given above.

Note also that the terms *condition* and *warranty* can be used in senses different from those indicated above. For example, a condition may refer to something that must be done before the contract can come into existence or for it to remain valid (e.g. 'It shall be a condition of this contract that the agent shall at all times hold a full driving licence'). A warranty may also be a form of guarantee by which a manufacturer specifies the extent to which it agrees to repair defective goods (e.g. 'The manufacturer warrants that the products shall be free from rust for seven years from the date of this contract').

In the USA, the term *warranty* covers both conditions and warranties.

The role of the lawyer

When a contract has been breached, the initial role of the lawyer is to ascertain the nature of the breach and advise the client on their legal rights and remedies. In some cases, as in the example letters below, it will be perfectly evident what the client's rights are. In other cases, the lawyer will have to present detailed argument and evidence to show that a breach has or has not occurred (depending on which party to the contract the lawyer is acting for).

Once it has been established that a breach of contract has occurred, the next question is whether the perpetrator of the breach can put matters right. If it is clear that this can be done, then it may be possible to resolve matters by negotiation through correspondence. For example, in the example letters below, the breach is non-payment of rent, and it is clear that this is something that the tenant can put right. If the breach of contract is not something that can be put right by the perpetrator, or if the perpetrator is unwilling to put matters right, then the only solution is for the lawyer to assist the client by bringing a claim in the civil courts in order to secure damages for the breach of contract.

The example correspondence

The letters that follow relate to a situation in which the tenant of leased commercial property has fallen so far in arrears with the payment of rent that the landlord has no option but to commence legal proceedings. Non-payment of rent is of course a fundamental breach of a lease agreement, and therefore the landlord is entitled to forfeit the agreement. The aim of the legal proceedings will be to regain possession of the property and obtain a money judgment against the tenant. The money judgment will secure repayment of the accrued arrears of rent.

7

Client to solicitor providing preliminary instructions

In this letter, the client (a landlord) provides preliminary instructions to the solicitor and encloses important documents which will be needed to support a claim.

The
Pemberton
Estate

2 The Stables, Shadwell Court, Penzance TR18 6FT
telephone: +44 (0) 1736 56341, fax: +44 (0) 1736 56342
email: info@pembertonestate.org

YOUR REF.

OUR REF.   AHB/LEA/TRE

10 March 20—

FAO Roger Ponsonby
Sandersons Solicitors
15 Tradescant Avenue
Penzance
TR18 7DP

Dear Roger

Re: Lease of 5A Barnhill Road

I write further to our discussions over the telephone yesterday, when I advised that the tenant of the above property, Tremaine Furnishings Ltd, is so far in arrears with the rent – despite frequent reminders and following broken promises of payment – that we now have no option but to commence possession proceedings.

I enclose a copy of the lease, a statement confirming the arrears of rent, and a copy of the memo confirming the recent increase in monthly rent.

I look forward to hearing from you.

Best wishes

Anna Bannister

Anna Bannister (Mrs)
Director

Enc.
1 Copy of lease
2 Statement of arrears
3 Memo confirming increase in monthly rent

Sandersons Solicitors

15 Tradescant Avenue
Penzance
TR18 7DP
telephone: +44 (0) 1736 55897
fax: +44 (0) 1736 55898
email: info@sandersons.com

Your reference	AHB/LEA/TRE
Our reference	REP/PEM.1–14
	14 March 20—

Mrs A. Bannister
The Pemberton Estate
2 The Stables
Shadwell Court
Penzance
TR18 6FT

Dear Anna

Lease of 5A Barnhill Road

Thank you for your letter of 10 March.

I should be grateful if you could forward to me the following further
information:

1 Copies of invoices referred to in the statement.
2 General rent statement showing the tenant's payment history since
   the lease began.
3 Any other documents confirming the increased rent.

I look forward to hearing from you.

Best wishes

Roger Ponsonby

Roger Ponsonby
Senior Partner

**Solicitor
requesting further
information
from client**

Having received
instructions and
documentation from
the client, the solicitor
must consider whether
he has everything
necessary to prove
the claim against the
tenant. He concludes
that certain pieces of
important information
are missing, and
accordingly requests
them.

Letter before action

The solicitor now writes a letter to the tenant advising that legal proceedings for forfeiture of the lease are about to be commenced. This is known as a LETTER BEFORE ACTION.

In view of the previous negotiations between the landlord and tenant, and the history of broken promises on the tenant's part, the solicitor does not waste time inviting the tenant to submit further proposals for settlement. In any case, there is nothing to prevent the tenant from putting forward proposals for settlement during the course of the legal proceedings.

Sandersons Solicitors

15 Tradescant Avenue
Penzance
TR18 7DP
telephone: +44 (0) 1736 55897
fax: +44 (0) 1736 55898
email: info@sandersons.com

Your reference

Our reference   REP/PEM.1–14

16 March 20—

Tremaine Furnishings Ltd
5A Barnhill Road
Penzance
TR18 5ZT

Dear Sirs

Lease of 5A Barnhill Road

Our client: The Pemberton Estate

We refer to previous correspondence from our client and confirm we are instructed to commence proceedings for forfeiture of the lease dated 31 April 1999.

Our client will seek possession of the premises and a judgment in respect of rent arrears and interest, together with costs.

If you are unsure of your position, we recommend that you seek independent legal advice.

Yours faithfully

Sandersons Solicitors

Sandersons Solicitors

1 When did the lease commence?

2 Who will pay Sandersons' fees if the Pemberton Estate is successful in its legal action against Tremaine Furnishings?

3 What do Sandersons recommend that Mr Tremaine does?

tremaine

MR G. TREMAINE

Tremaine Furnishings Ltd
5A Barnhill Road
Penzance
TR18 5ZT

📞 +44 (0) 1736 52338
🖨 +44 (0) 1736 52339
✉ info@tremfurnish.com

Your ref. REP/PEM.1–14

Our ref. PEM/LEASE

20 March 20—

Tenant seeking to delay proceedings

This is an example of a letter written purely for the purposes of buying time in the face of impending court proceedings.

Sandersons Solicitors
15 Tradescant Avenue
Penzance
TR18 7DP

Dear Sirs

Re: Lease of 5A Barnhill Road

Thank you for your letter of 16 March.

I would like to propose terms of settlement without the need for legal proceedings.

However, I will need to complete some financial calculations before writing again with specific proposals, and I would be grateful if you would delay issuing proceedings until you have heard again from me.

Yours faithfully

Gerald Tremaine

Mr G. Tremaine

Solicitor countering tenant's delaying tactics

The solicitor points out the obvious deficiencies in the proposal sent by the tenant. The aim here is to keep up the pressure on the tenant.

Sandersons Solicitors

15 Tradescant Avenue
Penzance
TR18 7DP
telephone: +44 (0) 1736 55897
fax: +44 (0) 1736 55898
email: info@sandersons.com

Your reference   PEM/LEASE
Our reference   REP/PEM.1–14

22 March 20—

Tremaine Furnishings Ltd
5A Barnhill Road
Penzance
TR18 5ZT

Dear Sirs

Lease of 5A Barnhill Road

Our client: The Pemberton Estate

Thank you for your letter of 20 March 20—.

You do not give any timescale within which we might expect to receive your proposals for settlement, nor do you give any indication of the nature of those proposals. There has been a prolonged history of rent arrears on your lease, during which our client has attempted to assist you by, for example, agreeing to accept payment on a quarterly basis.

In the circumstances, our client has no faith in your capacity or willingness to clear the arrears, and our instructions remain to issue proceedings.

Yours faithfully

Sandersons Solicitors

Sandersons Solicitors

1 What examples of assistance given by the landlord to the tenant do Sandersons cite?

2 What criticisms do Sandersons make about the tenant's proposal to offer proposals for settlement?

Sandersons Solicitors

15 Tradescant Avenue
Penzance
TR18 7DP
telephone: +44 (0) 1736 55897
fax: +44 (0) 1736 55898
email: info@sandersons.com

Your reference AHB/LEA/TRE
Our reference REP/PEM.1–14

24 March 20—

Mrs A. Bannister
The Pemberton Estate
2 The Stables
Shadwell Court
Penzance
TR18 6FT

Dear Anna

Lease of 5A Barnhill Road

I now enclose the draft particulars of claim for your consideration.
Please provide an up-to-date interest calculation for insertion into the
statement.

I also enclose copies of correspondence received from and sent to the tenant,
the contents of which are self-explanatory.

With best wishes

Roger Ponsonby

Roger Ponsonby
Senior Partner

Enc.
1 Draft particulars of claim
2 Copy correspondence

Solicitor forwarding particulars of claim for client's approval

This is the document which sets out the facts and arguments on which the client's claim is based.

7

Example letter

From client to solicitor regarding part-payment

In this letter, the client reports that a small part-payment has been received from the tenant. In the context of the scale of the outstanding arrears and the lack of any further proposals for payment, this is not sufficient to prevent legal proceedings from being issued. However, it does mean that the particulars of claim will need to be amended.

7

Example letter

The Pemberton Estate

2 The Stables, Shadwell Court, Penzance TR18 6FT
telephone: +44 (0) 1736 56341, fax: +44 (0) 1736 56342
email: info@pembertonestate.org

YOUR REF. REP/PEM.1–14
OUR REF. AHB/LEA/TRE
1 April 20—

FAO Roger Ponsonby
Sandersons Solicitors
15 Tradescant Avenue
Penzance
TR18 7DP

Dear Roger

Re: Lease of 5A Barnhill Road

I write to advise that we have now received a small part-payment in the sum of £4,000 from the tenant (against arrears of £30,000). However, we have not received any further proposals for the clearing of the arrears.

Kindly amend the particulars of claim and issue proceedings.

With best wishes

Anna Bannister

Anna Bannister (Mrs)
Director

Questions

1 Why will the particulars of claim need to be amended?

Sandersons Solicitors

15 Tradescant Avenue
Penzance
TR18 7DP
telephone: +44 (0) 1736 55897
fax: +44 (0) 1736 55898
email: info@sandersons.com

Your reference

Our reference REP/PEM.1–14

5 April 20—

Truro County Court
Courts of Justice
Edward Street
Truro
Cornwall
TR1 2PB

Dear Sirs

The Trustees of the Pemberton Estate v Tremaine Furnishings Ltd

We act for the Trustees of the Pemberton Estate and enclose the
following for issue:

1 Form N5 (Claim for Possession of Property)
2 Particulars of Claim with enclosures plus two copies for service
3 Issue fee of £120

Please issue the papers and serve the defendant in the usual way.

Yours faithfully

Sandersons Solicitors

Sandersons Solicitors

Solicitor sending documentation to county court

With this letter, the solicitor sends the documentation to the court for issue. This is the first step in the possession proceedings. The court will now open a file for the case, and serve the defendant with sealed copies of the claim.

From solicitor to client regarding court hearing

In this letter, the solicitor confirms that the proceedings have been issued and that a date for a preliminary court hearing has been set. The solicitor also advises that a member of staff at the office of the Pemberton Estate will need to make a statement in support of the claim and should be prepared to attend court if necessary.

Sandersons Solicitors

15 Tradescant Avenue
Penzance
TR18 7DP
telephone: +44 (0) 1736 55897
fax: +44 (0) 1736 55898
email: info@sandersons.com

Your reference   AHB/LEA/TRE
Our reference   REP/PEM.1–14

12 April 20—

Mrs A. Bannister
The Pemberton Estate
2 The Stables
Shadwell Court
Penzance
TR18 6FT

Dear Anna

Lease of 5A Barnhill Road

I write to confirm that the court has now issued proceedings and set a date for an initial hearing at 10 a.m. on 5 May 20—.

We will need to prepare a statement in support of the claim. You would be the most appropriate person to provide this statement in view of the fact that you conduct the estate's dealings with Mr Tremaine over this matter. It is desirable that you attend court on 5 May if no agreement is reached with Mr Tremaine in the meantime.

I will check with you before the hearing as to whether any further payments have been received.

Best wishes

Roger Ponsonby

Roger Ponsonby
Senior Partner

tremaine

MR G. TREMAINE

Tremaine Furnishings Ltd
5A Barnhill Road
Penzance
TR18 5ZT

📞 +44 (0) 1736 52338
🖨 +44 (0) 1736 52339
✉ info@tremfurnish.com

Your ref. REP/PEM.1–14
Our ref. PEM/LEASE

16 April 20—

Sandersons Solicitors
15 Tradescant Avenue
Penzance
TR18 7DP

Dear Sirs

Re: lease of 5A Barnhill Road

I write further in this matter, and am now in a position to put forward proposals for settlement. As a token of my good faith, I enclose a cheque in the sum of £5,000.

My proposal is to pay double rent for the next three months, and then make three payments of £5,000, which will clear the arrears within six months.

I would like to clarify that my recent difficulties with paying the rent have been entirely the fault of difficult business conditions. Business is now improving markedly. However, I would stress that I will only be able to make these payments if a possession order is not made, and therefore my potential to earn income to clear the arrears is not destroyed.

I look forward to hearing from you on this proposal.

Yours faithfully

Gerald Tremaine

Mr G. Tremaine

Enc.
Cheque

From tenant detailing proposals for settlement

In this letter, the tenant finally produces some concrete proposals for settlement. These will have a significant bearing on the way in which the landlord approaches the proceedings, as the subsequent letter from the solicitor to the landlord shows.

---

1 How does Mr Tremaine seek to establish his good faith?

2 To what does Mr Tremaine attribute his failure to pay the rent recently?

3 What argument does he put forward to the effect that a possession order would be counter-productive to the landlord's interests?

Solicitor to landlord advising on tenant's proposals

In this letter, the solicitor provides advice to the client in the light of the offer received from the tenant. He points out that the court will be unwilling to make an outright possession order given that the tenant has now made clear and concrete proposals for settlement, and suggests an alternative solution.

7

Example letter

Sandersons Solicitors

15 Tradescant Avenue
Penzance
TR18 7DP
telephone: +44 (0) 1736 55897
fax: +44 (0) 1736 55898
email: info@sandersons.com

Mrs A. Bannister
The Pemberton Estate
2 The Stables
Shadwell Court
Penzance
TR18 6FT

Your reference   AHB/LEA/TRE
Our reference   REP/PEM.1–14

20 April 20—

Dear Anna

Lease of 5A Barnhill Road

I have now received a letter from Mr Tremaine (copy enclosed) in which he offers to clear the arrears within six months.

The court is likely to be sympathetic to this proposal. The judge would balance the long history of arrears against the offer to clear the arrears within a relatively short period of time. The argument Mr Tremaine raises that he would lose his potential to earn income if an outright possession order were made would also be likely to prove persuasive. It is highly unlikely that the court would be prepared to make an outright possession order.

I suggest the correct approach would be to request an order for possession suspended on terms that Mr Tremaine must comply with the provisions of his proposed schedule of repayments. If such an order were made, and Tremaine subsequently defaulted, you would be able to ask the court bailiff to enforce the order without further notice. Tremaine would then have to apply to the court again to suspend the bailiff's warrant.

I enclose your statement for signature and look forward to hearing whether you are prepared to accept a suspended order as outlined above.

Best wishes

Roger Ponsonby

Roger Ponsonby
Senior Partner

Enc.   1 Copy letter   2 Statement

1 What factors does the solicitor believe the court will take into account when deciding what order to make?

2 What kind of order does the solicitor suggest should be sought?

3 How would such an order work in practice?

Sandersons Solicitors

15 Tradescant Avenue
Penzance
TR18 7DP
telephone: +44 (0) 1736 55897
fax: +44 (0) 1736 55898
email: info@sandersons.com

Solicitor to tenant regarding payment proposals

In this letter, the solicitor indicates to the tenant that his proposals are accepted. Note the forcefulness and clarity with which the solicitor points out the consequences of non-compliance with the order that the landlord is seeking.

Tremaine Furnishings Ltd
5A Barnhill Road
Penzance
TR18 5ZT

Your reference AHB/LEA/TRE

Our reference REP/PEM.1–14

20 April 20—

Dear Sirs

Lease of 5A Barnhill Road

Our client: The Pemberton Estate

Thank you for your letter of 16 April 20—, on which we have now had the opportunity of taking our client's instructions.

Our clients are prepared to accept your offer on the basis that they will be seeking a suspended order for possession. They will also be seeking costs.

We now enclose a draft order. As you will see this gives our client possession of the property but suspends it provided the payments set out in the order are made. If an order in these terms were made by the court, it would mean that if any of the payments specified in the order were not made, our client would be entitled to instruct bailiffs to recover possession of the property without further notice to you.

Conversely, if all the payments are made in accordance with the order, the claim will eventually be dismissed.

We propose to ask the court to make an order in the terms of the enclosed draft at the hearing on 5 May 20—. Kindly confirm that you are in agreement with this course of action.

Yours faithfully

Sandersons Solicitors

Sandersons Solicitors

Enc. Draft order

1 What will happen if the tenant does not keep up the payments specified in the proposed order?

2 What will happen if the tenant does keep up the payments specified in the proposed order?

3 What will the solicitor be asking the court to do?

Letter to court enclosing statement and schedule of costs

It is necessary for the claimant to file with the court and serve upon the defendant any witness statements which will be used in the court proceedings. The court also requires a statement of the legal costs incurred in working on the case. This is of particular importance in circumstances where – as in this case – the defendant is likely to have to pay the costs. In making an award for costs, the court will assess whether the costs are reasonable and may reduce them if appropriate.

Sandersons Solicitors

15 Tradescant Avenue
Penzance
TR18 7DP
telephone: +44 (0) 1736 55897
fax: +44 (0) 1736 55898
email: info@sandersons.com

Your reference

Our reference REP/PEM.1–14

28 April 20—

Truro County Court
Courts of Justice
Edward Street
Truro
Cornwall
TR1 2PB

Dear Sirs

The Trustees of the Pemberton Estate v Tremaine Furnishings Ltd

Case No: 17578/20—

We enclose the witness statement of Anna Bannister together with the schedule of our client's costs in readiness for the hearing on 5 May 20—.

Yours faithfully

Sandersons Solicitors

Sandersons Solicitors

Enc.
1 Witness statement of Anna Bannister
2 Schedule of costs

Sandersons Solicitors

15 Tradescant Avenue
Penzance
TR18 7DP
telephone: +44 (0) 1736 55897
fax: +44 (0) 1736 55898
email: info@sandersons.com

Your reference	PEM/LEASE
Our reference	REP/PEM.1–14
	24 April 20—

Tremaine Furnishings Ltd
5A Barnhill Road
Penzance
TR18 5ZT

Dear Sirs

Lease of 5A Barnhill Road
Our client: The Pemberton Estate

We enclose by way of service upon you the witness statement of Anna
Bannister in readiness for the hearing on 5 May 20—.

Yours faithfully

Sandersons Solicitors

Sandersons Solicitors

Enc.
Witness statement of Anna Bannister

From solicitor to tenant serving court documents

In addition to filing the witness statement and schedule of costs with the court, the solicitor must also serve these documents upon the defendant.

Breach of contract: possession proceedings

7

Example letter

7

Sandersons Solicitors

15 Tradescant Avenue
Penzance
TR18 7DP
telephone: +44 (0) 1736 55897
fax: +44 (0) 1736 55898
email: info@sandersons.com

Your reference AHB/LEA/TRE
Our reference REP/PEM.1–14

6 May 20—

Mrs A. Bannister
The Pemberton Estate
2 The Stables
Shadwell Court
Penzance
TR18 6FT

Dear Anna

Lease of 5A Barnhill Road

I confirm that I attended court yesterday for the hearing of the repossession proceedings in relation to this property.

The district judge made an order in the terms of the draft order we had prepared, and allowed our costs without deduction.

I will forward a sealed copy of the order to you as soon as I receive it from the court.

With best wishes

Roger Ponsonby

Roger Ponsonby
Senior Partner

1 Did the judge allow all the costs claimed by the Pemberton Estate?

2 What does the solicitor promise to do next?

Points to remember

1 The landlord's right to sue the tenant for non-payment of rent is based on breach of contract. Since non-payment of rent is a breach of a major term, the landlord is entitled to claim the unpaid rent plus interest.

2 Where a breach of contract can be remedied, it is preferable to try to negotiate settlement both before and during legal proceedings. The threat of legal proceedings acts as a spur to the defendant to remedy the breach of contract.

3 If a claimant succeeds in a court action against a defendant, it is usual for the defendant to have to pay the claimant's legal costs incurred in pursuing the case.

4 The court may be entitled to impose suspended orders in cases of non-payment of rent. Where a suspended order is made, the landlord cannot regain possession of the property provided the tenant makes the payments specified in the order.

7

Negligence claims: occupier's liability

NEGLIGENCE CLAIMS

Torts

Negligence is a tort, which is defined as:

> a wrongful act or omission for which damages can be obtained in a civil court by the person wronged, other than a wrong that is only a breach of contract (Oxford Dictionary of Law)

The law of tort brings together different areas of law which have in common that each gives rise to civil causes of action outside the law of contract. It is beyond the scope of this book to describe these in any detail, but they include the following:

1 Negligent interference with personal, proprietary, and economic interests (the tort of negligence).

2 Damage to interests in economic relations, business and trading interests (deceit, passing off, interference with contractual relations, conspiracy, and intimidation).

3 Damage to interests in intellectual property (copyright, patents).

4 Intentional invasion of personal and proprietary interests (interference with goods, trespass).

5 Infringement of further personal and proprietorial interests (nuisance; rule in *Rylands v Fletcher*; strict liability for injuries caused by defective and dangerous goods – from EU law).

6 Damage to reputation of individuals (defamation: libel and slander).

Negligence

The law of tort is mainly concerned with providing compensation for personal injury and property damage caused by negligence. Negligence has been defined as carelessness amounting to the culpable breach of a duty, giving rise to a right of action. The modern law of negligence stems from Lord Atkin's dicta in *Donoghue v Stevenson (1932)*:

> *The rule that you are to love your neighbour becomes in law, you must not injure your neighbour; and the lawyer's question, who is my neighbour? receives a restricted reply. You must take reasonable care to avoid acts or omissions which you can reasonably foresee would be likely to injure your neighbour. Who, then, is my neighbour? The answer seems to be – persons who are so closely and directly affected by my act that I ought reasonably to have them in contemplation as being so affected when I am directing my mind to the acts or omissions which are called in question.*

Accordingly, to succeed in a negligence claim usually involves being able to answer 'yes' to the following questions:
— Was there a duty of care?
— Has that duty been breached?
— Has damage been caused as a result?

In evaluating a claim, the court will look at a number of issues, including 1) whether the defendant owed a duty of care to the claimant, 2) whether it was reasonably foreseeable that the defendant's actions or omissions would lead to the harm suffered by the claimant, 3) whether there is a direct chain of causation between the negligent act and the damage caused, and 4) whether it is reasonable in all the circumstances to impose a duty of care.

The test of foreseeability is not what the defendant actually foresaw happening, but what a reasonable person could have been expected to foresee. The reasonable person – traditionally the 'reasonable man' – refers to the idea that where the court is trying to establish whether a duty of care has been breached in a negligence case, it will consider what an ordinary person might be expected to do considering the circumstances and the foreseeable consequences.

Damages

Damages is the name given to a sum of money awarded by the court for harm suffered by the claimant through either a breach of contract or a tort.

8

8

The purpose of damages in all tort cases is to put the claimant in the position he or she would have been if the tort had not been committed. *Recovery* is limited by the rules of remoteness of damage, and the plaintiff is under a duty to take all reasonable steps to *mitigate* the losses suffered.

Certain factors can either constitute a defence to a negligence claim or operate to reduce the amount of damages the claimant can recover. These include:

1 *Contributory negligence* on the part of the claimant – where the claimant's carelessness contributes to the damage suffered.

2 *Volenti non fit injuria* – where the claimant has consented to the risk prior to the incident occurring, i.e. had full knowledge of the risk and gave full and free consent.

Negligence claims arise in many different forms. Among the more common are: personal injury, damage to property, professional negligence, medical negligence, and occupier's liability.

Personal injury

Personal injury claims are probably the most common area of legal practice in which the doctrine of negligence is used. These claims arise where the defendant physically injures the claimant.

A claimant in a personal injury case seeks redress through damages. These fall into two categories:
— *General damages* are awarded for a loss that cannot be precisely estimated (e.g. for pain and suffering).
— *Special damages* are awarded for losses that can be quantified (e.g. loss of earnings).

The role of the lawyer

The role of the solicitors in a personal injury claim is largely adversarial. That is to say, they must seek to prove the case being fought by putting forward evidence in support of the contentions being made. The claimant's solicitor must first force the defendant to admit to being at fault, and then proceed to extract as much compensation as possible. On the other hand, the defendant's solicitor must seek to protect the defendant from liability where possible, and to limit the amount of compensation the defendant will have to pay where it is not feasible to deny liability.

In order to achieve this, the lawyer must first be capable of taking a realistic view of the client's chances of success, calmly identifying and weighing the weak and strong points of the case. All the available evidence must be gathered, and the relevant law researched and reviewed, before a realistic assessment of the strength of the case can be carried out. Once it is clear that the client has a good case, the lawyer must act as a forceful advocate on the client's behalf. To begin with, this will involve arguing the client's case clearly and persuasively in correspondence with a view to achieving settlement without the need for court proceedings. In the event that the prospective defendant is prepared to admit liability, the process then becomes one of bargaining. The lawyer must try to achieve as good a settlement as possible on the client's behalf, but must also be prepared to negotiate and to compromise where necessary.

If it is not possible to resolve matters through correspondence, it will be necessary to institute court proceedings. One of the key features of civil litigation (of all kinds) is the emphasis on procedure. Once court proceedings have been initiated, it is not sufficient for the lawyer merely to have a strong grip on the merits of the client's case and the arguments that support it. The lawyer must also be well organized, efficient, and have a thorough knowledge of the intricacies of court procedure. It is possible to lose a strong case purely on procedural grounds – for example, by missing deadlines for the institution of proceedings, the filing of evidence, and so on. The lawyer must ensure that all time limits under the Civil Procedure Rules for the taking of procedural steps in the processing of a claim are complied with – no easy matter when one bears in mind that a busy lawyer may have dozens of cases on the go at the same time. The key to success in this area is to have a foolproof diary system in which all important landmark dates and deadlines are logged in such a way that reminders will be produced automatically in good time before the relevant date or deadline arrives. The advent of advanced computer systems makes it much easier for the lawyer to establish an effective system – but equally, and for the same reason, the courts today are much less tolerant of missed deadlines than used to be the case.

In civil litigation it is usual for a successful claimant's legal fees to be paid by the defendant. In certain categories of cases, including personal injury claims, a solicitor may offer a CONDITIONAL FEE AGREEMENT, which must be in writing. The essence of these arrangements is that the client does not have to pay the solicitor any fees for carrying out the work. Of course, if the client fails to succeed in his or her claim, the solicitor loses out as well as the client, but if the claim succeeds, the lawyer is entitled to charge a higher fee ('no win, no fee'). It is therefore crucial that the solicitor accurately assesses the strength of the case at the outset.

The example correspondence

The letters that follow relate to a minor personal injury claim in which an elderly woman slipped on some yoghurt left on the floor of a supermarket, suffering minor injuries as a result. Such incidents, of course, happen frequently.

Supermarket owners have a duty of care towards persons using the supermarket to ensure that it is a reasonably safe and hazard-free environment. This means that the supermarket owners must take all reasonable steps in their power to ensure that hazards (such as spilt yoghurt) do not present themselves. Much hangs on the word 'reasonable' – it may not be enough simply for a claimant to prove that he or she slipped on something in the store and suffered injury as a result, if the supermarket can show that it had nevertheless taken 'reasonable' steps to prevent this happening.

Consequently, the solicitor must use all available evidence to press the case on the client's behalf, with a view to demonstrating that 'reasonable' steps have not been taken. Often in such cases, the defendant will start by trying to brush the claim aside, but if this tactic does not succeed the defendant may be prepared to come to terms fairly swiftly. The reason for this is that the value of the compensation involved in such cases is generally minor when weighed against the possible financial consequences of the adverse publicity that might be created if the claimant took the matter to court and won.

The case in these example letters concerns occupier's liability. Originally regulated by common law rules, this area is now largely governed by two statutes: the Occupier's Liability Act 1957 and the Occupier's Liability Act 1984. The 1957 act lays down rules about the duty of occupiers towards people who come on to their land or premises with permission; it applies in this case. The 1984 act sets out duties owed to those who enter without permission – i.e. trespassers. Negligence plays a large role in determining the liability of the occupier (the supermarket), since the main question to be determined is whether the supermarket had a duty of care towards Mrs Walker.

8

Advice letter to client

This is the first letter from the solicitor to the client following the initial client interview. In this case, since the client is rather elderly and unsophisticated, the solicitor explains matters at greater length and with more care than might be the case, for example, in a letter sent to a business client. Note the rather homely tone that the solicitor adopts at times, and the clear way in which the letter is divided into different sections.

Spandy, Harewood & Jagger Solicitors
23–25 Hills Road
Reading
RG1 9AX

telephone: +44 (0) 118 87332
fax: +44 (0) 118 87333
email: enq@sh&j.co.uk

Our ref.   MDL/WAL.5–1
Your ref.   —
3 February 20—

Mrs J.B. Walker
15A Railway Terrace
Tilehurst
Reading
RG31 6GJ

Dear Mrs Walker

Re: Your personal injury claim

I write further to our meeting yesterday when we discussed your accident in Gamleys Supermarket on 10 November last year.

Your instructions

You told me that you were in the supermarket picking up one or two things for dinner. You walked around the corner from the cheese display into the bakery aisle and slipped on something on the floor. This later turned out to be yoghurt. You fell and your right arm got painfully caught in the basket you were carrying. The basket wrapped itself around your arm as you fell.

A member of staff then came to help you up, and you later gave a statement to another member of staff, who asked how the accident had happened. However, due to the shock and pain you were experiencing, you signed the statement without reading it. You experienced significant pain in your right arm and shoulder, and this did not improve overnight. Therefore, you went to see your doctor, who referred you to the hospital for physiotherapy and put you on a course of painkillers. X-rays taken at the hospital showed that you had sustained damage to your arm and shoulder muscles.

The physiotherapy treatment is now finished, and you believe that you are about 75% recovered but continue to experience pain when raising your right arm above your shoulder – for example, when hanging out the washing.

You work as a cleaner at Fortmead School, and were off work as a result of the accident for six weeks. You were also unable to play bowls, your main hobby, during that period.

1

1 What medical treatment did Mrs Walker receive after her accident?

2 Who will be responsible for Mrs Walker's legal fees if she loses the case?

3 What opinion does the solicitor give about the amount of compensation Mrs Walker might receive?

4 What other sums might Mrs Walker be able to claim apart from compensation for the suffering caused by her accident?

My advice

In order for us to succeed in a claim against the supermarket, we must prove that the inspection system used by the supermarket was inadequate and that your accident happened as a result of this. To prove this we will need to obtain the inspection records from the supermarket to see whether the checks were carried out on a regular basis, as they should have been.

It is impossible at the moment to be sure about how much money you would get if we succeed. This depends to a great extent on the nature of your injuries, whether you make a good recovery, and whether you have suffered any permanent damage. We will need in due course to obtain a medical report to clarify these matters. If your claim succeeds, you will also be able to claim the cost of expenses incurred as a result of your accident – e.g. travel expenses, costs of medical prescriptions – in addition to obtaining a sum of money compensating you for the suffering caused by the accident. You would also be entitled to claim for any earnings lost as a result of the accident.

Conditional fee arrangement

If you are successful, our costs will be paid by the losing party (i.e. the owners of the supermarket). If, on the other hand, you lose, you will not have to pay our costs and we would not be able to recover any monies for work carried out.

If you win, we will be entitled to charge you what is known as a 'success fee'. This is a percentage of the costs that we obtain from the other side. It reflects the financial risk taken in pursuing the case on your behalf on this basis.

If you agree with this arrangement, we shall offer a written agreement for you to sign.

The next step

I will now write to the supermarket to obtain the accident book entry, cleaning records and the statement you signed. I will be in touch again shortly, but in the meantime if you have any questions please do not hesitate to contact me.

Yours sincerely

Marie Long

Marie Long (Ms)
Partner

2

To prospective defendant stating nature of claim

This is the first letter to the prospective defendant – the owners of the supermarket in which Mrs Walker's accident occurred. This letter is used to state the nature of the claim and why the supermarket is liable, and also to obtain evidence necessary to prove the claim.

8

Spandy, Harewood & Jagger Solicitors
23–25 Hills Road
Reading
RG1 9AX

telephone: +44 (0) 118 87332
fax: +44 (0) 118 87333
email: enq@sh&j.co.uk

Our ref.   MDL/WAL.5–1
Your ref.   —
3 February 20—

Gamleys Supermarkets plc
10–15 The Groves
Bracknell
Berks
RG42 4PN

Dear Sirs

Our client: Mrs Julie Belinda Walker
Accident in Reading store on 10 November 20—

We are instructed by the above-named client in relation to an accident that took place in your store on 10 November 20—.

We are instructed that the circumstances of the accident were that our client was in the store picking up one or two things for dinner, when she walked around the corner from the cheese display into the bakery aisle and slipped on something on the floor. This later turned out to be yoghurt. She fell and her right arm became entangled in the shopping basket she was carrying, which wrapped itself around her arm as she fell.

A member of staff attended at the scene of the accident and our client later gave a statement to another member of staff, but since she was in some pain and shock at the time, signed it without having read it. She was then told that the substance she had slipped on was yoghurt.

Our client experienced significant pain in her right arm and shoulder following the accident, and this did not improve overnight. Therefore, she went to see her doctor, who referred her to the hospital for physiotherapy and put her on a course of painkillers. X-rays taken at the hospital showed that she had sustained damage to her arm and shoulder muscles. The treatment is now finished, and our client is 75% recovered but is unlikely to recover 100% movement.

1

1 What legislation is cited to support Mrs Walker's claim?

2 What conclusions does Mrs Walker's solicitor draw from the circumstances of Mrs Walker's accident?

3 What part of the letter is pure speculation on the solicitor's part, and why?

4 Which words used in the letter have the same meaning as the following?
a regain
b recreation
c genuine
d ameliorate

As a result of the accident our client was off work for six weeks and was unable to play bowls, which is her main hobby, during that period.

As you know, under the Occupier's Liability Act 1957 you have a duty to use reasonable care to ensure that the shop floor is kept reasonably safe and clear of spillages. The circumstances of our client's accident flow from a clear failure to do so. It follows that our client has a valid claim in negligence against you.

In order that we can advise our client further, please provide:

1 Accident book entry.
2 Cleaning records for the date of our client's accident.
3 A copy of the store's policy for cleaning the shop floor.
4 The statement signed by our client.

Please also provide details of your insurers.

We look forward to hearing from you.

Yours faithfully

Spandy, Harewood & Jagger Solicitors

Spandy, Harewood & Jagger Solicitors

2

From prospective defendant playing for time

In this letter, the supermarket avoids dealing with the question of liability and also fails to provide the information requested. The letter confines itself to administrative details.

GAMLEYS

Gamleys Supermarkets plc
Customer Relations Department

10–15 The Groves
Bracknell RG42 4PN
Berkshire
telephone: +44 (0) 1344 23660
fax: +44 (0) 1344 23661
email: custrel@gamleys.co.uk

Our ref TL/CL00424

Your ref MDL/WAL.5–1

10 February 20—

Spandy, Harewood & Jagger Solicitors
23–25 Hills Road
Reading
RG1 9AX

Dear Sirs

Re: Mrs Julie Belinda Walker
Accident in Reading store on 10 November 20—

We confirm receipt of your letter dated 3 February 20—.

Our insurers are Branksome Ltd of 1 Tandley Drive, Solihull, W Midlands.

We are required under the Social Security (Recovery of Benefits) Act 1997 to inform the Compensation Recovery Unit (CRU) of the Department of Works & Pensions about your client's claim. We therefore require the following information:

1 Your client's National Insurance number.
2 Your client's date of birth.
3 Details of the nature and extent of your client's injuries.

Yours faithfully

Trina López

Ms Trina López
Manager

Spandy, Harewood & Jagger Solicitors
23–25 Hills Road
Reading
RG1 9AX

telephone: +44 (0) 118 87332
fax: +44 (0) 118 87333
email: enq@sh&j.co.uk

Our ref.   MDL/WAL.5–1
Your ref. TL/CL00424
12 February 20—

Gamleys Supermarkets plc
10–15 The Groves
Bracknell
Berks
RG42 4PN

Dear Sirs

Our client: Mrs Julie Belinda Walker
Accident in Reading store on 10 November 20—

Thank you for your letter. We enclose the information you have requested.

We look forward to receiving the information requested in our letter of 3 February 20—.

Yours faithfully

Spandy, Harewood & Jagger Solicitors

Spandy, Harewood & Jagger Solicitors

Enc.
Information sheet

To prospective defendant renewing request for information

Having not received the information requested, Mrs Walker's solicitors renew their request while also providing the information requested by the supermarket.

From prospective defendant denying liability

In this letter, the supermarket finally provides the information requested, and also attempts to brush aside the claim that Mrs Walker is making. There are obvious weaknesses in the argument made by the supermarket in this letter. The solicitor will study this letter carefully and separate clear statements of fact from unsupported assertions. The latter will then be attacked and exposed.

8

Example letter

GAMLEYS

Gamleys Supermarkets plc
Customer Relations Department

10–15 The Groves
Bracknell RG42 4PN
Berkshire
telephone: +44 (0) 1344 23660
fax: +44 (0) 1344 23661
email: custrel@gamleys.co.uk

Our ref   TL/CL00424

Your ref   MDL/WAL.5–1

20 February 20—

Spandy, Harewood & Jagger Solicitors
23–25 Hills Road
Reading
RG1 9AX

Dear Sirs

Re: Mrs Julie Belinda Walker
Accident in Reading store on 10 November 20—

Thank you for your letter of 12 February 20—.

We now enclose the documents you have requested.

We would advise that our cleaning system is that once a day the whole store is thoroughly cleaned by contract cleaners, and during peak hours a member of staff is on site touring round the store and spot-cleaning where necessary. In addition, all staff are trained to be vigilant and to deal immediately with any spillages discovered.

We are advised by the store management that a member of staff would have been working in the area where the incident happened. Some customers may cause a spillage and fail to report it to staff for their immediate attention. The offending yoghurt could only have been spilled moments before your client slipped on it.

Therefore, we regret that we cannot accept liability in this case.

Yours faithfully

Trina López

Ms Trina López
Manager

Enc.
1 Copy accident book entry
2 Copy cleaning records
3 Copy store cleaning policy
4 Copy statement of Julie Belinda Walker

1 How often is the store cleaned?

2 There are two unsupported assertions in the letter. What are they?

3 What is the supermarket's conclusion about Mrs Walker's claim?

Spandy, Harewood & Jagger Solicitors
23–25 Hills Road
Reading
RG1 9AX

telephone: +44 (0) 118 87332
fax: +44 (0) 118 87333
email: enq@sh&j.co.uk

Our ref.   MDL/WAL.5–1
Your ref.   TL/CL00424
25 February 20—

Gamleys Supermarkets plc
10–15 The Groves
Bracknell
Berks
 RG42 4PN

Dear Sirs

Our client: Mrs Julie Belinda Walker
Accident in Reading store on 10 November 20—

Thank you for your letter of 20 February 20—.

You have failed to specify when the particular aisle where our client fell was cleaned, nor have you provided evidence showing that a member of staff was actually on duty at the time as you state.

In addition, you have produced no evidence to support your assertion that the yoghurt could only have been dropped minutes before our client fell. We would draw your attention to the case of *Ward v Tesco Stores (1975)* in which it was held that it is the defendant's responsibility to give an explanation to show that the accident had not arisen from want of care on their part, and that in the absence of such explanation the judge was entitled to conclude that the accident occurred because the defendant had failed to take reasonable care.

Yours faithfully

Spandy, Harewood & Jagger Solicitors

Spandy, Harewood & Jagger Solicitors

To prospective defendant rejecting denial of liability

In this letter, the solicitor attacks the prospective defendant's denial of liability by exposing its failure to produce evidence to support its assertions, and by citing case law which supports Mrs Walker's claim.

To client advising on progress

In this letter, the solicitor reports to the client on progress made with the case so far.

Spandy, Harewood & Jagger Solicitors
23–25 Hills Road
Reading
RG1 9AX

telephone: +44 (0) 118 87332
fax: +44 (0) 118 87333
email: enq@sh&j.co.uk

Our ref. MDL/WAL.5–1
Your ref.

25 February 20—

Mrs J.B. Walker
15A Railway Terrace
Tilehurst
Reading
RG31 6GJ

Dear Mrs Walker

Re: Your personal injury claim

I write further in this matter, and now enclose a copy of a letter recently received from the supermarket, together with a copy of my reply. Briefly, if the supermarket cannot show that proper and adequate checks were made, we should be able to prove negligence.

What I would expect to happen next is that the supermarket will hand the matter over to solicitors to deal with. I will let you know as soon as I hear anything further.

Yours sincerely

Marie Long

Marie Long (Ms)
Partner

Enc. 2 × copy letters

Proctor & Peel Solicitors

The Station House
The Cuttings
Bracknell
RG42 2FR

telephone: +44 (0) 1344 26745
fax: +44 (0) 1344 26746
email: info@p&p.com

our reference GAM/TL/CL00424
your reference MDL/WAL.5–1
10 March 20—

Spandy, Harewood & Jagger Solicitors
23–25 Hills Road
Reading
RG1 9AX

Dear Sirs

Re: Mrs Julie Belinda Walker
Accident in Reading store on 10 November 20—

We write to advise that this matter has been referred to us. All further correspondence should be sent to the above address.

We can confirm that we have now completed our investigations into this matter, and liability is admitted.

Yours faithfully

Proctor & Peel Solicitors

Proctor & Peel Solicitors

From prospective defendant's solicitors admitting liability

This letter is of critical importance. In it the prospective defendant admits liability for Mrs Walker's accident. In effect, therefore, the supermarket admits that it will have to pay compensation. The remaining question is how much compensation should be paid. Although liability is no longer disputed, Mrs Walker is still entitled to take legal proceedings if a reasonable amount of compensation is not offered. The next stage is to put together the evidence that will support her claim for compensation and then to negotiate settlement.

8

Example letter

To client confirming that liability is admitted

In this letter, the solicitor advises that liability is admitted and outlines the next step that needs to be taken.

8

Spandy, Harewood & Jagger Solicitors
23–25 Hills Road
Reading
RG1 9AX

telephone: +44 (0) 118 87332
fax: +44 (0) 118 87333
email: enq@sh&j.co.uk

Our ref. MDL/WAL.5–1
Your ref.

12 March 20—

Mrs J.B. Walker
15A Railway Terrace
Tilehurst
Reading
RG31 6GJ

Dear Mrs Walker

Re: Your personal injury claim

I enclose a copy of a letter received from solicitors appointed to act for Gamleys Supermarkets and am pleased to be able to confirm that Gamleys have admitted responsibility for your injuries.

We now need to obtain medical evidence to support your claim, and I would be grateful if you would telephone my secretary to make an appointment to come in and see me.

Yours sincerely

Marie Long

Marie Long (Ms)
Partner

Enc.
Letter from Proctor & Peel

Spandy, Harewood & Jagger Solicitors
23–25 Hills Road
Reading
RG1 9AX

telephone: +44 (0) 118 87332
fax: +44 (0) 118 87333
email: enq@sh&j.co.uk

Our ref.   MDL/WAL.5–1
Your ref.

12 March 20—

Medical Records Department
Lakemead Hospital
Crowley Drive
Reading
RG1 8NP

Dear Sirs

Re: Mrs Julia Belinda Walker
Date of birth: 23.7.41
Address: 15A Railway Terrace, Tilehurst, Reading

We act for the above-named client who is pursuing a personal injury claim, and enclose a signed form of authorization.

Please provide a full set of our client's medical notes.

Yours faithfully

Spandy, Harewood & Jagger Solicitors

Spandy, Harewood & Jagger Solicitors

Enc.
Form of authorization

To hospital to obtain medical records

The purpose of this letter is to obtain copies of the client's medical records. These will be needed so that a medical expert can be instructed to prepare a report on the client's injuries. The client's specific authority is required in order for the hospital to release the notes to the solicitor.

8

Example letter

To prospective defendant's solicitors: choice of medical expert

The purpose of this letter is to enquire whether the prospective defendant's solicitors are prepared to agree to Mrs Walker's solicitors' choice of medical expert. Note that a deadline is included in the letter in order to prevent the case dragging on unnecessarily, and to keep some pressure on the other side.

Spandy, Harewood & Jagger Solicitors
23–25 Hills Road
Reading
RG1 9AX

telephone: +44 (0) 118 87332
fax: +44 (0) 118 87333
email: enq@sh&j.co.uk

Our ref.	MDL/WAL.5–1
Your ref.	GAM/TL/CL00424
	22 March 20—

Proctor & Peel Solicitors
The Station House
The Cuttings
Bracknell
RG42 2FR

Dear Sirs

Our client: Mrs Julie Belinda Walker
Your client: Gamley Supermarkets plc
Re: Accident in Reading store on 10 November 20—

We thank you for your letter of 10 March 20—, the contents of which we are pleased to note.

We have now obtained our client's medical notes and propose to instruct either Mr Granville Davis or Mr Jasbinder Singh, both of whom are orthopaedic surgeons at the Foundation Hospital.

Please contact us within the next 14 days to advise whether you have any objection to the instruction of either of these experts.

Yours faithfully

Spandy, Harewood & Jagger Solicitors

Spandy, Harewood & Jagger Solicitors

Spandy, Harewood & Jagger Solicitors
23–25 Hills Road
Reading
RG1 9AX

telephone: +44 (0) 118 87332
fax: +44 (0) 118 87333
email: enq@sh&j.co.uk

Our ref.   MDL/WAL.5–1
Your ref.

10 April 20—

Mr Granville Davis
Orthopaedic Surgeon
The Foundation Hospital
Reading
Berks
RG1 8ZR

Dear Sir

Our client: Mrs Julie Belinda Walker
Address: 15A Railway Terrace, Tilehurst, Reading
Re: Accident in Reading store on 10 November 20—

We refer to our telephone conversation on 8 April 20— and thank you for accepting instructions to prepare a report on our client.

Details of accident

We are instructed that the circumstances of the accident were that our client was in the store picking up one or two things for dinner, when she walked around a corner and slipped on something on the floor. This later turned out to be yoghurt. She fell and her right arm became entangled in the shopping basket she was carrying, which wrapped itself around her arm as she fell.

Our client experienced significant pain in her right arm and shoulder following the accident, and this did not improve overnight. Therefore, she went to see her doctor, who referred her to the hospital for physiotherapy and put her on a course of painkillers. X-rays taken at the hospital showed that she had sustained damage to her arm and shoulder muscles. The treatment is now finished.

As a result of the accident our client was off work for six weeks and was unable to play bowls, which is her main hobby, during that period.

Our client believes that she is about 75% recovered but she continues to experience pain when raising her right arm above her shoulder – for example, when hanging out the washing.

1

Letter of instruction to orthopaedic surgeon

This is a letter of instruction to a medical expert to prepare a report on Mrs Walker's injuries. The report will be of critical importance in establishing the amount of compensation that Mrs Walker can expect to receive. Since it is not in dispute that the accident was the direct cause of Mrs Walker's injuries, the instructions focus on the seriousness of the injuries themselves. Mrs Walker's previous medical history may be relevant to this investigation if she happened to suffer from any condition that would be aggravated by the injuries sustained in the accident. One of the key factors in determining the amount of compensation she can expect to receive is whether the accident has led to any permanent damage.

1 Will Mrs Walker's solicitors pay Mr Davis's fees in any event?

2 When must Mr Davis deliver his report?

3 Does Mrs Walker herself believe that she has made a full recovery from her accident?

Our instructions

We should be grateful if you would examine our client and provide a full and detailed report dealing with:

1 Our client's relevant pre-accident medical history.
2 The injuries she sustained.
3 Her present condition.
4 The likely extent and duration of any continuing disability, complaint, or impact on daily living.

Please contact our client direct to arrange the appointment. We confirm that we will be responsible for your reasonable professional fees in preparing the report.

We enclose our client's medical records for your consideration, and look forward to receiving your report within eight weeks of today's date. In the meantime, if you have any queries, please do not hesitate to contact the writer.

Yours faithfully

Marie Long

Marie Long (Ms)
Partner

Enc.
Medical records

2

Spandy, Harewood & Jagger Solicitors
23–25 Hills Road
Reading
RG1 9AX

telephone: +44 (0) 118 87332
fax: +44 (0) 118 87333
email: enq@sh&j.co.uk

Our ref.   MDL/WAL.5–1
Your ref.   GAM/TL/CL00424
15 June 20—

Proctor & Peel Solicitors
The Station House
The Cuttings
Bracknell
RG42 2FR

Dear Sirs

Our client: Mrs Julie Belinda Walker
Your client: Gamley Supermarkets plc
Re: Accident in Reading store on 10 November 20—

We write further in this matter and now enclose by way of service the following:

1 Witness statement of Julie Belinda Walker dated 10 June 20—.
2 Schedule of special damages.
3 Medical report prepared by Granville Davis.

We look forward to receiving proposals for settlement within the course of the next 14 days, failing which we will take steps to issue proceedings.

Yours faithfully

Spandy, Harewood & Jagger Solicitors

Spandy, Harewood & Jagger Solicitors

To prospective defendant's solicitors serving documentation

After the medical report has been prepared, Mrs Walker's solicitor will prepare a schedule of special damages. This is a document which sets out any costs which Mrs Walker has incurred or sums lost as a result of the accident (e.g. lost earnings, medical and travel expenses). In addition, Mrs Walker will make a witness statement. This is in effect a narrative setting out the circumstances of the accident and the progress of Mrs Walker's recovery from it. These are then served upon the prospective defendant's solicitors, who are invited to make proposals for settlement – i.e. to offer a specific sum of money as compensation. Again, Mrs Walker's solicitors use the threat of court proceedings to maintain pressure on the prospective defendants to respond swiftly with a realistic offer.

Points to remember

1 Personal injury litigation and negotiation falls into two parts. The first is to prove liability. The second is to produce evidence as to the amount of damages that should be paid.

2 Different kinds of language are needed in correspondence in this area. When dealing with clients, it is important to find a sympathetic and human tone. When dealing with the opponent in the litigation process, the tone should be formal, clear, and to the point.

3 Personal injury litigation is heavily dependent on obtaining evidence, medical or otherwise. The evidence that can be obtained is often only as good as the instructions provided by the solicitor to the experts. Therefore, all letters of instruction should be clear, detailed, and specific as to what information is required.

8

Residential property: buying a house

9

Introduction

In legal practice, residential property work is concerned with the buying, selling, leasing, and licensing of properties in which people actually live, whereas commercial property work is concerned with business and commercial property.

The underlying law is the same for residential as for commercial property work. **(For an introduction to this, ▶ see Unit 3.)** However, it should be noted that the clients are private individuals rather than business people. Therefore, a slightly different (less formal, more sympathetic) approach may be required. In addition, it may be necessary to explain in much greater detail the legal steps that must be taken in order to complete the sale or purchase of the property.

The role of the lawyer

The role of the lawyer in the process of buying and selling residential property is to guide the buyer or seller through the somewhat complicated sale procedure. A lawyer engaged in this area of work must combine an acute attention to detail with an ability to work to strict timetables, and be able to communicate with clients (who often find the process of buying or selling property stressful), estate agents, and other lawyers.

The legal work involved in the process of buying a residential property can be divided into several stages:

1 Preliminary investigations. These include:

  a The local authority search. The results of this search contain information on any restrictions or conditions that may apply to the property, i.e. financial charges, conditional PLANNING CONSENTS, TREE PRESERVATION ORDERS, LISTED BUILDING status, conservation areas, etc.

  b Investigation of the seller's title to the property and any ENCUMBRANCES affecting the property.

2 Exchange of contracts and payment of the DEPOSIT.

3 Completion of the purchase: payment of the purchase price and obtaining the signed TRANSFER DEED and the keys to the property.

4 Registration of the client's ownership of the property (and any MORTGAGE) with the LAND REGISTRY.

The example correspondence

The example letters that follow relate to the purchase of a residential property and show the lawyer's involvement in the process.

DANWORTH

Danworth & Co.
1 Cooper's Yard. Ely
Cambridgeshire, CB6 3BN
telephone: +44 (0) 1353 74467
fax: +44 (0) 1353 74468
email: info@dan&co.com

YOUR REF

OUR REF   DRT/BAX.1–2

4 February 20—

Armstrong & Jones
5 Larwood Avenue
Hayes
UB3 4FR

Dear Sirs

Re: 55 Dryden Road, Hayes
Our client: Jemima Baxter
Your client: Jimmy Garcia

We confirm that we act for Ms Jemina Baxter regarding her proposed purchase of the above property for the sum of £160,000 subject to contract, and look forward to receiving draft documentation from you in due course.

Yours faithfully

Danworth & Co.

Danworth & Co.

Opening letter from buyer's solicitor to seller's solicitor

The opening letter from the buyer's solicitor to the seller's solicitor confirms that the firm has been instructed by the buyer in relation to the proposed purchase. It is usually the seller's solicitor who prepares the sales documentation (including the contract and transfer deed).

To buyer advising on progress of purchase

In this letter, the buyer's solicitor Della Thomas informs the buyer as to the progress made on the purchase. She also advises the buyer on two issues relevant to the sale – the local authority search and the property survey.

Danworth & Co.
1 Cooper's Yard. Ely
Cambridgeshire, CB6 3BN
telephone: +44 (0) 1353 74467
fax: +44 (0) 1353 74468
email: info@dan&co.com

Ms J.G. Baxter
32 Granville Terrace
Ely
Cambridgeshire, CB6 6GR

YOUR REF

OUR REF DRT/BAX.1–2

4 February 20—

Dear Ms Baxter

Re: 55 Dryden Road, Hayes

I write to confirm that I have now received the agent's particulars and have written to the other side to request that they forward the draft sales documentation to me.

I have also received the results of the local authority search (copy enclosed) and confirm that this does not reveal any matters of undue concern. However, please note that the search does not give information regarding adjacent land, including any planning applications that may affect it. It is of course possible to carry out searches in respect of the adjacent land, although this will give rise to further charges.

I note that you have now received a mortgage offer. As you know, it has been agreed that a deposit equalling 5% of the sale price will be paid on exchange of contracts. The remaining 95% will be paid on completion.

One question that you will need to consider is whether there should be a full structural survey of the property. The mortgagees will carry out a survey of the property, and a copy of this will be provided to you. However, this survey is simply to ensure that the property will provide a good security for the money loaned. It does not amount to a full structural survey. We would strongly recommend that you have your own survey conducted. If you wish we can put you in touch with a firm of surveyors with whom we deal frequently.

I will be in touch again as soon as I hear from the seller's solicitors. However, please do not hesitate to contact me if you have any queries in the meantime.

Yours sincerely

Della Thomas

Della Thomas (Ms)
Partner

Enc. Local authority search results

1 What important information is not included in the local authority search?

2 What preliminary payment is made prior to completion of the purchase?

3 Why do the mortgagees carry out a survey of the property?

ARMSTRONG & JONES

5 Larwood Avenue, Hayes, UB3 4FR
Telephone: +44 (0) 1895 60336, Fax: +44 (0) 1895 60337
Email: enq@a&j.co.uk

Our ref: PHB/GAR.3–2

Your ref: DRT/BAX.1–2

15 February 20—

Danworth & Co
1 Cooper's Yard
Ely
Cambridgeshire
CB6 3BN

Dear Sirs

Re: 55 Dryden Road, Hayes
Our client: Jimmy Garcia
Your client: Jemima Baxter

Thank you for your letter of 4 February 20—. We confirm that we are instructed by the above-named client to act on the sale of this property.

We now enclose the following:

1 Draft contract in duplicate.
2 Up-to-date office copy entries.
3 Completed Fixture, Fittings, and Property Information forms.
4 Copy Water Services & Council Tax bills.
5 Copy planning documents.

Kindly acknowledge receipt.

Yours faithfully

Armstrong & Jones

Armstrong & Jones

From seller's solicitor to buyer's solicitor: sale documentation

In this letter, the seller's solicitor writes to the buyer's solicitor enclosing the necessary sales documents. The 'office copy entries' are a copy of the details of the property contained in the Land Registry entry. These are important, since they confirm the identity of the owner of the property as well as the identity of the owner of any rights over the property (e.g. charges, easements, etc.).

Buyer's solicitor to buyer forwarding documents

In this letter, the buyer's solicitor forwards to the buyer relevant documents received from the seller's solicitor. She explains what the documents are about and advises on certain issues which need further clarification.

The solicitor asks Ms Baxter not to date the contract. This is because the date on the contract should be the date the contracts are exchanged between the solicitors handling the sale (see letter dated 25 February). The solicitors themselves will insert the dates on each part of the contract.

DANWORTH

Danworth & Co.
1 Cooper's Yard. Ely
Cambridgeshire, CB6 3BN
telephone: +44 (0) 1353 74467
fax: +44 (0) 1353 74468
email: info@dan&co.com

Ms J.G. Baxter
32 Granville Terrace
Ely
Cambridgeshire, CB6 6GR

YOUR REF

OUR REF DRT/BAX.1–2

17 February 20—

Dear Ms Baxter

Re: 55 Dryden Road, Hayes

I have now received the draft sales documentation from the seller's solicitor, and I enclose copies of the following documents for your consideration:

1 Office copy entries: these are issued by the Land Registry, and show the ownership of the property together with any third party rights which affect the property (e.g. loans secured against the property, rights of way across the property, etc). They show that Mr Garcia is the sole owner of the property, subject to a mortgage in favour of NatWest bank which will be paid off on sale of the property. There are no third party rights affecting the property.

2 Fixtures, Fittings and Property Information forms: these forms are completed by the seller and give information about the property. I think it would be sensible to clarify certain details – in particular we should obtain the completion certificate in respect of the conservatory which was added to the property in 1999.

3 Planning documents: these show that permission was granted for the building of the conservatory.

4 Water service and council tax bills: these are paid up to the present date.

5 Contract in duplicate: please sign – but do not date – both copies and return them to me.

I will now write to the seller's solicitors with some additional enquiries. Provided we receive satisfactory replies to these, we should be able to exchange contracts fairly shortly.

Yours sincerely

Della Thomas

Della Thomas (Ms)
Partner

---

1 What further information does Della Thomas think should be obtained from the seller's solicitor?

2 Are there any loans secured against 55 Dryden Road?

3 What does Della Thomas ask her client to do?

4 What words used in the letter are synonyms for the following?
   a given
   b questions
   c only

DANWORTH

Danworth & Co.
1 Cooper's Yard. Ely
Cambridgeshire, CB6 3BN
telephone: +44 (0) 1353 74467
fax: +44 (0) 1353 74468
email: info@dan&co.com

YOUR REF PHB/GAR. 3–2

OUR REF DRT/BAX.1–2

17 February 20—

Armstrong & Jones
5 Larwood Avenue
Hayes
UB3 4FR

Dear Sirs

Re: 55 Dryden Road, Hayes
Our client: Jemima Baxter
Your client: Jimmy Garcia

Thank you for your letter of 15 February 20— and the enclosed documentation.

By way of additional enquiries before contract, kindly provide copies of the following:

1 Building regulation approvals.
2 Completion certificate relating to the conservatory.

Yours faithfully

Danworth & Co.

Danworth & Co.

cc. Ms J.G. Baxter

Buyer's solicitor to seller's solicitor making further enquiries

If the buyer's solicitor is not entirely happy with any aspect of the information about the property provided by the seller's solicitor prior to contracts being exchanged, it is standard practice to raise additional enquiries with a view to clarifying any matters which remain unclear. In this case, the letter is copied to the client so that she knows precisely what enquiries are being raised.

Seller's solicitor responding to enquiries

The seller's solicitor now writes to the buyer's solicitor and provides the documents requested.

ARMSTRONG & JONES

5 Larwood Avenue, Hayes, UB3 4FR
Telephone: +44 (0) 1895 60336, Fax: +44 (0) 1895 60337
Email: enq@a&j.co.uk

Our ref: PHB/GAR.3–2

Your ref: DRT/BAX.1–2

21 February 20—

Danworth & Co
1 Cooper's Yard
Ely
Cambridgeshire
CB6 3BN

Dear Sirs

Re: 55 Dryden Road, Hayes
Our client: Jimmy Garcia
Your client: Jemima Baxter

Thank you for your letter of 17 February 20—.

We now enclose the following:

1   Building regulation approvals.

2   Completion certificate relating to the conservatory.

Yours faithfully

Armstrong & Jones

Armstrong & Jones

DANWORTH

Danworth & Co.

1 Cooper's Yard. Ely
Cambridgeshire, CB6 3BN
telephone: +44 (0) 1353 74467
fax: +44 (0) 1353 74468
email: info@dan&co.com

YOUR REF

OUR REF   DRT/BAX.1–2

23 February 20—

Ms J.G. Baxter
32 Granville Terrace
Ely
Cambridgeshire
CB6 6GR

Dear Ms Baxter

Re: 55 Dryden Road, Hayes

I write to advise that I have now received the information requested from the seller's solicitor (copies enclosed).

Since you have now signed the contract and mortgage papers, we are now able to exchange contracts. Unless you have any objections, I would suggest we try to exchange contracts on 25 February with completion set for 11 March.

Yours sincerely

Della Thomas

Della Thomas (Ms)
Partner

Enc.
1 Building regulation approvals
2 Completion certificate relating to the conservatory

Advice from buyer's solicitor to buyer

The buyer's solicitor now writes to her client forwarding the information received and advising as to the further procedural steps that need to be taken.

9

Example letter

Buyer's solicitor to seller's solicitor confirming exchange of contracts

Exchange of contracts is done over the telephone between the respective solicitors for the buyer and seller in accordance with a protocol laid down by the Law Society. Each party holds a version of the contract signed by their respective clients: hence the reference to 'exchange' of contracts. This is the 'Formula B' referred to in the letter. On exchange of contracts the buyer formally commits to buying the property and the seller to selling it. A deposit is now paid by the buyer to the seller. It is typically around 5% or 10% of the purchase price. The remainder of the purchase price is paid at completion, immediately after the transfer deed has been signed.

The buyer's solicitor also sends requisitions on title. These are enquiries about the seller's title to the property, designed to ascertain whether there have been any important changes to it since earlier searches were done.

Danworth & Co.
1 Cooper's Yard. Ely
Cambridgeshire, CB6 3BN
telephone: +44 (0) 1353 74467
fax: +44 (0) 1353 74468
email: info@dan&co.com

YOUR REF   PHB/GAR. 3–2

OUR REF   DRT/BAX.1–2

25 February 20—

Armstrong & Jones
5 Larwood Avenue
Hayes
UB3 4FR

Dear Sirs

Re: 55 Dryden Road, Hayes
Our client: Jemima Baxter
Your client: Jimmy Garcia

We refer to the telephone conversation today between our Della Thomas and your Mr Spencer when contracts were exchanged under Formula B at 3.26 p.m. with completion fixed for 11 March 20—.

We enclose our client's signed part of the contract and look forward to receiving your client's signed part. We also enclose a cheque in respect of the deposit together with requisitions on title.

Yours faithfully

Danworth & Co.

Danworth & Co.

Enc.
1 Signed contract
2 Cheque for deposit
3 Requisitions on title

Seller's solicitor confirming exchange of contracts

The seller's solicitor confirms exchange of contracts and returns the requisitions on title.

ARMSTRONG
& JONES

5 Larwood Avenue, Hayes, UB3 4FR
Telephone: +44 (0) 1895 60336, Fax: +44 (0) 1895 60337
Email: enq@a&j.co.uk

Our ref: PHB/GAR.3–2

Your ref: DRT/BAX.1–2

28 February 20—

Danworth & Co
1 Cooper's Yard
Ely
Cambridgeshire
CB6 3BN

Dear Sirs

Re: 55 Dryden Road, Hayes
Our client: Jimmy Garcia
Your client: Jemima Baxter

We write further to the telephone conversation on 25 February between your Della Thomson and our Philip Spencer when contracts were exchanged under Formula B at 3.26 p.m. with completion fixed for 11 March 20—.

We enclose our client's signed part of the contract and acknowledge receipt of your cheque in respect of the deposit.

We now enclose requisitions on title duly completed.

Yours faithfully

Armstrong & Jones

Armstrong & Jones

Enc.
1 Signed contract.
2 Requisitions on title

Buyer's solicitor to buyer advising on completion date

The buyer's solicitor now writes to her client confirming that contracts have been exchanged and that completion will take place on 11 March.

DANWORTH

Danworth & Co.
1 Cooper's Yard. Ely
Cambridgeshire, CB6 3BN
telephone: +44 (0) 1353 74467
fax: +44 (0) 1353 74468
email: info@dan&co.com

Ms J.G. Baxter
32 Granville Terrace
Ely
Cambridgeshire
CB6 6GR

YOUR REF

OUR REF   DRT/BAX.1–2

28 February 20—

Dear Ms Baxter

Re: 55 Dryden Road, Hayes

I write to confirm that contracts were exchanged on 25 February and completion has been set for 11 March 20—.

Yours sincerely

Della Thomas

Della Thomas (Ms)
Partner

Buyer's solicitor to seller's solicitor confirming purchase price paid

This letter reminds the seller's solicitor to forward the transfer deeds and other title deeds. The buyer's solicitor is obliged to register both the buyer's ownership of the property and the charge on the property in favour of the mortgage company with the Land Registry. It will not be possible to do this until the transfer deeds and other title deeds have been received. Once the registration procedure has been completed, the deeds must be handed over to the mortgage company until such time as the mortgage is paid off.

DANWORTH

Danworth & Co.
1 Cooper's Yard. Ely
Cambridgeshire, CB6 3BN
telephone: +44 (0) 1353 74467
fax: +44 (0) 1353 74468
email: info@dan&co.com

Armstrong & Jones
5 Larwood Avenue
Hayes
UB3 4FR

YOUR REF   PHB/GAR.3–2

OUR REF   DRT/BAX.1–2

11 March 20—

BY FAX AND MAIL: 456789

Dear Sirs

Re: 55 Dryden Road, Hayes
Our client: Jemima Baxter
Your client: Jimmy Garcia

We write to confirm that the funds for completion were sent by telegraphic transfer to your bank today and that our client has received the keys to the property.

We look forward to receiving the signed transfer deed, title deeds and supporting documents, and any applicable undertakings.

Yours faithfully

Danworth & Co.

Danworth & Co.

ARMSTRONG
& JONES

5 Larwood Avenue, Hayes, UB3 4FR
Telephone: +44 (0) 1895 60336, Fax: +44 (0) 1895 60337
Email: enq@a&j.co.uk

Our ref: PHB/GAR.3–2

Your ref: DRT/BAX.1–2

13 March 20—

Danworth & Co
1 Cooper's Yard
Ely
Cambridgeshire
CB6 3BN

Dear Sirs

Re: 55 Dryden Road, Hayes
Our client: Jimmy Garcia
Your client: Jemima Baxter

We confirm receipt of the purchase funds by telegraphic transfer and now enclose the following:

1 Transfer deed executed by our client.
2 Title deeds
3 Charge certificate.

We hereby undertake to discharge the mortgage with NatWest bank and to forward form DS1 as soon as it is received.

Yours faithfully

Armstrong & Jones

Armstrong & Jones

Seller's solicitor forwarding signed transfer deed

In this letter, the seller's solicitor confirms that the purchase monies have been paid in full, and forwards the signed transfer deed. It remains for the seller's solicitor to arrange for the balance of the seller's mortgage to be paid off out of the purchase funds – clearly a matter of the utmost importance both to the buyer and to the buyer's mortgage lender. The form DS1 to which the seller's solicitor refers is the Land Registry form which will confirm that the property is free of mortgage. Once this is received, the buyer's solicitor will be able to register both the buyer's ownership and the mortgage lender's charge over the property.

Points to remember

1 When acting for a buyer of a property, a solicitor's most important function (as well as handling the paperwork and procedure) is to obtain evidence that the seller actually has good title to the property being sold – i.e. has full rights of ownership, and that there are no other persons who might be able to claim competing ownership rights. It is important to check all Land Registry entries with extreme care. In addition, the solicitor needs to verify insofar as possible that the property is in the condition that the buyer has a right to expect it to be, and that it is not going to be adversely affected by any local authority plans.

2 When acting for a seller in connection with the sale of property, the solicitor's main concern is to verify that the buyer is actually in a position to purchase the property. It is important to gain evidence at an early stage about the buyer's proposed funding – usually a mortgage – and whether this has been secured. The seller's main concern in most, although perhaps not all, cases will be to transact the sale quickly and secure the funds as soon as possible, and the solicitor will accordingly be expected to be brisk and proactive in seeking to conclude the transaction.

3 Property law contains a great deal of obscure legal terminology. It is important to grasp the meaning of these peculiar terms, since many of them relate to matters which have a strong practical impact on the purchase of land (▶ see Unit 3).

4 The lawyer involved in assisting clients in the buying and selling of land needs to combine an acute attention to detail with an ability to work to strict timetables and communicate effectively with clients and others.

Inheritance law: estate administration

10

WILLS AND PROBATE

Inheritance law – sometimes called wills and probate – is concerned with the distribution of a person's property following their death. This may occur either in accordance with the provisions of a will which that person has made, or under the applicable rules relating to INTESTACY (i.e. when a person dies without having made a will).

The property of a deceased person is known as their ESTATE. It may comprise freehold and leasehold land (together known as REAL PROPERTY, *real estate*, or *realty*) and all other property (known as PERSONAL PROPERTY or *personalty*). ▸**see page 45**.

Wills

The document by which a person directs what should happen to their property after their death is known as a will. A will must be 1) in writing, 2) signed by the TESTATOR (the person making the will), and 3) witnessed by at least two witnesses.

In order for a will to be valid, the testator must be over eighteen when the will is made and of sound mind. The will must appoint one or more persons to carry out the terms of the will. These persons are known as EXECUTORS. A person who inherits property under a will is known as a BENEFICIARY.

Revocation and alteration of wills

A will can be REVOKED or altered in the following ways:

1 By making a new will that makes it clear that the previous will(s) is / are revoked ('I revoke all former wills and codicils made by me').

2 By total destruction of the previous will.

3 By marriage. Revocation is automatic on the marriage of the testator. The only exception to this is where the will is clearly made with the forthcoming marriage in mind. Such wills should clearly state this to be the case and set down the time-limit within which the marriage is due to take place.

4 By divorce. Divorce does not invalidate a will but is likely to make it largely ineffective because any gift to the former SPOUSE (i.e. husband or wife) will no longer take effect.

5 By amendment. Amendments to a will can be made using a CODICIL. This is a document prepared and signed with all the formalities of a will, which is then attached to the original will.

Intestacy

A person who dies without having made a will is said to have died *intestate*. If this occurs, that person's property is distributed in accordance with the intestacy rules. These rules set out the order of priority applied when distributing the estate to the possible beneficiaries. The person who is appointed by a court to distribute the property of someone who has died intestate is known as an ADMINISTRATOR.

The collective term covering both administrators and executors is PERSONAL REPRESENTATIVE. The word TRUSTEE is also used.

Probate

Probate has two meanings:

1 It is the official document which confirms that the will is valid and states who the executors are. This is obtained from the Probate Registry and the procedure is known as grant of probate. Where the grant is made to an administrator (on intestacy), it is known as a GRANT OF LETTERS OF ADMINISTRATION.

2 Generally, the term probate is used to refer to the various laws and courts which deal with wills, intestacy, succession, inheritance, administration, and disputes over estates.

Contentious probate

Sometimes a person's estate becomes the subject of litigation. This typically occurs when a person has made a will which fails to provide for persons who arguably should have been left property in it, usually spouses, children, and other dependants. In most legal systems, the persons not so provided for are entitled to bring legal claims to secure a share of the estate.

This branch of legal work is known as CONTENTIOUS PROBATE. In England and Wales, the majority of such claims are brought under the Inheritance (Provision for Family and Dependants) Act 1975.

The role of the lawyer

Aside from contentious probate, when the lawyer must bring or defend claims against an estate, the role of the lawyer is to advise and assist the client in drawing up a suitable will and to administer the estate after a person's death. The basic steps in this latter instance are as follows:

1 Ascertain the extent of the estate.

2 Notify relevant authorities of the death.

3 Draw up a list of people who owed money to the deceased (debtors).

4 Draw up a list of people to be paid money from the estate (creditors).

5 Apply for grant of probate.

6 Collect any debts owed, sums payable on insurance policies, sums in banks, etc.

7 Pay debts owed by the estate.

8 Advertise for creditors.

9 Sell assets not specifically devised or bequeathed in the will.

10 Draw up an estate distribution account.

11 Distribute the estate to the beneficiaries.

The example correspondence

The example letters that follow relate to the administration of the estate of an elderly client who has recently died. The main purposes of the correspondence are 1) to advise the relevant parties of the death, 2) to ascertain the extent of the estate, 3) to gather in the estate, 4) to pay any outstanding debts from the money gathered in, and 5) to distribute the remaining assets to the beneficiaries. In a simple case, such as the one outlined below, the majority of the letters written are routine in nature.

10

To bank confirming death of client

The purpose of this letter is to inform the bank that the client has died and to ascertain the level of funds in the bank account. A copy of the death certificate is included with the letter as evidence that the client has actually died.

Example letter

12 ARTHURSGATE ▪ SHEFFIELD ▪ S1 2TL ▪ SOUTH YORKS
TELEPHONE: +44 (0) 114 843351 ▪ FAX: +44 (0) 114 843352
EMAIL: info@pb&co.com

▪ OUR REF RMF/WAT.2–2

▪ YOUR REF

22 September 20—

Barclays Bank
5 Market Street
Sheffield
S1 4NX

Dear Sirs

Re: George Hubert Waterford
Account number: 03456128
Sort Code: 05-08-12

We act for the executors of the late George Hubert Waterford, who died on 30 August 20—. We enclose a copy of the death certificate.

We should be grateful if you would provide us with a probate valuation for the account together with forms of withdrawal for the executors to encash the account when probate is granted.

If you require any further information please do not hesitate to contact us at this office.

Yours faithfully

Pond, Barnsley & Co.

Pond, Barnsley & Co.

Enc.
Copy of death certificate

Questions

1 By whom are Pond, Barnsley & Co. instructed?

2 Why are the forms of withdrawal needed?

12 ARTHURSGATE ▪ SHEFFIELD ▪ S1 2TL ▪ SOUTH YORKS
TELEPHONE: +44 (0) 114 843351 ▪ FAX: +44 (0) 114 843352
EMAIL: info@pb&co.com

▪ OUR REF RMF/WAT.2–2

▪ YOUR REF

22 September 20—

The Inland Revenue
Concept House
5 Young Street
Sheffield
S1 4LA

Dear Sirs

Re: George Hubert Waterford
National Insurance number: SM 06 84 21 D

We act for the executors of the late George Hubert Waterford, who died on 30 August 20—, and enclose a copy of the death certificate.

We should be obliged if you would advise us whether any repayment of overpaid income tax is due to the estate. If so, please send us a claim form for repayment of income tax for the period 1 April 20— to 30 August 20—.

We confirm that we will be applying for grant of probate in due course.

Yours faithfully

Pond, Barnsley & Co.

Pond, Barnsley & Co.

Enc.
Copy of death certificate

To the Inland Revenue

The Inland Revenue is the tax office in Britain. It is a requirement that the Inland Revenue be notified of any deaths that have occurred, in order that the tax situation of the deceased person be clarified and concluded. The 'NI number' is the National Insurance number – which is the social security number allocated to citizens and permanent residents in Britain.

1 What information do Pond, Barnsley & Co. want from the Inland Revenue?

2 What application do Pond, Barnsley & Co. intend to make?

To the Department of Work and Pensions (DWP)

The Department of Work and Pensions (DWP) is the government department in charge of administering social benefits, including state pensions and unemployment benefit, in the UK.

Example letter

12 ARTHURSGATE ▪ SHEFFIELD ▪ S1 2TL ▪ SOUTH YORKS
TELEPHONE: +44 (0) 114 843351 ▪ FAX: +44 (0) 114 843352
EMAIL: info@pb&co.com

▪ OUR REF RMF/WAT.2–2

▪ YOUR REF

22 September 20—

Department of Work and Pensions
L2 Kings Court
80 Hanover Way
Sheffield
S3 7UF

Dear Sirs

Re: George Hubert Waterford
National Insurance number: SM 06 84 21 D

We act for the executors of the late George Hubert Waterford, who died on 30 August 20—, and enclose a copy of the death certificate. We are in receipt of instructions to administer the estate.

Please find enclosed Form of Registration or Notification of Death. We should be obliged if you would notify us as to the amount of retirement pension owing.

Yours faithfully

Pond, Barnsley & Co.

Pond, Barnsley & Co.

Enc.
1 Copy of death certificate
2 Form of Registration or Notification of Death

Questions

1 Which words used in the letter are synonyms for the following?
a advise
b quantity
c due
d grateful

12 ARTHURSGATE ■ SHEFFIELD ■ S1 2TL ■ SOUTH YORKS
TELEPHONE: +44 (0) 114 843351 ■ FAX: +44 (0) 114 843352
EMAIL: info@pb&co.com

■ OUR REF   RMF/WAT.2–2

■ YOUR REF

22 September 20—

The Homecare Agency
1 Friar's Walk
Sheffield
S1 4LT

Dear Sirs

Re: George Hubert Waterford
19A King's Crescent, Sheffield

We act for the executors of the late George Hubert Waterford, who died on 30 August 20—, and enclose a copy of the death certificate.

We should be grateful if you would let us have a note of any money either due to or owed by the estate to your organization in respect of services provided to Mr Waterford. Please also send a copy of Mr Waterford's account.

Yours faithfully

Pond, Barnsley & Co.

Pond, Barnsley & Co.

Enc.
Copy of death certificate

To care provider

In this case, the deceased person was an elderly man who required some degree of daily nursing assistance. This was carried out by a private organization, the Homecare Agency

To Inland Revenue Capital Taxes Office

Taxes fall roughly into two categories: taxes on income and taxes on capital. Capital taxes relate to gains on disposal of assets. Income tax is levied on a person's regular income. In the UK, income tax and capital gains tax are the prime examples of the two types of tax. Form IHT 200 is the form used by the UK tax authorities to record a person's assets and liabilities for inheritance tax purposes.

12 ARTHURSGATE ■ SHEFFIELD ■ S1 2TL ■ SOUTH YORKS
TELEPHONE: +44 (0) 114 843351 ■ FAX: +44 (0) 114 843352
EMAIL: info@pb&co.com

■ OUR REF RMF/WAT.2–2

■ YOUR REF

22 September 20—

The Inland Revenue Capital Taxes Office
Walsh Court
10 Bell Square
Sheffield
S1 2FY

Dear Sirs

Re: George Hubert Waterford
National Insurance Number: SM 06 84 21 D

We act for the executors of the late George Hubert Waterford, who died on 30 August 20—, and enclose a copy of the death certificate.

We also enclose form IHT 200 detailing Mr Waterford's assets and liabilities.

We confirm that we shall be applying for grant of probate at Sheffield Probate Registry in due course.

Yours faithfully

Pond, Barnsley & Co.

Pond, Barnsley & Co.

Enc.
1 Copy of death certificate
2 Form IHT 200

12 ARTHURSGATE ▪ SHEFFIELD ▪ S1 2TL ▪ SOUTH YORKS
TELEPHONE: +44 (0) 114 843351 ▪ FAX: +44 (0) 114 843352
EMAIL: info@pb&co.com

▪ OUR REF RMF/WAT.2–2

▪ YOUR REF

22 September 20—

Sheffield Probate Registry
PO Box 832
The Law Courts
50 West Bar
Sheffield
S3 8YR

Dear Sirs

Re: George Hubert Waterford

We act for the executors of the above-named deceased, and enclose the following:

1 Oath for executors
2 Original last will and testament
3 Probate Summary
4 Cheque in the sum of £55 for probate fees and office copy entries of grant.

Yours faithfully

Pond, Barnsley & Co.

Pond, Barnsley & Co.

To Probate Registry

Once the assets and liabilities in the estate have been fully ascertained, a probate summary is completed. This is a document which sets out the assets and liabilities and indicates the value of the estate. This document is then sent to the Probate Registry. Provided no difficulties arise, probate will then be granted. This means that the assets in the estate can be gathered in.

To deceased's landlord

In this case, the deceased person lived in rented accommodation. Therefore, it is necessary for the lawyers to communicate with the landlords to advise them of the tenant's death and to establish whether any further payment must be made to the landlord in respect of rent or other fees, or conversely whether any reimbursement is due in respect of rent and fees paid in advance.

12 ARTHURSGATE ▪ SHEFFIELD ▪ S1 2TL ▪ SOUTH YORKS
TELEPHONE: +44 (0) 114 843351 ▪ FAX: +44 (0) 114 843352
EMAIL: info@pb&co.com

▪ OUR REF RMF/WAT.2–2
▪ YOUR REF
10 October 20—

Ronan Housing Group
44 Westway
Sheffield
S10 6TB

Dear Sirs

Re: George Hubert Waterford
19A King's Crescent, Sheffield

We act for the executors of the late George Hubert Waterford, who died on 30 August 20—, and enclose a copy of the death certificate.

We note that Mr Waterford was a tenant of the above property held on lease from your organization. The property was cleared on 5 September 20—.

We should be grateful if you would forward to us a statement showing monies due or owing, e.g. in respect of reimbursement of rent or other fees paid in advance. In the event that rent has been paid in advance covering a period beyond 5 September 20—, a rebate will of course be expected.

We look forward to hearing from you.

Yours faithfully

Pond, Barnsley & Co.

Pond, Barnsley & Co.

Enc.
Copy of death certificate

Questions

1 In what circumstances will Ronan Housing Group have to pay money back to Mr Waterford's estate?

2 What is the significance of the date 5 September 20—?

3 Which words used in the letter are synonyms for the following?
a repayment
b lessee
c anticipated

12 ARTHURSGATE ▪ SHEFFIELD ▪ S1 2TL ▪ SOUTH YORKS
TELEPHONE: +44 (0) 114 843351 ▪ FAX: +44 (0) 114 843352
EMAIL: info@pb&co.com

▪ OUR REF   RMF/WAT.2–2

▪ YOUR REF

17 October 20—

Barclays Bank
5 Market Street
Sheffield
S1 4NX

Dear Sirs

Re: George Hubert Waterford
Account number: 03456128
Sort Code: 05-08-12

We write further in this matter and enclose an office copy of the grant of probate and a withdrawal request to close the account and repay the proceeds to us on behalf of the executors.

Yours faithfully

Pond, Barnsley & Co.

Pond, Barnsley & Co.

Enc.
1 Office copy grant of probate
2 Withdrawal request

To bank

Now probate has been granted, the executors are entitled to begin gathering in the money in the estate. The purpose of this letter to the bank is to request payment of the funds and to close the account.

Chaser letter to landlord

From time to time in legal practice it is necessary to send chaser letters, when correspondence has not been replied to. These letters must strike a careful balance between firmly emphasizing the importance of a response being obtained and maintaining high standards of professional courtesy.

10

Example letter

12 ARTHURSGATE ■ SHEFFIELD ■ S1 2TL ■ SOUTH YORKS
TELEPHONE: +44 (0) 114 843351 ■ FAX: +44 (0) 114 843352
EMAIL: info@pb&co.com

■ OUR REF RMF/WAT.2–2

■ YOUR REF

15 November 20

Ronan Housing Group
44 Westway
Sheffield
S10 6TB

Dear Sirs

Re: George Hubert Waterford
19A King's Crescent, Sheffield

We write further to our letter of 10 October, to which we have not received a response. We trust this is an oversight on your part and look forward to receiving a statement showing monies due or owing as previously requested.

Yours faithfully

Pond, Barnsley & Co.

Pond, Barnsley & Co.

12 ARTHURSGATE ▪ SHEFFIELD ▪ S1 2TL ▪ SOUTH YORKS
TELEPHONE: +44 (0) 114 843351 ▪ FAX: +44 (0) 114 843352
EMAIL: info@pb&co.com

Pond
Barnsley
& Co.

▪ OUR REF   RMF/WAT.2–2

▪ YOUR REF

28 November 20—

The Homecare Agency
1 Friar's Walk
Sheffield
S1 4LT

Dear Sirs

Re: George Hubert Waterford
19A King's Crescent, Sheffield

We write further in this matter and now enclose a cheque in the sum of £1,110.50 in settlement of Mr Waterford's account. Kindly acknowledge receipt.

Yours faithfully

Pond, Barnsley & Co.

Pond, Barnsley & Co.

Enc.
Cheque

To care agency settling account

Once all the money in the estate has been gathered in, it is the role of the lawyer to ensure that all outstanding debts owed by the estate to third parties are settled before the residue of the estate is distributed to the beneficiaries. In the UK, cheques remain in frequent use for making such payments.

To executors concerning distribution of residual funds

Once the estate has been gathered in and all debts paid, the lawyer will report to the executors regarding the distribution of the residual funds to the beneficiaries. It is customary for a person making a will (the testator) to appoint two executors, of whom one is likely to be a lawyer and the other a member of the testator's family.

10

Example letter

12 ARTHURSGATE ■ SHEFFIELD ■ S1 2TL ■ SOUTH YORKS
TELEPHONE: +44 (0) 114 843351 ■ FAX: +44 (0) 114 843352
EMAIL: info@pb&co.com

■ OUR REF RMF/WAT.2–2

■ YOUR REF

19 December 20—

Mr G. Waterford
24B The Larches
Luton
Beds
LU1 9BY

Dear Mr Waterford

Estate of George Hubert Waterford
National Insurance number: SM 06 84 21 D

I write to confirm that I have now completed the administration of your father's estate.

I enclose a copy of the estate distribution account together with a cheque representing your share of the residual estate. I confirm that payments as shown in the account have also been made to the other beneficiaries. You will note that this firm's fees have been deducted from the estate in the usual way as shown in the distribution account, and I enclose a fee note for your records.

This now brings matters to a conclusion. However, if you have any questions please do not hesitate to contact me.

Yours sincerely

Roger Freeman

Roger Freeman
Senior Partner

Enc.
1 Copy of estate distribution account
2 Cheque
3 Fee note

1 Will Mr Waterford have to pay Pond, Barnsley & Co.'s fees?

2 What payments has Roger Freeman arranged?

3 What words or phrases used in the letter are synonyms for the following?
   a subtracted
   b invoice
   c queries

Points to remember

1 Inheritance law is full of obscure terminology. It is important to use this correctly – for example, to differentiate between an *executor* and an *administrator*, between *realty* and *personalty*, etc.

2 Inheritance law is largely procedural. The administration of an estate requires painstaking thoroughness and attention to detail.

3 In comparison with other branches of the law, inheritance law calls for a greater degree of numeracy – for example, when drawing up estate accounts and dealing with tax issues affecting the estate.

4 Like divorce law, inheritance law often involves dealing with persons who may be upset, either through grief or for less noble reasons (such as not being provided for in a will). The drafting of letters to such people often calls for a delicate touch.

10

Family: getting divorced

11

FAMILY LAW

Family law regulates the legal aspects of relationships between married couples, unmarried COHABITANTS, and, increasingly, same-sex partners who live together.

This unit is concerned with the law in relation to married couples. As a general rule, cohabitants are often not granted the same rights as married couples, and homosexual couples enjoy fewer rights than heterosexual couples. However, note that the Civil Partnerships Act 2004 came into force in Britain in December 2005. This allows same-sex couples to obtain legal recognition of their relationship and also provides them with parity of treatment with opposite-sex married couples on a wide range of legal matters.

Family law deals with three main issues:

1 Regulation of the legal aspects of the couple's relationship itself.

2 Regulation of arrangements for children.

3 Regulation of property rights relating to the relationship.

Ending the relationship itself

One area of family law is concerned with providing solutions to problems between parties which may arise either during the course of a relationship or after the relationship has ended. It includes provision for divorce or JUDICIAL SEPARATION proceedings where a marriage has broken down. In order to apply for a divorce in England and Wales it is necessary to show that the marriage has irretrievably broken down. This can be proved in five different ways:

1 Adultery: the PETITIONER must satisfy the court that the RESPONDENT has committed adultery and that it is therefore intolerable to live with them.

2 Unreasonable behaviour: the petitioner must satisfy the court that the respondent has behaved in such a way that the petitioner cannot reasonably be expected to live with them.

3 Two years separation and consent: if the parties have lived apart for a continuous period of at least two years and the respondent consents to a divorce, the petitioner is entitled to a divorce.

4 Desertion: the petitioner must satisfy the court that the respondent has deserted them for a continuous period of at least two years.

5 Five years separation: if the parties have lived apart for a continuous period of at least five years, the petitioner is entitled to a divorce, whether or not the respondent agrees.

There are two stages involved in obtaining a divorce. The DECREE NISI is the first stage. This occurs when the court is satisfied that the petitioner is entitled to a divorce. Once this is granted, the petitioner must wait for a minimum period of six weeks before applying for the DECREE ABSOLUTE, which is the final stage in the divorce.

In England and Wales, the Family Law Act 1996 is designed to deal with problems associated with the breakdown of relationships. It provides protection for married persons, cohabitants, and certain other categories of persons against DOMESTIC VIOLENCE and HARASSMENT, and also regulates rights of occupation of property. If domestic violence or harassment has occurred or is likely to occur, such persons can apply to the court for a non-molestation order. The same categories of persons may also be entitled to apply for an occupation order. This is an order which governs who is allowed to enter and remain in the property, or, conversely, who must keep away from it.

Arrangements for children

The welfare of any children is of paramount importance in the breakdown of a relationship. In England and Wales, the majority of legal issues relating to the care of children are contained in the Children Act 1989. Under this Act, the court can make a variety of orders regarding children. The main types of order include:

11

— *Contact order*: this requires the party with whom a child is living to allow the child to visit or stay with another party or parties (usually the child's other parent and family members) on a regular basis.
— *Residence order*: this settles arrangements about where the child is to live.
— *Prohibited steps order*: this is designed to prevent a party from taking certain steps in relation to the children which might be to their detriment (e.g. taking them abroad to live permanently).
— *Specific issues order*: this determines specific issues that have arisen regarding care of the child (e.g. medical treatment).

The court has to take certain factors into account when considering what kind of order to make. These include: the wishes of the child; his or her physical, emotional, and educational needs; the likely effect of any change; the child's age, background, and characteristics; any harm the child has suffered or might suffer in the future; and how capable the parents are of meeting the child's needs.

When applying for a divorce in a marriage in which there is a child or children, the petitioner must also send a STATEMENT OF ARRANGEMENTS for the children to the court. This document sets out the arrangements proposed for the children after the divorce.

Property rights

The court has extensive powers to make financial orders within the context of divorce proceedings, and also has more limited powers regarding financial arrangements for unmarried couples. The following notes relate to divorce proceedings.

The petitioner or the respondent in divorce proceedings may apply for ANCILLARY RELIEF, which is the name given to the financial provision orders which the court is entitled to make. The most common orders which the court may make include:

— *Property adjustment order*: an order affecting the rights of ownership of property of either spouse, or both, e.g. the transfer of the matrimonial home to one party or the other.
— *Periodical payments order*: an order that one party must pay a regular sum of money to the other party.
— *Pension sharing order*: an order providing for one party to claim a share of the other party's pension entitlement.
— *Lump sum order*: an order for the payment of a specified sum of money.
— *Order for sale of property*.
— *Consent order*: usually in the case of an 'amicable' divorce; see the introduction to the first example letter below.

When considering which orders should be made, the court takes into account a range of factors. These include: the income and earning capacity of the parties; the financial needs and obligations of each party; the standard of living enjoyed by the family during the marriage; the age of each party and the length of the marriage; any disabilities from which either party may suffer; and the contributions made by each party during the marriage. The conduct of the parties does not usually have a bearing on the nature of the financial settlement.

The role of the lawyer

The skills needed by the family lawyer tend to differ somewhat from those needed, for example, by a business lawyer. There are three main reasons for this:

1 Unlike other areas of legal practice, the context in which family law operates is one where emotions often run high. The family lawyer has to deal with clients whose personal lives may be literally falling apart, and who are therefore in a state of emotional distress. Such clients tend to base their decisions on emotional considerations rather than logic, and may even wish to act against their own best interest. Therefore, in addition to providing sound legal advice, the family lawyer has to use considerable patience, interpersonal skills, and subtle persuasion. They must master the art of demonstrating empathy with the client's difficult personal circumstances, without losing legal objectivity.

2 Family law places strong emphasis on the need for mediation and negotiation between the parties, as an alternative to solutions imposed by the court. The thinking behind this is that it is better for all the parties – particularly for the children of a relationship – that issues are settled by mutual agreement rather than by court proceedings, which tend to raise the emotional temperature and encourage divisiveness. Therefore, the family lawyer must be a skilled negotiator and persuader as well as a good court advocate. He or she must be able to use subtle tactics of persuasion as well as assertive deal-making skills on the client's behalf.

3 In order to encourage mediation and negotiation between the parties, family law is not for the main part written in black and white. It tends to work on the basis of guidelines to follow and factors that should be taken into account when making decisions, rather than on the basis of strict rules to follow. Therefore, the family lawyer must adopt slightly different methods of legal interpretation than may be required in other areas of the law. They must become skilled in applying guidelines, which may be general or somewhat vague, to a particular case, and in making an educated guess as to how that case would be treated in court, by comparing it to previous cases with similar features that have gone to court.

The example correspondence

The correspondence below illustrates how these issues affect the way in which letters in this area are composed.

11

Initial letter from petitioner's solicitor to client

This is the first letter written by the lawyer to her client after the initial meeting with the client. The lawyer uses this letter to record the information provided by the client, to provide advice to the client, and to outline what steps will be taken on the client's behalf. At this stage, the lawyer also sends a client care letter to the client. This is a standard letter which sets out the terms and conditions on which the lawyer will carry out work for the client. In effect, it forms a contract between the lawyer and client. For an example client care letter, ▶ **see page 16.**

Note how Ms Marsh uses empathetic language at certain sensitive points in the letter. She notes that Mrs Greaves has 'sadly' come to the view that her marriage has irretrievably broken down, and that she is 'understandably' concerned about the stability of Mr Greaves's relationship with Ms Lampton. This language is designed to make the client feel that the lawyer cares about her problems.

TURNER
JONES
SMITH
& CO.

7 Old Hall Street
Oxford
OX1 7PB
telephone: +44 (0) 1865 37522
fax: +44 (0) 1865 37523
email: info@tjs&co.com

Your reference
Our reference   NLM/GRE.1–1
Date   17 April 20—

Mrs M. Greaves
35 Rington Crescent
Oxford
OX4 6RR

Dear Mrs Greaves

Your marriage

Thank you for coming in to see me on 14 April when we discussed your matrimonial situation. The purpose of this letter is to summarize the issues we discussed and to outline what steps should be taken next.

You informed me that you have sadly come to the view that your marriage has irretrievably broken down. Your husband, Anthony Greaves, has admitted to you that he is having an affair with a work colleague called Michelle Lampton. You wish to divorce Mr Greaves on the basis of his adultery. He accepts this.

There are two children of the marriage, Hayley (10) and Nathan (8). You have always been the main carer for the children and it is agreed between you and Mr Greaves that they will continue to live with you at 35 Rington Crescent after the divorce. You are happy for the children to have regular contact with Mr Greaves, perhaps every Saturday. This should initially take place at 35 Rington Crescent, as you are understandably concerned about the stability of Mr Greaves's relationship with Ms Lampton. You would prefer the children not to be introduced to her until they feel more settled with the new arrangements.

Both you and Mr Greaves are 38 years old, and you married in June 1992. Mr Greaves is employed as a chartered accountant and earns around £40,000 per year. You are a branch manager for Go! Travel agents and earn around £25,000 per year. The matrimonial home at 35 Rington

1

1 What assets are there in the marriage?

2 What is Ms Marsh's advice about financial settlement?

3 What does Ms Marsh ask Mrs Greaves to do?

4 What is Ms Marsh going to do next?

Crescent is currently held in joint names. You believe that it is probably worth around £200,000. There is a mortgage on the property on which there is around £150,000 outstanding. The other assets in the marriage include a sum of £5,000 in a joint savings account. Both you and Mr Greaves are members of work pension schemes.

My advice was that provided Mr Greaves is prepared to admit to the adultery, there should be no difficulty in securing a divorce on that basis. As far as the children are concerned, we will need to complete the statement of arrangement for the children, which is a document setting out what arrangement is to be made for the children following the divorce. The court will examine this, and has the right to delay the divorce proceedings if it is not satisfied that adequate arrangements have been made for the children. However, that is highly unlikely to occur, as the arrangements you propose are very sensible.

As far as the financial aspects of the divorce are concerned, I advised that it will be necessary to have full and frank disclosure of both your and Mr Greaves's means before final advice can be given. Mr Greaves will be obliged to disclose his means separately and I will write to his solicitors in due course on this point. In the meantime, I should be grateful if you would provide the following information:

1 Bank statements for the past twelve months in respect of all bank accounts held either by you or jointly with Mr Greaves
2 Mortgage statement in respect of the Alliance & Leicester mortgage on 35 Rington Crescent
3 Valuation of 35 Rington Crescent prepared by a reputable firm of estate agents
4 Statement in respect of your pension fund arranged by Go! Travel showing the current transfer value
5 Salary advice slips for the past twelve months in respect of your employment with Go! Travel
6 Statement of your monthly expenditure (please complete the enclosed form)

I advised that Mr Greaves will in any event need to pay maintenance at a sum to be agreed until the children leave school. You told me that you had in fact discussed this matter and he fully accepts his responsibilities in this respect. As far as the house is concerned, one option would be for the house to be transferred to you on the basis that it could be sold when the children leave school, and Mr Greaves would then be entitled to a certain proportion of the proceeds of sale.

2

In an 'amicable' divorce such as the one referred to in these letters, there is no need for court hearings. Most aspects of the divorce can be settled in correspondence between lawyers. However, it is the court that grants the divorce, approves the arrangements for the children, and may also approve the financial arrangements between the parties in the form of a 'consent order'. It is therefore advisable to apply to the court for a consent order. The consent order is usually drawn up by a solicitor (usually the petitioner's) but it has to be formally approved by the court.

11

You informed me that Mr Greaves's solicitor is Mr M. Devire at Hatton, Moor & Lesley in Reading, and I have written to Mr Devire advising that we act for you and enquiring whether Mr Greaves is prepared to admit to the adultery for the purposes of the divorce petition. I enclose a copy of this letter, together with our standard client care letter in duplicate. I should be grateful if you would sign, date, and return the duplicate copy.

I will be in touch as soon as I hear anything from Hatton, Moor & Lesley. In the meantime, if you have any queries please do not hesitate to contact me.

Yours sincerely

Nicola Marsh

Nicola Marsh (Ms)
Partner

Enc.
1 Statement of outgoings form
2 Copy of letter to Hatton, Moor & Lesley
3 Client care letter

3

7 Old Hall Street
Oxford
OX1 7PB
telephone: +44 (0) 1865 37522
fax: +44 (0) 1865 37523
email: info@tjs&co.com

Your reference
Our reference NLM/GRE.1–1
Date 17 April 20—

Messrs Hatton, Moor & Lesley
35 Franklin Road
Reading
RG1 9DZ
FAO Frank Barnstaple

Dear Sirs

Our client: Mary Greaves
Your client: Anthony Greaves

We have been instructed by Mrs Greaves in relation to matrimonial matters and understand that you are in receipt of instructions to act for Mr Greaves. Kindly confirm that this is the case.

Our client has come to the view that the marriage has irretrievably broken down. She wishes to petition for divorce on the grounds of your client's adultery with Michelle Lampton. We understand that your client is prepared to admit to this for the purposes of the divorce petition. Kindly confirm.

We understand that it is agreed between our respective clients that the children will continue to live with our client at 35 Rington Crescent after the divorce, and that your client will have regular contact with them, perhaps every Saturday. This should initially take place at 35 Rington Crescent, and our client does not wish the children to be introduced to Ms Lampton until they feel more settled with the new arrangements.

With regard to financial settlement, please provide full disclosure of your client's income, outgoings, and assets. We have asked our client to collate her financial documentation and will revert to you with this shortly.

We look forward to hearing from you.

Yours faithfully

Turner, Jones, Smith & Co.

Turner, Jones, Smith & Co.

Initial letter from petitioner's solicitor to respondent's solicitor

In this letter, Ms Marsh advises that her firm acts for Mrs Greaves. She asks Hatton, Moor & Lesley to confirm that they act for Mr Greaves and enquires whether Mr Greaves is prepared to admit to the adultery. She also asks for financial disclosure.

1 What specific agreement do Turner, Jones, Smith & Co. seek?

2 What information do they request?

3 What do they promise to send?

4 When might the children be introduced to Ms Lampton?

Reply from respondent's solicitor

Note how Mr Greaves's solicitors link the issue of his admitting to the adultery to Mrs Greaves granting a concession on the legal costs of the divorce – a classic negotiation tactic. In most cases, if the court accepts the allegations made by the petitioner in the divorce petition and accordingly grants a divorce, the respondent will be obliged to pay the legal costs incurred by the petitioner in applying for the divorce. These include the solicitor's fees as well as the court fees. Mr Greaves's lawyers choose to tabulate their responses to the questions raised in Ms Marsh's letter, which makes it easier to read and understand at a glance.

The letter is 'without prejudice' because it ensures that, in the event that Mrs Greaves does not agree to the 50/50 division of the divorce costs, Mrs Greaves's solicitors will not be able to present this letter to the court as circumstantial evidence of his adultery.

11

Hatton, Moor & Lesley

35 Franklin Road
Reading
RG1 9DZ
telephone: +44 (0) 118 673770
fax: +44 (0) 118 673771
email: enq@hm&les.co.uk

▶ your ref. NLM/GRE.1–1
▶ our ref. FWB/GRE.2–1
23 April 20—

Messrs Turner, Jones, Smith & Co
7 Old Hall Street
Oxford
OX1 7PB

WITHOUT PREJUDICE

Dear Sirs

Our client: Anthony Greaves
Your client: Mary Greaves

Thank you for your letter of 17 April 20—. We confirm we are in receipt of instructions to act for Mr Greaves.

With regard to the specific points you raise:

1 Our client is prepared to admit to adultery provided that your client agrees to the divorce costs being split 50/50.
2 Contact proposals: these are agreed by our client.
3 Financial disclosure. Our client's financial documentation is enclosed. Kindly acknowledge receipt. We look forward to receiving reciprocal disclosure in due course.

Yours faithfully

Hatton, Moor & Lesley

Hatton, Moor & Lesley

Enc. Financial documents

7 Old Hall Street
Oxford
OX1 7PB
telephone: +44 (0) 1865 37522
fax: +44 (0) 1865 37523
email: info@tjs&co.com

Your reference
Our reference   NLM/GRE.1–1
Date   27 April 20—

Mrs M. Greaves
35 Rington Crescent
Oxford
OX4 6RR

Dear Mrs Greaves

Your marriage

I write further to my letter of 17 April and now enclose a copy of a letter
I have received from Mr Greaves's solicitors.

You will note that Mr Greaves is prepared to admit to adultery on the basis
that the divorce costs are split 50/50. The successful petitioner in a divorce case
is able to claim the costs of the divorce from the other party. However, in order
to obtain a divorce based on Mr Greaves's adultery you either need a clear
admission from him, or alternatively some evidence that he has committed
adultery. Such evidence might include, for example, love letters received from
or written to Ms Lampton. In the circumstances, it may be better to accept the
compromise put forward by Mr Greaves's solicitors.

You will see that Mr Greaves confirms that the arrangements for contact with
the children are accepted, and that he has provided financial disclosure. This
seems to correspond closely with what you told me about the family finances.
Once you have collated the financial documents I requested from you, we will
need to discuss financial settlement.

I also enclose the statement of arrangements for children. Please read this
through carefully, and if you are happy with it, sign and date it and return it
to me. Please let me know if there is anything in it that needs to be changed.

Yours sincerely

Nicola Marsh

Nicola Marsh (Ms)
Partner

Enc.
1   Statement of arrangement for children
2   Copy letter from Hatton, Moor & Lesley

**Advice letter
from petitioner's
solicitor to client**

Mrs Greaves's solicitor
encloses a copy of the
letter received from
Mr Greaves's solicitors
and provides advice
upon the matters
contained within it.

11

Example letter

---

1   What reason does
Ms Marsh give for
Mrs Greaves to agree
to split the divorce
costs 50/50 with
Mr Greaves?

2   What information
does Ms Marsh
provide to
Mrs Greaves?

3   What does she ask
Mrs Greaves to do?

4   Why does Ms Marsh
want another
meeting with
Mrs Greaves?

From petitioner's solicitor to the court

Mrs Greaves's lawyer has now received all the information needed to send the divorce papers to the court. The court will now issue the papers by processing them, allocating a case number to the divorce petition, and opening a case file. It will also serve the papers upon Mr Greaves by sending the papers to him in the post. The 'Notice of Acting' is a document which notifies the court that Turner, Jones, Smith & Co. have been appointed to act for Mrs Greaves and that therefore all official court documents should be sent to them.

TURNER JONES SMITH & CO.

7 Old Hall Street
Oxford
OX1 7PB
telephone: +44 (0) 1865 37522
fax: +44 (0) 1865 37523
email: info@tjs&co.com

Your reference
Our reference   NLM/GRE.1–1
Date   2 May 20—

The Chief Clerk
Oxford County Court
St Aldate's
Oxford
OX1 1TL

Dear Sir

Our client: Mary Greaves

We act for Mary Greaves and now enclose for issue and service upon the respondent the following:

1 Divorce petition in duplicate
2 Statement of arrangements for children in duplicate
3 Notice of Acting
4 Cheque for court fee

Yours faithfully

Turner, Jones, Smith & Co.

Turner, Jones, Smith & Co.

TURNER JONES SMITH & CO.

7 Old Hall Street
Oxford
OX1 7PB
telephone: +44 (0) 1865 37522
fax: +44 (0) 1865 37523
email: info@tjs&co.com

Your reference
Our reference   NLM/GRE.1–1
Date   10 May 20—

Mrs M. Greaves
35 Rington Crescent
Oxford
OX4 6RR

Dear Mrs Greaves

Your marriage

I write further to our meeting on 8 May when we discussed financial settlement. I enclose a copy of a letter to Mr Greaves's solicitors which contains the proposal we discussed, and will let you know when I receive a response.

As advised, if this proposal is acceptable to Mr Greaves, the next stage is to draw up a consent order. This is a document that records the agreement between you and Mr Greaves and is then submitted to the court for approval. Once approved, it takes effect as a court order, even though there will be no need for a court hearing. This means that if the order is breached, you will be entitled to apply to the court for enforcement of the order in the same way as an order made after a full court hearing.

I can also advise that I have received a telephone call from Mr Greaves's solicitor, who told me that Mr Greaves has been served with the divorce petition and has completed and returned the necessary paperwork to the court. This means that I should shortly receive notification from the court that you are entitled to apply for decree nisi. Once decree nisi is granted, we will also be able to finalize the financial settlement.

I will let you know as soon as I hear anything from Mr Greaves's solicitors.

Yours sincerely

Nicola Marsh

Nicola Marsh (Ms)
Partner

Enc. Copy of letter to Hatton, Moor & Lesley

Informing the client of progress

Ms Marsh keeps her client up to date with what is going on in the case. She explains in simple terms what is being done, but does not burden the client with excessive legal detail.

1 How does a consent order differ from an ordinary court order?

2 What has Ms Marsh heard from Mr Greaves' solicitors?

3 What is the significance of this news?

Petitioner's solicitor proposing terms of financial settlement

In this letter, Mrs Greaves's lawyer puts forward a proposal for financial settlement to Mr Greaves's solicitors. Quite a lot of legal terminology is used in the letter, because Mrs Greaves's lawyer needs to make reference to concepts which will be included in the consent order, and which cannot easily be explained in other ways. All of the terminology she uses would be familiar to a lawyer, but perhaps not to a layperson. (See Glossary.)

TURNER
JONES
SMITH
& CO.

7 Old Hall Street
Oxford
OX1 7PB
telephone: +44 (0) 1865 37522
fax: +44 (0) 1865 37523
email: info@tjs&co.com

Your reference   FWB/GRE.2–1
Our reference   NLM/GRE.1–1
Date   10 May 20—

Messrs Hatton, Moor & Lesley
35 Franklin Road
Reading
RG1 9DZ

Dear Sirs

Our client: Mary Greaves
Your client: Anthony Greaves

We write further in this matter, having now had the opportunity of taking our client's instructions in relation to financial settlement. We enclose our client's financial disclosure – kindly acknowledge receipt.

We are instructed to put forward the following proposal for financial settlement:

1 Matrimonial home to be transferred into our client's name, subject to a charge securing 30% of the net proceeds on sale for your client. Our client will use her best endeavours to have your client released from liability under the mortgage.

2 The property will be sold when Nathan reaches the age of seventeen or ceases full-time secondary education, whichever is the later. Our client will have the option to buy out your client's share as an alternative to sale.

3 Your client to pay maintenance at the rate of £800 per month until (2) above, subject to increase at RPI rate.

4 Our client to retain the sum in the joint savings account.

5 No claims on pensions by either party.

We should be grateful to hear from you in relation to this proposal. We confirm that our client will apply for decree nisi as soon as we receive notification from the court.

Yours faithfully

Turner, Jones, Smith & Co.

Turner, Jones, Smith & Co.

1 Would the house definitely be sold when Nathan leaves school?

2 Would the maintenance that Mr Greaves would pay always be £800 per month?

3 What does the letter say about the progress of the divorce proceedings?

Hatton, Moor & Lesley

35 Franklin Road
Reading
RG1 9DZ
telephone: +44 (0) 118 673770
fax: +44 (0) 118 673771
email: enq@hm&les.co.uk

▶ your ref. NLM/GRE.1–1
▶ our ref. FWB/GRE.2–1

14 May 20—

Messrs Turner, Jones, Smith & Co
7 Old Hall Street
Oxford
OX1 7PB

Dear Sirs

Our client: Anthony Greaves
Your client: Mary Greaves

Thank you for your letter of 10 May, on which we have now had the opportunity of taking our client's instructions.

Our client is prepared to accept the suggested proposals for settlement, with the following amendments:

1 The charge on the former matrimonial home should secure 35% of the proceeds of sale. We note that the maintenance sought is somewhere in excess of what the court would be likely to consider reasonable, bearing in mind our client's financial commitments. He is prepared to pay it, however, provided your client is prepared to compromise on the split of the proceeds of sale.

2 Our client requires the sum in the joint savings account. This is needed in order for him to rehouse himself in rental property, which will necessitate purchasing furniture and putting down a deposit on the rent.

If your client is in agreement with these proposed amendments, kindly let us have a draft consent order for consideration.

Yours faithfully

Turner, Jones, Smith & Co.

Turner, Jones, Smith & Co.

Respondent's solicitor's reply to financial proposals

In this letter, Mr Greaves's lawyer responds to the proposal sent by Mrs Greaves's lawyer. It is clear that Mr Greaves is basically in agreement with what has been suggested but is seeking to make the settlement a little more advantageous to himself. In order to assist him in this, his lawyers link issues together, demanding concessions on one issue in exchange for concessions on another, and they make reference to what they say the court would decide on the matter. These are typical, and perfectly legitimate, negotiation ploys used by family lawyers.

---

1 What issue does Mr Greaves's solicitors link to the issue of the split of the proceeds of sale of the former matrimonial home?

2 What other argument does Mr Greaves's solicitors use on this point?

3 Why does Mr Greaves need the money in the joint savings account?

4 What document does Mr Greaves's solicitors want from Mrs Greaves's solicitors?

Petitioner's solicitor to client

This simple letter is primarily a covering letter used to send Mr Greaves's lawyer's response to Mrs Greaves, and to update her about the divorce proceedings. Since the amendments proposed to the original proposal are easy to understand, Mrs Greaves's lawyer suggests a discussion over the telephone rather than a further appointment in the office.

TURNER
JONES
SMITH
& CO.

7 Old Hall Street
Oxford
OX1 7PB
telephone: +44 (0) 1865 37522
fax: +44 (0) 1865 37523
email: info@tjs&co.com

Your reference	
Our reference	NLM/GRE.1–1
Date	18 May 20—

Mrs M. Greaves
35 Rington Crescent
Oxford
OX4 6RR

Dear Mrs Greaves

Your marriage

I enclose a copy of a letter received from Mr Greaves's solicitors, the contents of which are self-explanatory. Perhaps you could telephone me to discuss this matter.

I have also received the acknowledgement of service from the court. This means that you can now apply for decree nisi. I will draw up the necessary documents in this regard.

Yours sincerely

Nicola Marsh

Nicola Marsh (Ms)
Partner

7 Old Hall Street
Oxford
OX1 7PB
telephone: +44 (0) 1865 37522
fax: +44 (0) 1865 37523
email: info@tjs&co.com

Your reference	FWB/GRE.2–1
Our reference	NLM/GRE.1–1
Date	18 May 20—

Messrs Hatton, Moor & Lesley
35 Franklin Road
Reading
RG1 9DZ

Dear Sirs

Our client: Mary Greaves
Your client: Anthony Greaves

Thank you for your letter of 14 May. We have now had the opportunity of taking our client's instructions, and can advise that the requested amendments are acceptable to our client.

In the circumstances, we enclose a draft consent order, which incorporates your suggestions, for your consideration and look forward to hearing from you at your earliest convenience. We can also indicate that an application for decree nisi has now been submitted to the court.

Yours faithfully

Turner, Jones, Smith & Co.

Turner, Jones, Smith & Co.

Enc. Draft consent order

Petitioner's solicitor enclosing draft consent order

Having taken instructions, Mrs Greaves's lawyer replies to Mr Greaves's lawyer enclosing a draft consent order. Ms Marsh notes that Mrs Greaves has now applied for decree nisi. Provided the consent order is agreed, it simply remains for the consent order to be submitted to the court for approval (although the court does have the power to refuse to approve such an order). Once the consent order is approved by the court, Mrs Greaves can apply for the decree absolute, which formally brings her marriage to an end.

11

Example letter

Points to remember

1 Remember that letters written to clients in family law cases often need to show greater empathy with the client than in other types of case. This can be achieved by using certain adjectives and adverbs (e.g. *understandable*, *sadly*, *sensible*, *difficult*, etc.).

2 The practice of family law places great emphasis on negotiation skills, both in writing and orally.

3 In UK (as in US and Canadian) jurisdictions, the courts often have much greater powers to make orders in divorce proceedings than is common in other jurisdictions. This is particularly the case where financial settlement is concerned.

4 In UK (as in US and Canadian) family law, divorce procedure is still to a great extent 'fault based'. This means that a person wanting a divorce often has to give some evidence that their wife or husband has done something wrong during the marriage, such as committing adultery or behaving unreasonably.

11

Memoranda, file notes, brief and instructions to counsel

12

INTERNAL COMMUNICATIONS

This unit considers three different kinds of what may be regarded as internal communications:

1 Memoranda created within a law firm for distribution among the staff of the firm to advise about new policies, procedures, or events.

2 File notes created by lawyers which relate to a particular case which the lawyer is handling and which are kept on the file relating to that case.

3 A document by which a solicitor briefs a barrister to represent a client in court.

MEMORANDA

A memorandum (usually known as a *memo*) is a written internal communication, not email, which advises or informs staff of new policies, procedures, events, or decisions. It is usually quite formal and impersonal in style.

Memos may be addressed to one other person or to a number of persons. They may be put on a noticeboard for everyone to see, or circulated in internal mail.

Layout

Firms often use headed paper for memos. This gives less information about the firm than the letterhead for external correspondence, but may indicate which department has issued the memo.

A memo should state at the top of the first page:
— the person(s) to whom it is addressed
— the person who wrote the memorandum
— the date
— the subject

Important points or long lists of points are usually best presented using bullets (●), dashes (–), or numbers.

Content

A typical memo might be structured as follows:
— Appropriate title – one that accurately reflects the content of the memo, and preferably one for which a file can easily be selected.
— The first paragraph of the memo may be used to explain the background to the issue that the memo refers to.
— The main part of the memo should be used to explain concisely:
  — what is going to happen
  — why it is going to happen
  — when it is going to happen
  — how it will affect people
  — who will be affected
— The next part of the memo should explain what should be done by anyone affected.
— The last part of the memo should advise staff where they can go for an explanation and how to communicate their comments or complaints.
— The memorandum should be signed by the writer.

Smith, Billings & Co.
23 Grange Road
Liverpool

To: All employees
Date: 13 March 2003
From: Michael Empson
Subject: Litigation department move

You have no doubt heard that due to pressures on our office space resulting from the firm's rapid expansion it has become necessary to move some staff members to another location.

The partners have decided that the whole of the litigation department will be moved to new premises at 35 Smithson Avenue, Liverpool. The relevant details of the move are as follows:

1   The move will take place over the weekend of 12 / 13 April.
2   The members of staff who will be moving include John Stiles, Emily Lane, Bernard Hill, Giles Flaxton, Mary Peebles, and Larissa May.
3   Staff affected by the move are asked to pack their computers, books, and other work items into the storage boxes provided by the removal firm no later than 4 p.m. on Friday 11 April. If needed, more boxes can be obtained from Jane Baxter.
4   An external IT contracting firm will visit the premises at 35 Smithson Avenue on Monday 14 April to set up the computers and establish the internal network. While this work is going on there will be a training day for the whole firm, details of which will be announced later.

If anyone has any questions regarding the move, please contact me.

Michael Empson

Senior Partner

Memorandum

This memo informs staff of a forthcoming office move, and gives details of the people affected and the day, and other matters concerning the relocation.

Memoranda, file notes, brief and instructions to counsel

12

Example memorandum

FILE NOTES

File notes are commonly used in legal practice. They are created by lawyers and usually relate to a particular case which the lawyer is handling. They are kept on the file relating to that case.

There are three main categories of file notes: attendance notes, research notes, and notes which record miscellaneous work done on the case.

No particular formalities need to be used for notes, since they are usually created for the writer's own use. The language used in file notes may therefore be slightly less formal than in letters and emails, and abbreviations may be used. It should be borne in mind, however, that such notes may ultimately be read by third parties and by the client, who has a general right to the papers in his or her file. Impolite references to the client or anyone else are therefore unwise.

File notes should always specify:
— the date of the attendance, meeting, or event to which the note refers
— the name of the client and case to which it relates
— the reference number of the case if applicable (this is an important safeguard against the misfiling of the file note)
— the subject of the note

Attendance notes

Attendance notes are used to record the contents of interviews with clients, telephone conversations with clients or other lawyers, and attendances at court or at external meetings. An attendance note should set out the following:
— date
— client's name
— file name
— topic of discussion
— the names of the parties involved in the discussion or event (e.g. the names of the judge and other lawyers present at a court hearing)

— matters discussed between the parties, including any specific information given by either party
— any advice given by the lawyer (in the case of a note relating to a lawyer-client discussion)
— any agreements reached by the parties
— any action to be taken as a result of the attendance

File notes are of crucial importance in legal practice for a variety of reasons. These can be summarized as follows:
— File notes act as memory aids. A lawyer may have up to one hundred or even more 'live' cases in hand at any one time. These will be in various stages of completion, and will run over different periods. Some cases are completed in a couple of weeks, a few may even run for the best part of a decade. No lawyer can expect to be able to recall exactly what stage a case has reached or what discussions have been held about it with different parties. Making a clear written record will help recollection.
— File notes protect the solicitor. We live in an increasingly litigious age, and lawyers are not exempt from being sued by dissatisfied clients. One issue that typically arises in professional negligence cases is that a client will allege that he or she was not advised by the lawyer about some important legal point or fact which would have had a great bearing on the case. There is little difficulty in verifying whether such information was given if it was given in writing. It is more problematic if oral advice was given. However, if the file relating to the case contains comprehensive file notes, it is possible to check whether the advice or information in dispute was given or not and to produce evidence about the matter. This evidence may literally win or lose a professional negligence case.
— File notes provide a full picture of the case. In long-running cases, it may be necessary for the file to be passed from one lawyer to another, perhaps because the first lawyer is leaving the law firm or retiring. The new

lawyer will have to familiarize him or herself with the details of the case by reference to the documents contained in the case file. If these are limited to letters and formal court documents, the lawyer will have little idea of the upshot of many important discussions which may have taken place during the case, including advice given and information received during these conversations. This is likely to prove to be a disadvantage.

— File notes also act as a time record of the work done on the case. Most lawyers base their bills on the amount of time actually spent working on each case. This is usually recorded electronically, but file notes are also used to record time spent on particular pieces of work on the case. This aspect of file notes can become particularly significant in litigation matters in which the other party may have to pay the lawyer's costs. The party that has to pay the costs is usually entitled to complain if the costs are too high. It becomes more difficult for that party to complain if there is an accurate record showing exactly what work has been carried out and how long was spent on it. Time is generally recorded in units of six minutes, making 10 units to the hour. This explains the rather odd indications in breakdowns of lawyers' time recording, in which they state that they have spent, for example, 6, 12, 18, or 42 minutes on a particular piece of work.

Research notes

Research notes set out the results of legal research carried out by lawyers into issues relevant to cases on which they are working.

The content of a research note will vary according to the nature of the research to be carried out, but should contain the following:
— which research sources were consulted
— the specific references for any findings (i.e. volume, page, and paragraph numbers), so that these can be quickly found again if needed
— a summary of the main findings
— any matters which might cast doubt on the conclusions of the research
— who has done the research (lawyers typically use their initials to indicate the identity of the writer)
— what needs to be done as a result of the research findings

Attendance note 1

This is a typical attendance note which records the matters discussed during an interview with a client. (New technical terms are in the glossary.)

Attendance note

Date:	22 February 20—
Client:	Hatchford Sports Ltd
File:	HAT.11–2
Re:	New matter: distribution agreement with Sharpers Ltd

RBD attending Gerald Hatchford of Hatchford Sports Ltd in the office regarding a new matter. Mr Hatchford explained that his company (which owns a local chain of sports shops) had entered into a distribution agreement with Sharpers Ltd. The intention of the agreement is that Sharpers will supply Hatchford with its current range of sports shoes (these include football boots, squash shoes, and basketball boots) for distribution in a defined territory. It is an exclusive agreement, as far as these products are concerned.

Gerald Hatchford has been informed that the current range of shoes produced by Sharpers is shortly to be discontinued and replaced by a new range of updated models. Gerald has been informed verbally by Sharpers' managing director, Sheila Prynn, that Sharpers intend to discontinue the contract, and appoint new distributors. Apparently, there is no question of Sharpers being dissatisfied with Hatchford's performance (there is a minimum sales stipulation in the termination clause) – it is more down to personal relationships, as Gerald and Sheila Prynn do not get along well.

Gerald wanted to know whether Sharpers were entitled to terminate the contract in these circumstances. RBD perusing the contract & noting that the definition of 'the products' falling under the agreement – in clause 5 – includes any 'similar products manufactured for sale by Sharpers within the currency of this agreement'. Therefore, in the absence of any other factor that might entitle Sharpers to terminate the contract, it seems that they are not entitled to terminate it. Explaining to Gerald the importance of clause 5, as it effectively means that Hatchford has a right to distribute the new range of shoes on the same terms as agreed for the old range – i.e. as exclusive distributors. Also noting the arbitration clause, which states that any disagreement regarding the construction of the contract should be referred to arbitration if it cannot be resolved amicably.

Leaving it that RBD would write to Sharpers in the first instance to indicate that the contract obliges them to offer the new products to Hatchford for distribution, and that they are not entitled to terminate the contract. If this did not have the desired effect, Hatchford would have to consider taking the case to arbitration.

Engaged – 30 minutes

1 What does Mr Hatchford want advice about?

2 Why are Sharpers not entitled to terminate the contract?

3 What does RBD suggest should be done as a first step?

4 What will happen if this first step does not work?

Attendance note

Date:	15 January 20—
Client:	Frances Miller
File:	MIL.7–2
Re:	Divorce file – client interview

MDF attending Mrs Miller on the telephone when she called to discuss Mr Miller's contact with the children (Sam aged 9 and Clare aged 7). She explained that since the decree absolute came through, Mr Miller has become very uncooperative regarding contact with the children, and was refusing to stick to the times previously agreed (i.e. alternate weekends). He was turning up at the house unannounced at all sorts of times demanding to see them. She wanted to know what she could do – she wanted to stop contact altogether.

Advised Mrs Miller re the welfare checklist in the Children Act 1989 and advised that in the circumstances there were no grounds to stop contact altogether, but certainly it was in everyone's interests for contact to proceed on a regular basis. Advised that in the last resort it would be possible to apply to the court for a defined contact order which Mr Miller would have to stick to. However, this should only be a last resort.

Agreed that to begin with we would write a letter to his solicitors indicating what was going on and reminding them of the agreement about contact reached in correspondence (letter dated 23 November). If this did not have the desired effect, we could think again.

Engaged: 12 minutes

Attendance note 2

This is a typical telephone attendance note which records a discussion between lawyer and client over the telephone.

1 What does Mrs Miller want advice about?

2 What is MDF's advice to her?

3 What is MDF going to do for Mrs Miller?

Research note

Here is a typical research note, giving an account of the lawyer's legal research work, action to be taken, and time taken doing the work.

Research note

Date: 9 July 20—
Client: Willis Tool Company
File: WIL.5–1
Re: Defective product – contract claim

GRH engaged researching re. letter received by Willis Tool Company from a third party to a sales contract claiming entitlement to damages under the Contracts (Rights of Third Parties) Act 1999 for an injury caused by a hedge strimmer purchased from Willis.

Noting that the basic effect of this legislation is to allow a third party to enforce a contractual term where the contract either expressly states that the term or contract benefits a third party, or where the particular term purports to benefit a third party.

Looking up the Act on the HMSO website and noting as follows:
(1) Subject to the provisions of this Act, a person who is not a party to a contract (a 'third party') may in his own right enforce a term of the contract if:
   (a) the contract expressly provides that he may, or
   (b) subject to subsection (2), the term purports to confer a benefit on him.
(2) Subsection (1)(b) does not apply if on a proper construction of the contract it appears that the parties did not intend the term to be enforceable by the third party.

GRH taking the view that the wording of subsection (2) provides a comprehensive defence to any claim brought on this basis.

We need to write to the prospective claimant immediately denying liability on this basis.

Engaged – 18 minutes

1 What is meant by a 'third party'?

2 What is the Contracts (Rights of Third Parties) Act 1999 intended to achieve?

3 Under what circumstances is a third party not allowed to enforce a term in the contract?

4 What is GRH's conclusion?

Time record note

The purpose of such notes is to provide a running record of what work has been done on the file which relates to a particular case, and how long it took.

File note

Date: 5 June 20—
Client: Felicity George
File: GEO.5–1
Re: Divorce

JBT engaged drafting divorce petition (on basis of unreasonable behaviour) and statement of arrangements for children, for issue in Oxford County Court.

Engaged – 30 minutes

BRIEF AND INSTRUCTIONS TO COUNSEL

A brief to counsel (i.e. a barrister) is a document by which a solicitor briefs a barrister to represent a client in court. Note that in some circumstances a solicitor will not ask a barrister actually to represent the client in court, but merely to provide advice on the case – for instance, on whether it would be likely to succeed in court or not in the event that an application to court was made. Where this occurs, the document the solicitor sends to the barrister is not known as a brief to counsel but as *instructions to counsel*.

When briefing counsel to represent a client in court, the solicitor will include with the brief itself copies of all the documents which the barrister will need in order to represent the client effectively in court. These include copies of the documents submitted to the court (such as applications and statements), in addition to all the documents issued by the court (such as notices of court hearings and court orders themselves). The solicitor will also include all documents which will assist the barrister in understanding the course and merits of the case. For example, in a long-running case it is usual to enclose copies of the most important correspondence that has been exchanged between the parties to the case.

In the case to which the example brief overleaf relates, the client wishes to apply for a non-molestation order. This is an order made under Part IV of the Family Law Act 1996 the effect of which will be to forbid the respondent to harass, pester, or use violence against the applicant. A power of arrest is also sought. This is a document which is lodged with the local police station and allows the police to arrest the respondent if he breaches the order and to produce him before the court which issued the order. The court will then reconsider the case and decide what is to be done with the respondent.

Since barristers employ clerks, who in effect manage the allocation of work to the barristers, the solicitor sends the brief to the clerk at the barrister's chambers.

IN THE OXFORD COUNTY COURT   CASE NO. OX0500356

BETWEEN: Maria Rachel Danworth   Applicant
AND Darren John Skinner   Respondent

BRIEF TO COUNSEL

Counsel will find enclosed copies of the following:

1 Application for a non-molestation order in form FL401 dated 14.3.05
2 Applicant's sworn statement in support of application (with two exhibits) dated 14.3.05
3 Letter from Dr Jane Baxter dated 16.3.05
4 Statement of service in form FL415 dated 16.3.05
5 Notice of hearing listed for 21.3.05

Your instructing solicitors act for the applicant, Maria Danworth, in respect of her application for a non-molestation order against the respondent, Darren Skinner, who is her ex-boyfriend.

Our client informs us that she met Mr Skinner at a New Year's Eve party at the end of 2004, and started a relationship with him a week later. The relationship was stormy and our client decided to end it two weeks ago when she discovered syringes in Mr Skinner's flat. On confronting him, he admitted that he was a heroin addict. Our client lives in her own flat which is only about quarter of a mile from Mr Skinner's.

Mr Skinner has not taken the breakup of the relationship well, and has harassed our client on an almost daily basis. Details of this harassment are set out in detail in our client's sworn statement, but include uninvited visits to our client's flat, verbal abuse, and nuisance phone calls. There has also been one incidence of violence. This occurred on the night of Saturday 12 March. Mr Skinner came to our client's flat uninvited at about 11 p.m., and, when she answered the door, made an unprovoked attack upon her, punching her and causing a deep cut to her left cheek. Our client saw her doctor the following day, and counsel is referred to the letter from Dr Baxter in this regard. This details the nature of the injury suffered by our client.

1

1 What kind of order is Maria Danworth seeking?

2 Why did she end her relationship with Darren Skinner?

3 What evidence of the violent incident which occurred on Saturday 12 March is provided with the brief?

4 What will happen on Monday 21 March 2005?

Following this violent incident, our client consulted this firm. Counsel is accordingly instructed to attend Oxford County Court at 10 a.m. on Monday 21 March 2005 and represent our client on the hearing of her application for a non-molestation order against the respondent. A power of arrest should also be obtained if possible. If counsel requires any further information she should contact our John Talbot.

SIGNED ————————————————————————

DATED ————————————————————————

TO: The Clerk to Ms Jane Standford, Park Chambers,
        1 Bell Tower Buildings, Leeds LS1 4LB

FROM: Barton & Co. Solicitors, 3 Green Road, Leeds LS1 8JY

2

Points to remember

1 Memoranda (or memos) are written to staff in a law firm to inform them about, e.g. new policies, procedures, or events.

2 A file note usually relates to a particular legal case. It can be
   — an attendance note that records the contents of interviews with clients, telephone conversations with clients or other lawyers, and attendance at court or external meetings.
   — a research note recording the results of legal research carried out.
   — a time note to help provide a running record of work done on a file and the time spent on it.

3 A brief to counsel is a document by which a solicitor briefs a barrister to represent a client in court. If the intention of the solicitor is merely to seek advice, then the document is known as instructions to counsel.

Personnel appointments

13

Introduction

The purpose of this unit is to familiarize the student with the kind of correspondence involved in obtaining a job. The example of applying for a job in a law firm has been taken, as some students may wish or need to pursue this course of action. The sample correspondence includes responding to a job advertisement, registering with a recruitment consultant, an unsolicited job application, preparing a curriculum vitae (cv), filling out application forms, and subsequent correspondence relating to an interview, turning down an application, and the offer and acceptance or rejection of a job.

APPLYING FOR A JOB

Job advertisements

Advertisements (often shortened to *ads*) for employment appear in all the media, including radio, television, and the Internet, as well as in newspapers and periodicals. However, for legal appointments the best place to begin your search for employment may be in a professional legal publication. In most countries the national law society (solicitors) or bar association (barristers) has its own magazine, which is likely to appear at least monthly and which will generally contain a large section reserved for advertisements for all kinds of legal positions and for legal services.

Most advertisements contain a number of abbreviations, which are usually well understood in the profession. They are included primarily to save space, and therefore money, on the advertisement. A typical advertisement for a general commercial lawyer might read as follows:

> *Wanted, 3 yrs + PQE gen. comm. practitioner. Caseload to include co-co, comm. Prop. & IPR. Large city-centre practice. Must have own transport. Salary negotiable. FT position, assistant with partner potential. Apply with cv to Mr J.M. Stokes by 13.04.05.*

A full-length version of this would read:

> *Wanted, a general commercial practitioner with more than three years of post-qualified experience. The caseload will include company commercial, commercial property, and intellectual property rights. Large city-centre practice. Must have own transport. Salary negotiable. A full-time position for an assistant lawyer with potential to become a partner. Apply with your curriculum vitae to Mr J.M. Stokes by 13 April 2005.*

Recruitment consultants

The role of a recruitment consultant is to find suitable candidates to fill posts offered by particular firms or organizations. The recruitment consultant is typically engaged

by a firm or organization that wishes to fill a particular position. The consultant will then:
— Advertise the position.
— Receive applications from all those who are interested in the position.
— Select a number of the most qualified candidates (the shortlist) and propose them to the firm or organization that it interviews.
— Act as a liaison point between the firm or organization and the candidates during the negotiations regarding the terms of employment.

The value of the recruitment consultant's services to a firm is that the firm does not have to deal with the time-consuming process of advertising the position and sorting through large numbers of applications. Instead, it can rely on the recruitment consultant's expertise in finding the best-qualified candidates for the position.

In most cases, recruitment consultants are happy to receive and store on their databases the personal details of any persons looking for jobs, whether or not there is an immediately available suitable position for that person. Therefore, the value of the recruitment consultant to persons applying for jobs is that they can register their details with a number of recruitment consultants, along with details of the kind of position they are looking for, in the knowledge that they will be contacted if any suitable positions arise. Of course, it helps if the person looking for a job makes the effort to contact from time to time any recruitment consultants with whom that person has registered. In that way, the job seeker will remain fresh in the minds of the consultants with whom he or she is dealing.

Recruitment consultants generally advertise the positions they have been asked to help fill in professional legal publications, alongside advertisements placed by individual firms and organizations themselves.

How to apply

There are basically three kinds of job application:
— An application for a specific advertised position
— An application to a recruitment consultant to register your details in case a suitable position arises
— An unsolicited application – i.e. a general application to a firm in circumstances where no specific position has been advertised

The kind of letter you write will depend on the kind of application you make, but in all cases you should:
— Find out whether the application must be made on a special application form or by sending your curriculum vitae (cv) and a covering letter. If an application form is required, telephone or write to the firm to which you are applying to obtain it.
— Find out the name and job title of the person to whom you should send your application. Many job applications are disregarded because they are not addressed to a particular person. Many big law firms nowadays have personnel departments (also called human resources departments) which deal with job applications. If it is not clear to whom an application should be addressed, phone the personnel department to find out.
— Do your research. Find out as much as possible about the firm or organization you are applying to before sending your application. In this way you can 1) save yourself the trouble of sending out any applications which are highly unlikely to be successful, and 2) adapt your application to the needs of the particular firm or organization to which you are writing.
— Remember to quote any reference numbers mentioned in an advertisement.

When applying for a legal position, always ensure that your letter and cv or application form are free from grammatical errors and spelling mistakes. Lawyers are trained to pay attention to detail, and mistakes will make a very poor impression.

13

Applying for an advertised position

Your letter should have a beginning, middle, and end. Generally, the terms *vacancy*, *post*, *position*, or *appointment* are used instead of the word job in advertisements.

At the beginning of your letter, explain what you are applying for and mention any documents that you have enclosed. For example:

> *I wish to apply for the vacancy for a commercial lawyer advertised in this month's edition of* Legal News. *I enclose a copy of my curriculum vitae [OR the relevant application form duly completed].*

Use the middle of the letter to state what appeals to you about the position you are applying for, and why you think that you would be particularly well-suited to it. You can use this part of the letter 1) to demonstrate knowledge about the firm or organization to which you are writing, and 2) to give some indication of your expertise and experience. For example:

> *This position is of particular interest to me since I note that your firm is well known for its work for IT companies. I have had over three years of experience in IT law in my present position, and am keen to develop my expertise in this area further.*

At the end of the letter, offer to supply more information if necessary:

> *I look forward to hearing from you. However, if there is any further information you require in the meantime, please let me know.*

Applying to a recruitment consultant to register details

The main purpose of this letter is to indicate what kind of position you are seeking and what kind of previous experience you have. However, it is important to make a good impression on the recruitment consultant to whom you write, since the consultant is only likely to put your name forward to firms looking for new employees if he or she has confidence in your abilities.

When dealing with recruitment consultants, it is important to remind them periodically that you are still looking for work. Most consultants have large databases of people who have at one time or other registered their details, and those who have been silent for a long period of time tend to get forgotten. Phone the recruitment consultant either shortly before or shortly after you have sent them your details, and let them know exactly what you are looking for and why you are a suitable candidate. After this initial conversation, if you hear nothing for a week or so, phone again to check on progress.

In your initial letter, state what kind of position you are looking for, the geographical area in which your ideal job should be located, the salary range you are seeking, and mention any documents that you have enclosed. For example:

> *I am looking for a position as an assistant commercial lawyer, mainly specializing in company commercial matters, in a large commercially oriented law firm. Ideally, I would like to remain in the London area, but would be prepared to consider relocating for an exceptional position. I am looking for a salary in the region of £30,000–£40,000 per annum.*

You should then state any particular qualities or experience you have that will make you especially attractive to employers. For example:

> *I have had over five years of experience in the field of company commercial law and also have significant experience in IT law. I am fluent in German and spent one year during my current employment working at the firm's branch office in Munich, where I headed the company commercial department.*

At the end of your letter, you should indicate that you will be proactive in pursuing your job search. A suitably worded ending will communicate to the recruitment consultant that you are a serious applicant worthy of being strongly marketed to prospective employers. For example:

If there is any further information you require, please let me know. I am keen to pursue this matter vigorously, and will telephone your Ms Smith on Friday 12 June to discuss progress. I can be contacted at any time on my mobile, number 07845 746 939.

Unsolicited applications

When sending an unsolicited application, you should start by asking whether the firm you are writing to might have a vacancy that you could fill. For example:

I am writing to enquire whether you might have a vacancy in your company commercial department for an assistant lawyer. I enclose a copy of my curriculum vitae.

If someone associated with the firm you are writing to suggested that you write to them, mention this in your opening:

I was recommended by Clive Enright, who I understand has a long association with your firm, to contact you regarding a possible position in your company commercial department.

In either case, you should then explain why you are applying to the firm – state what it is about the firm that particularly attracts you, and why you would be a suitable employee for the firm. For example:

I am particularly interested by the possibility of working for your firm, since I note that you have strong expertise in the field of intellectual property. I have three years post-qualified experience working in the commercial department of my present firm, and have primarily focused on patent and industrial design rights. I am keen to further my expertise and experience in this area.

At the end of the letter, offer to supply more information if necessary:

I look forward to hearing from you. If there is any further information you require in the meantime, please let me know.

Application forms and cvs

When you receive an application form, always read it through carefully so that you know exactly what information is required. It is a good idea to photocopy it, complete the photocopy, and when you are happy with it, copy the information onto the actual form.

Some firms or organizations prefer a curriculum vitae (cv; *résumé* in American English). A curriculum vitae should contain your personal and working history.

Application forms and cvs may be emailed, faxed, or sent by post. It is best to try to find out from the firm or organization to which you are applying which method they prefer before you send your application.

There are a number of ways of presenting information in a cv. Traditionally, the sequence was name, address, contact details, marital status, education, qualifications, work experience, referees, and interests. However, it is now more common to begin with brief personal details, followed by a short profile or description of yourself (sometimes also called a career summary). After that, the most important information is recent employment history, and skills and qualifications. In the interests of completeness, you should account for all years since leaving school, but if the information is irrelevant to the position you are applying for or is some years old, you should summarize it as briefly as possible.

These days, it is generally unnecessary to mention marital status, children, age, health, or current salary unless specifically asked to do so, but this will vary according to the law and customs in different countries.

13

Example cv

Curriculum vitae (cv) 1

This is a typical curriculum vitae of a trainee lawyer with experience.

13

Richard Hambleton

Address	33 Arundel Road Oxford OX4 7TR
Telephone	01865 773051
Mobile	032 976 1459
Email	richard.hambleton@elt.com
Profile	– Five years' qualified commercial lawyer with wide experience in company commercial and IT law. – Experience of supervising and coordinating a team of lawyers – Excellent communication and client skills – Analytical, innovative, self-motivating, confident – Fluent in German and French – Computer literate

Employment

2000-present **Cranford & Marchand**
Assistant lawyer, commercial department

Caseload comprised company commercial and IT matters. Worked on several large merger cases under the supervision of the partner in charge of the department. Helped build up the IT law practice and was personally involved in supervising, coordinating, and training a team of junior assistant lawyers.

1998–2000 **Burns, Arthurs & Frank**
Trainee

Undertook training contract, gaining experience in company commercial, commercial property, commercial litigation, and criminal litigation departments. Co-wrote article, 'Recent developments in IT law', published in the June 2000 edition of *New Law*.

Qualifications

1997	Diploma of Legal Practice, College of Law
1996	LL B, University of Bristol

Abigail Empson

Date of birth:	12 July 19—
Address:	19 Bradley Terrace, Birmingham B18 2FD
Telephone:	0121 4214 6891
Mobile:	045 382 6619
Email:	abigail.empson@freeserve.net.uk
Profile:	A highly motivated and well-travelled law graduate with high academic qualifications and extensive practical work experience.

Education:

19—–19—   Founder School, Warwick

GCSEs: Maths (A), English (A), French (A), History (A), Spanish (A), Art (B), Geography (B), Chemistry (C), Physics (C), Biology (C)

A levels: Law (A)   English (B)   Spanish (B)

20—–20—   College of Law, York
Diploma of Legal Practice

October 20—   Oxford Language Training Institute
TEFL certificate

20—–20—   Bristol University
LL B   2:1

Work experience:

July–September 20—   Paralegal work at Brabham, Thorpe & Partners, York, mainly assisting the civil litigation department.

November 20—–July 20—   Worked as TEFL tutor at J.P. English School, Santiago, Chile and at The Business English College in Barcelona, Spain.

Other information:

September 20—–July 20—   Spent part of my LL B degree course studying Private International Law at Salamanca University, Spain.

Interests: My main interest outside work is Spanish language and culture, and I have travelled extensively both in Spain and in South America. I also enjoy cinema and playing tennis and badminton.

References:

Professor J.T. Mercer   Ms R.M. Taylor
School of Law   Partner
Bristol University   Brabham, Thorpe & Partners
Bristol BS1 4CD   10 Yarl Street
                         York YO1 4JY

1 What kinds of work experience has Abigail had?

2 What is Abigail's main interest?

3 Where did Abigail graduate from?

4 Who is Ms R. M. Taylor?

Application for an advertised position

Notice that the applicant starts off by referring to the job advertisement. He goes on to expand on his present duties and gives other information that he believes to be relevant to the post. He explains why he is applying for this particular vacancy and demonstrates knowledge of the firm to which he is applying. If on his cv, he gives his current employers as referees, he could also mention that he would prefer Small & Fanshawe not to approach them until after an interview.

23 Wakefield Terrace
Cambridge
CB2 1AP

16 May 20—

Ms G. Summers
Human Resources Coordinator
Small & Fanshawe
1 Garfield Road
Oxford
OX1 4BE
Your Ref: GS 311/09

Dear Ms Summers

I wish to apply for the vacancy advertised in Legal News on 10 May 20— for an assistant commercial lawyer. I enclose a copy of my curriculum vitae.

I am currently employed as an assistant lawyer at Bring & Fewster in Cambridge and have had four years of post-qualified experience, primarily in company commercial and IT law. In addition to handling a substantial caseload, I am also heavily involved in helping to co-ordinate my firm's marketing strategy with regard to IT clients. I am particularly interested by the position on offer at your firm, since I am aware that the firm has extensive expertise in this area.

I speak fluent French, and use the language daily in the course of my work.

If there is any further information you require, please contact me. I look forward to hearing from you.

Yours sincerely

Michael Arthurs

Michael Arthurs

Enc. cv

Small & Fanshawe

1 Garfield Road
Oxford
OX1 4BE

telephone	+44 (0) 1865 42689
fax	+44 (0) 1865 42690
email	enq@s&f.co.uk
our reference	GS 311/09

30 May 20—

Mr Michael Arthurs
23 Wakefield Terrace
Cambridge
CB2 1AP

Dear Mr Arthurs

Thank you for your letter of 16 May.

We would like you to come for an interview on Thursday 8 June at 11.00 a.m. Could you please phone me on ext. 214 to confirm that you will be able to attend?

I look forward to hearing from you.

Yours sincerely

Gill Summers

Ms G. Summers
Human Resources Co-ordinator

Application to a recruitment consultant to register

The applicant gives specific information about the kind of post she is looking for. In this way, she ensures both that the recruitment consultants will not waste her time by suggesting her for posts that do not meet her expectations, and that the recruitment consultant's job is made easier by defining the terms of the employment that they should try to find for her. The applicant signals her seriousness about the job search by telephoning the recruitment consultants before sending her letter and by promising to phone again soon to check on progress.

Recruitment consultants do not usually send written acknowledgements that they have received applicants' details, but may telephone to discuss any aspects of the application that need to be clarified. They may also make alterations to the presentation (but not to the content) of an applicant's cv in order to maximize their chances of obtaining a suitable post.

23 The Glebe
Wantage
OX12 9PZ

10 September 20—

Ms M.R. Talbot
A1 Legal Recruiting
17A March Street
London
WC1 4HS

BY FAX: 020 456 2389

Dear Ms Talbot

I refer to our telephone conversation this morning and now enclose a copy of my curriculum vitae.

As discussed, I am looking for a position as an assistant lawyer in the company commercial department of a commercially oriented practice in the south-east of the UK. I have three years of post-qualified experience in the commercial department of Hamble, Jones & Partners in Oxford, and have particular expertise in the fields of corporate acquisitions and IT law. I am strongly motivated, have advanced computer skills, and I also have experience of supervising other lawyers and trainees. I seek a salary in the range £30,000 – £40,000 and a post with real partnership potential.

I will telephone you on Friday 28 September to check on progress.

Yours sincerely

Vanessa Ledworth

Vanessa Ledworth

14 Grenville Road
Coventry
CV1 5PT
27 May 20—

Mr J.C. Norton
Thompson & Grimes
35 Anfield Way
Coventry
CV1 9RS

Dear Mr Norton

I am writing to you on the recommendation of Jill Masterton, assistant lawyer in your commercial litigation department. We met last month on a legal skills training course in London and she suggested that I should contact your firm and mention her name.

I am at present employed as a trainee solicitor at Burns, Gartner & Co. in Warwick. My training contract is due to finish in September of this year, and I am seeking a post as an assistant solicitor. During the course of my training contract I have gained experience in various types of commercial work, including company commercial, commercial litigation, and commercial property. I am keen to specialize in commercial property in my future career and am particularly interested in applying to your firm since I am aware that the firm has a strong national reputation in this area of work and is seeking to expand its commercial property team.

I am a highly motivated person with good academic credentials. I graduated in law from Southampton University with a 2:1 and speak fluent German and Swedish. During the course of my training contract I have handled a number of important commercial property cases on my own, and have particular experience in drafting commercial leases and options. I have also co-written articles on commercial leases which have appeared in *Legal News*, and have assisted in creating a library of commercial precedents for in-house use at my present firm.

I would be grateful if you could send me an application form and further information about the posts currently available. If you require any further information, please contact me.

Yours sincerely

James Thorne

James Thorne

An unsolicited job application

In this letter the applicant first mentions how he knows of Thompson & Grimes, gives brief details about his education and experience, and then requests an application form. Of course, he could also include a cv with the letter, but in this case he knows that the firm's practice is to send application forms.

1 How did James Thorne hear about Thompson & Grimes?

2 What is his present position?

3 What are his qualifications?

4 Why does he want to work for Thompson & Grimes?

5 What experience does he have that is particularly relevant to the post he is seeking?

13

THOMPSON & GRIMES

35 Anfield Way • Coventry • CV1 9RS
Telephone: +44 (0) 24 743325 • Fax: +44 (0) 24 743326
Email: info@t&g.co.uk

Our ref. JN/VAC/6.01

5 June 20—

Mr J. Thorne
14 Grenville Road
Coventry
CV1 5PT

Dear Mr Thorne

Thank you for your letter of 27 May. I can confirm that we do have a vacancy for a newly qualified lawyer in our commercial property department.

I enclose our application form together with a copy of this firm's brochure. I should be grateful if you would complete the application form and send it to Mr M.B. Turner, Human Resources Manager, at the above address.

You will see from the form that we require two referees. I suggest that you include the names and contact addresses of your supervising partner at your present firm, and one academic referee from Southampton University.

We look forward to hearing from you.

Yours sincerely

Helen Baxter

p.p. Jim Norton
Partner

Enc.
1 Application form
2 Brochure

ATTENDING AN INTERVIEW

If you are invited to an interview, remember the following:

— Make sure you know in advance where the venue for the interview is and how you are going to get there. Leave yourself plenty of time – arriving late will create a very bad impression.

— Look the part. When applying for most legal jobs, you will be expected to be smartly but conservatively dressed.

— Do your research: find out as much as possible about the firm or organization to which you have applied, and the position you are seeking.

— Review your application. Be prepared for things you have mentioned in your application to be brought up and questioned by the interviewer. Therefore, do not mention anything in your application unless it can be supported by solid evidence.

— Be prepared for difficult questions. Always answer all questions frankly and fully. Try to discern the underlying objective of the interviewer in asking certain questions. The following are interview favourites:

—*'Where do you see yourself in five years' time?'* The interviewer is testing your ambition, sense of purpose, and career planning.

—*'Why do you want to work for us?'* The interviewer is checking for motivation *and* your understanding of the position on offer.

—*'Tell me about yourself.'* The interviewer is checking mainly for confident self-presentation and for your ability to present relevant information succinctly.

—*'Why do you want to leave your current job?'* The interviewer is looking for positive motivation. Never say that you want to leave in order to obtain a better-paid position or that your job is boring (even if either of those is true), and avoid direct criticism of your present or past employers or colleagues.

— If you do not get the job after being interviewed, do not be scared to telephone the firm to which you applied to ask the reason for this. If there is something in your style of presentation that you can correct, it is worth learning about it. Most reasonable firms will discuss with candidates over the telephone why they were rejected.

13

MAKING A DECISION

Being turned down / turning down an applicant

Firms reject applicants for a variety of reasons, the most common of which are lack of relevant qualifications or experience. However, it is unusual for a candidate to be told in the rejection letter the specific reason why he or she has been rejected.

Thank you for attending an interview on ——. We regret to inform you that you were unsuccessful in your application, and hope that you are successful in finding a suitable post elsewhere.

We regret that we are unable to offer you the position of —— for which you were interviewed on ——. Thank you for your interest in XYZ & Partners.

We have decided not to appoint any of the applicants who were interviewed for the post of —— on —— and will be re-advertising the vacancy.

Being offered / offering a post

Letters to successful applicants can vary in length and detail, depending on the type of job, whether the firm has a standard printed contract, or if for some reason it is necessary to give details of the terms of employment. Such letters will often be conditional upon satisfactory references being provided by the referees mentioned in your application or cv.

Opening

We are pleased to inform you that you were successful in your interview for the post of ——.

We would like to offer you the post of ——.

The firm is pleased to be able to offer you the post of trainee, subject to provision of satisfactory references ——.

Details of employment

As discussed during your interview, you will be working in the —— department under the supervision of ——. You are entitled to 20 days' annual leave plus all public holidays. There is a staff contributory pension scheme which you will be eligible to join on successful completion of a six-month probationary period. Four weeks' notice of termination of employment is required by both you and the partnership.

Closing

A letter offering a job would invite questions if anything is unclear, and ask for written confirmation of acceptance. In the UK, and in many other countries, the law requires that employees are provided with a written statement of the conditions of employment. The common practice therefore is that firms will draw up a formal contract of employment, and two copies of this are often sent with the letter (usually referred to as being *in duplicate*). The applicant is generally asked to return one signed copy, and keep the other copy for their own records. The letter often closes by proposing a starting date for the employment and welcoming the applicant to the firm.

ACCEPTING A POST

Letters confirming that you accept a post can be brief, as long as they cover all the relevant points.

Thank you for your letter of 15 March 20—— offering me the post of ——. I am delighted to accept, and look forward to seeing you at 9 a.m. on Monday 20 April. As requested, I enclose one signed copy of the contract of employment.

I am returning a signed copy of the contract of employment, which you sent me with your letter of 15 March. I confirm that I will be able to begin work on Monday 20 April at 9 a.m. and look forward to seeing you then.

32 Priory Road, London, SE17 6TR
telephone: +44 (0) 20 311568
fax: +44 (0) 20 311569
email: info@barnsandfew.com

Our ref. KB/013.6

17 April 20—

Ms J.R. Ampney
23A Crumley Drive
Reading
RG2 7XW

Dear Ms Ampney

Thank you for attending an interview on 15 April. We regret to inform you that you were unsuccessful in your application.

We would remark that all the candidates that we interviewed for this post were of a very high calibre, and we wish you every success in finding a suitable post elsewhere.

Yours sincerely

Kevin Brackley

Mr K. Brackley
Human Resources Manager

BARNSLEY AND FEWINGS

32 Priory Road, London, **SE17 6TR**
telephone: +44 (0) 20 311568
fax: +44 (0) 20 311569
email: info@barnsandfew.com

Our ref. KB/013.4

17 April 20—

Ms M.G. Cranford
81 Derwent Drive
Slough
SL5 3WE

Dear Ms Cranford

We are pleased to inform you that you were successful in your interview for the post of assistant lawyer in this firm's civil litigation department.

As discussed during your interview, you will be working under the supervision of John Arndale, partner in charge of civil litigation.

You are entitled to twenty days' annual leave plus all public holidays. There is a staff contributory pension scheme which you will be eligible to join on successful completion of a six-month probationary period. Four weeks' notice of termination of employment is required by both you and the partnership.

We enclose our standard terms and conditions of employment in duplicate and request that you read through these carefully, and, if you are happy with them, kindly sign and date both copies and return one copy to us with your letter of acceptance. We would like you to start at 9 a.m. on Monday 20 May and look forward to welcoming you to the firm.

Yours sincerely

Kevin Brackley

Mr K. Brackley
Human Resources Manager

Enc. Employment contract

81 Derwent Drive
Slough
SL5 3WE

24 April 20—
Your ref. KB/013.4

Mr K. Brackley
Barnsley and Fewings
32 Priory Road
London
SE17 6TR

Dear Mr Brackley

Thank you for your letter of 17 April 20— offering me the post of
assistant solicitor. I am delighted to accept, and look forward to
seeing you at 9 a.m. on Monday 20 May. As requested, I enclose one
signed copy of the contract of employment.

Yours sincerely

Mary Cranford

Mary Cranford

Enc. Employment contract

Points to remember

1 The word *job* is not usually used either in advertisements or applications. The terms *vacancy*, *post*, *position*, or *appointment* are more appropriate.

2 When applying for a job, use your covering letter to make an impression on the prospective employer. Explain why you want to work for that employer and what particular skills or experience you can bring to the post offered.

3 Make sure that your letter and cv are free from grammatical errors and spelling mistakes. Lawyers are trained to pay attention to detail, and mistakes will make a very poor impression.

13

Unit 1

▶ **page 16**

1 If members of staff carry out urgent or complex work or work after 8 p.m. or overnight or at weekends.

2 Where a matter is long-running or where significant costs will be incurred.

3 Yes, if it believes that the level of invoices unpaid is unacceptable.

4 Only provide financial services, where they form an incidental part of professional services the firm is engaged to provide.

5 At least seven years.

6 No. If the client continues to instruct the solicitor, the solicitor shall deem the client to have agreed the terms and conditions set out in the letter.

Unit 3

▶ **page 51**

1 Once the refurbishment works are finished.

2 To reply to the letter either himself or through solicitors.

3 a circulate b fair copies c refurbishment

▶ **page 52**

1 per annum, yearly, annual

2 On the date it is executed; *the date hereof* means the date of execution.

3 They say they will not be able to proceed to completion of the lease unless clauses 4 and 5 are amended.

4 The north boundary of the plot is incorrectly drawn.

▶ **page 54**

1 Quarterly: i.e. four times a year.

2 Three, in 2006, 2008, and 2010.

3 That a simple error was made. She confirms that the lease will expire on 31 March 2012 rather than 31 March 2010.

Unit 4

▶ **page 64**

1 He has carried out a search at Companies House.

2 The memorandum and articles of association.

3 £100: 100 £1 shares.

4 Brian Finchley and Graham Shorter.

5 Because it can be used to protect the shareholders' individual interests in the company in ways which cannot be achieved through the articles of association.

▶ **page 66**

1 That certain restrictions should be included in the shareholders' agreement.

2 That a provision be included in the shareholders' agreement according to which this could only be done by mutual agreement of the shareholders.

3 a firing b restriction c provision d staff

▶ **page 69**

1 Yes, but they must offer them for sale to the other shareholder first.

2 The other shareholder or the deceased shareholder's estate.

3 The parties must apply to the company's auditors to resolve the dispute.

4 Yes, provided both shareholders agree.

▶ **page 70**

1 Director and company secretary.

2 It is a legal requirement under the Companies Act 1985.

3 They are at the solicitor's office.

4 £900.

Unit 5

▶ **page 76**

1 The post was awarded to an outside applicant.

2 The position of Sales Representative.

3 Mr Parker recently praised Mr Griffiths for the exceptional sales figures he had achieved during the second quarter of this year.

4 Through a meeting with the Human Resources Department, or, if this fails, by bringing a claim before the Employment Tribunal.

5 a allocated b position c awarded d proposals

▶ **page 78**

1 That he has a valid claim for constructive dismissal and could bring a claim for compensation before the Employment Tribunal.

2 To sign, date, and return the duplicate copy of the client care letter.

▶ **page 79**

1 On the basis that it is not materially different to his current position and that it is only a proposal at this stage.

2 That at no stage did Mr Griffiths show any intention of applying for this position, and that it required skills that he does not possess.

3 That he should have used the company's internal grievance procedure.

▶ **page 81**

1 That he did not know about the position's existence until it was actually filled.

2 Because at his meeting with James Parker on 28 August, Mr Griffiths was explicitly told that his existing position would be lost and he would be designated to a new position.

3 That it must be treated as a fundamental breach of his employment contract, amounting to constructive dismissal.

Unit 6

▶ **page 89**

1 While they were registering trademarks.
2 London Institute could argue that it has acquired rights over the name by long-term use.
3 1) The client's options, 2) the prospects of success, and 3) the likely costs involved.

▶ **page 91**

1 An individual called Roy Miller.
2 Check 1) what else Roy Miller has registered, and 2) whether he has been a defendant in legal proceedings concerning domain names.
3 The cost of the initial action will be £500 plus VAT.

▶ **page 93**

1 That Mr Miller owns ten different combinations of 'london-institute.com' and that he is not involved in any other domain name disputes.
2 Because his portfolio of domain names is rather small and select and he is not involved in other disputes.
3 Because his infringement is probably not deliberate (i.e. he may not be seeking to make a profit from registering these names).
4 a dispute   b draft   c deliberately   d exploit   e amenable

▶ **page 94**

1 a legal proceedings   b instructed   c alumni   d proprietary   e goodwill
2 It supports the argument that London Institute has acquired proprietary rights in its name.
3 To contact them in person or through solicitors within fourteen days to discuss transfer of the domain name.

▶ **page 96**

1 He wants to receive 'appropriate compensation' in exchange for transferring the domain name.
2 By mobile phone after 11 a.m. on weekdays.
3 Because it is now simply a matter of agreeing a price through negotiation (i.e. no specialist legal knowledge is required).

Unit 7

▶ **page 104**

1 On 31 April 1999.
2 The tenant (Tremaine Furnishings Ltd).
3 Seek independent legal advice if unsure of his position.

▶ **page 106**

1 The landlord has agreed to accept payments on a quarterly basis.
2 No timescale is given for payment, nor does the tenant give any indication of the nature of his proposals.

▶ **page 108**

1 Because a part-payment of £4,000 has been received, thus lowering the total amount of the arrears that will need to be claimed.

▶ **page 111**

1 By enclosing a cheque for £5,000.
2 To difficult business conditions.
3 It would destroy his potential to earn income to clear the arrears.

▶ **page 112**

1 The court would balance the long history of arrears against the offer to clear the arrears within a relatively short period of time.
2 An order for possession suspended on condition that the tenant complies with the terms of his proposed schedule of repayments.
3 The landlord would not get possession of the property provided the tenant kept up the payments specified in the order. If the tenant defaulted, the landlord would be able to ask the court bailiff to enforce the order without further notice.

▶ **page 113**

1 The landlord would be entitled to instruct bailiffs to recover possession of the property without further notice to the tenant.
2 The claim will eventually be dismissed.
3 To make a suspended order (in the terms of an enclosed draft order) for possession and to order Mr Tremaine to pay the landlord's costs.

▶ **page 116**

1 Yes.
2 To forward a sealed copy of the order as soon as it is received from the court.

Unit 8

▶ **page 122**

1 Physiotherapy and a course of painkillers.
2 Her solicitors.
3 That it is impossible at the moment to be sure about how much money she would get if she succeeded. It would depend on the nature of her injuries, whether she makes a good recovery, and whether she has suffered any permanent damage.
4 The cost of expenses incurred as a result of her accident as well as compensation for any earnings lost.

▶ **page 124**

1 The Occupier's Liability Act 1957.
2 That the accident was the result of the supermarket's failure to use reasonable care to ensure that the shop floor is kept reasonably safe and clear of spillages.
3 The assertion that Mrs Walker is 75% recovered but is unlikely to recover 100% movement.
4 a recover   b hobby   c valid   d improve

► **page 128**

1 It is thoroughly cleaned once per day, with spot-cleaning when necessary.
2 That a member of staff would have been working in the area where the incident happened, and that the yoghurt could only have been spilled moments before the accident.
3 That it does not accept liability for the claim.

► **page 135**

1 Yes, but they state that the fees must be 'reasonable'.
2 Within eight weeks of the date of the letter of instruction.
3 No. She believes that she is about 75% recovered.

Unit 9

► **page 142**

1 Information regarding adjacent land, including planning applications that may affect it.
2 A deposit equalling 5% of the sale price.
3 To ensure that the property will provide a good security for the money loaned.

► **page 144**

1 The completion certificate in respect of the conservatory.
2 There is a mortgage in favour of NatWest bank.
3 Sign but not date both copies of the contract and return them.
4 a granted   b enquiries   c sole

Unit 10

► **page 156**

1 By the executors of the late George Hubert Waterford.
2 To withdraw the funds from the account when probate is granted (to encash the account).

► **page 157**

1 Whether any repayment of overpaid income tax is due to the estate.
2 A grant of probate.

► **page 158**

1 a notify   b amount   c owing   d obliged

► **page 162**

1 If rent or other fees were paid in advance, covering the period after Mr Waterford's home was cleared.
2 It is when Mr Waterford's home was cleared. Reimbursement of rent or other fees would only relate to payments made in advance to cover the period after this date.
3 a reimbursement   b tenant   c expected

► **page 166**

1 No. The firm's fees have been deducted from the estate.
2 Payments to the other beneficiaries.
3 a deducted   b fee note   c questions

Unit 11

► **page 172**

1 The matrimonial home and £5,000 in a joint savings account.
2 That Mr Greaves will have to pay maintenance until the children leave school, and that the house could be transferred to Mrs Greaves and then sold when the children leave school, and Mr Greaves would then be entitled to a proportion of the proceeds of sale.
3 To complete the statement of monthly outgoings and sign, date, and return the duplicate copy of the client care letter.
4 She will contact Mrs Greaves again as soon as she hears anything from Mr Greaves' solicitors.

► **page 175**

1 That Mr Greaves is prepared to admit to adultery with Michelle Lampton for the purposes of the divorce petition.
2 Confirmation that Hatton, Moor & Lesley are instructed by Mr Greaves, and full disclosure of Mr Greaves' income, outgoings, and assets.
3 Mrs Greaves' financial documentation.
4 When they feel more settled with the new arrangements.

► **page 177**

1 Since Mrs Greaves does not have a clear admission from Mr Greaves of his adultery, or some evidence of it, in order to prove his adultery to the court, it would be better to compromise on the divorce costs in order to obtain his admission to adultery.
2 That Mr Greaves confirms that the arrangements for contact with the children are accepted, and that he has provided financial disclosure.
3 To read through the statement of arrangements for children and, if happy with it, to sign, date, and return it.
4 To put together a proposal regarding financial settlement.

► **page 179**

1 It is agreed by the parties and then ratified by the court rather than being imposed by the court.
2 That Mr Greaves has been served with the divorce petition and has completed and returned the necessary paperwork to the court.
3 That Mrs Greaves will soon be able to apply for decree nisi.

► **page 180**

1 No. It would be sold when he reaches seventeen or when he ceases full-time secondary education, whichever is later.
2 No. It would rise in line with the RPI.
3 That Mrs Greaves will apply for decree nisi as soon as notification is received from the court.

▸ **page 181**

1 The issue of maintenance for the children.
2 That the maintenance sought is in excess of what the court would be likely to consider reasonable.
3 In order for him to rehouse himself in rental property.
4 A draft consent order.

Unit 12

▸ **page 190**

1 Whether the termination of a distribution agreement between Hatchford Sports Ltd and Sharpers Ltd is lawful.
2 Because clause 5 of the agreement states that if similar products are manufactured for sale by Sharpers Ltd during the course of the agreement then Hatchford Sports Ltd will be entitled to distribute them.
3 Write to Sharpers Ltd pointing out that the agreement obliges them to offer the new products to Hatchford for distribution, and that therefore they are not entitled to terminate the contract.
4 Hatchford Sports Ltd could take the matter to arbitration.

▸ **page 191**

1 About her ex-husband's contact with the children: in particular whether she can stop contact altogether on account of his erratic behaviour.
2 That there are no grounds to stop contact altogether, but it is in everyone's interests for contact to proceed on a regular basis.
3 Write a letter to Mr Miller's solicitors indicating what is going on and reminding them of the agreement about contact reached in correspondence.

▸ **page 192**

1 Someone who is not a party to the contract.
2 Allow a third party to enforce a contractual term where the contract either expressly states that the term or contract benefits a third party, or where the particular term purports to benefit a third party.
3 Where it appears from the contract that the parties did not intend the term to be enforceable by the third party.
4 That the wording of subsection 2 of the Contracts (Rights of Third Parties) Act 1999 provides a comprehensive defence to any claim brought on this basis.

▸ **page 194**

1 Maria Danworth is seeking a non-molestation order together with a power of arrest.
2 Because he admitted that he was a heroin addict after she found syringes at his flat and confronted him about them.
3 The letter from the client's GP Dr Jane Baxter dated 16.3.05 which details the nature of the injury.
4 The hearing of Maria Danworth's application for a non-molestation order.

Unit 13

▸ **page 203**

1 She has worked as a paralegal, assisting the civil litigation department, and also as a TEFL tutor abroad.
2 Her main interest is Spanish language and culture.
3 Bristol University.
4 She is a partner at Brabham, Thorpe & Partners.

▸ **page 207**

1 Through Jill Masterton, an assistant lawyer in the firm's commercial litigation department.
2 He is a trainee solicitor at Burns, Gartner & Co. in Warwick,
3 He has an upper second class (2:1) law degree from Southampton University.
4 He wishes to specialize in commercial property and is interested in applying to Thompson & Grimes since he knows that the firm has a strong national reputation in this area and is seeking to expand its commercial property team.
5 He has handled a number of important commercial property cases on his own and has experience in drafting commercial leases and options. He has also co-written articles on commercial leases which have appeared in *Legal News*, and helped create a library of commercial precedents for in-house use.

ab initio (Latin): from the beginning. For example, 'this contract is void *ab initio*'.

account of profits A remedy that a litigant can claim as an alternative to damages in certain circumstances, e.g. in an action for breach of copyright. A successful claimant is entitled to a sum of money equal to the profit the defendant has made through wronging the claimant (e.g. by infringing the claimant's copyright).

administrator A person appointed by the court to collect and distribute a deceased person's estate when the deceased died *intestate*.

affidavit A sworn written statement generally used to support certain applications, and also sometimes used as evidence in court proceedings. Now usually known as a *sworn statement*.

agent A person who is employed to act on behalf of another person who is known as the *principal*. The work of an agent is to conclude contracts with third parties on behalf of the principal.

allotment A method of acquiring previously unissued shares in a limited company in exchange for a capital contribution.

ancillary relief A court order incidental to another order or application, e.g. financial provision applications and orders made in the context of divorce proceedings.

annul To declare a contract to be no longer valid.

appellant A person who makes an appeal to a court that has the jurisdiction to hear appeals, such as the Court of Appeal in the UK.

arbitration The determination of a dispute by one or more independent third parties (the arbitrators) rather than by a court. Arbitrators are appointed by the parties in accordance with the terms of the *arbitration clause* in an agreement between them or in default by court.

arbitration clause A clause in a contract in which the parties agree to submit to *arbitration* if disputes arise between them.

arbitrator An independent person who is appointed by agreement between parties to a contract or by a court to hear and decide a dispute. The process is known as *arbitration*.

arrears The accumulation of financial liabilities that have not been settled by their due dates. For example, rent arrears occur when rent has not been paid as it falls due.

articles of association Regulations for the management of registered companies. They form, together with the provisions of the *memorandum of association*, the company's constitution.

asset Property; anything which can be turned into cash.

assignment The transfer of a legal right by one legal person to another.

audit A detailed inspection of a company's accounts by outside accountants, usually in connection with the preparation of the annual accounts of the company at the end of the year. Hence *auditor*: a person who carries out such an inspection.

authorized capital (nominal capital) The total value of the shares that a registered company is authorized to issue in order to raise capital.

bankruptcy petition An application to the court for a bankruptcy order to be made against an insolvent debtor.

barrister A professional court advocate who is admitted to plead in all the courts. Barristers may work in law firms or as legal advisers in commercial companies, but more often work in chambers, which group barristers acting as independent court advocates.

beneficiary One who inherits money or property under a will.

best endeavours Best efforts. An *undertaking* to use best endeavours to do something means that the person giving the undertaking must try to do what he or she has undertaken to do, but is not absolutely obliged to achieve it.

bill of lading A document acknowledging the shipment of a consignor's goods for carriage by sea.

breach The infringing or violation of a right, duty, or law. For example, 'Statchem have breached paragraph 14 of the contract by their actions.'

brief As a noun, means the document by which a solicitor provides instructions to a barrister to appear as an advocate in court. A brief typically includes copies of documents relevant to the case, a short narrative explaining the background to the case, and specific instructions on what the solicitor wishes the barrister to achieve in court. As a verb, *brief* means to instruct a barrister (done by a solicitor) to appear as an advocate in court. See *instructions to counsel*.

capital (share capital) A fund which represents the nominal value of shares issued by a company.

charge 1) An interest in land securing the payment of money (see also *mortgage*). Note that a charge is often used as a means of securing an interest in the former matrimonial home in divorce cases. 2) An interest in company property created in favour of a creditor to secure the amount owing.

chattel Any property other than *freehold property*.

chose in action A right (e.g. to recover a debt) that can be enforced by legal action.

clause. A sentence or paragraph in a contract.

client care letter A letter written by a solicitor to a new client setting out the terms of business on which the solicitor will provide legal services to the client. In effect, it forms the contract between the solicitor and the client according to which the solicitor provides professional services and the client pays for them.

codicil A document supplementary to a *will*, in which changes or additions to a will are made.

cohabitant A person who lives with another person in an intimate relationship analogous to marriage.

collateral Security that is additional to the main security for a debt. For example, a lender may require as collateral the assignment of an insurance policy in addition to the principal security of a mortgage on the borrower's home.

Companies House See *Registrar of Companies*.

condition A major term of a contract, which is regarded as being of the essence of the contract. *Breach* of a condition is a fundamental breach of contract which entitles the injured party to treat the contract as discharged. Contrast with *warranty*.

conditional fee agreement An agreement whereby in certain civil cases (e.g. a personal injury claim) the claimant does not pay the solicitor a fee: if the claim fails, the solicitor pays the defendant's costs; if it succeeds, the solicitor charges a higher fee ('no win, no fee'). See pages 121–23.

confidentiality Refers to information – generally important commercial secrets – that is given in confidence and may not be disclosed to specified classes of people, generally persons outside the firm. Hence *confidentiality agreement* – an agreement whereby a person agrees not to disclose specified information.

consent Agreement or compliance with a course of action or proposal. For example, 'No assignment shall be valid unless both parties have given their consent in writing prior to the proposed assignment being made.'

consent order A court order made by agreement between the parties and ratified by the court.

consideration An act, forbearance, or promise by one party to a contract that constitutes the price for which the promise of the other party is bought. Consideration is essential to the validity of any contract other than one made by deed.

construction Interpretation. For example, 'On proper construction of this clause, it appears to mean that assignment is not permitted under the contract.'

construe Interpret. For example, 'paragraph 10 shall be construed in the light of the provisions of paragraph 17.'

contentious Relating to litigation. Contentious business means the work of a solicitor where there is a contest between the parties involved. See also *non-contentious*.

corporeal hereditament A tangible item of property, such as a building or piece of land, that can be inherited.

correspondence Letters, memoranda, notes, messages. For example, 'There has been considerable correspondence between the parties.'

costs Sums payable for legal services. In civil litigation, the court generally orders the losing party to pay the costs of the winning party.

counsel As a noun, another word for a *barrister*, particularly used as jargon by solicitors. As a verb, it means 'advise'.

court bailiff An officer of the court whose role is to serve court documents and to enforce court orders.

creditor One to whom a debt is owed. See also *debtor*.

curriculum vitae A brief account of a person's previous career (and often education and qualifications), usually submitted with a job application. (US *résumé*.)

damages A sum of money awarded by a court as compensation for a *tort* or a *breach* of contract. See *general damages; special damages*.

debtor One who owes a debt. See also *creditor*.

decree absolute A decree of divorce that brings the marriage to a legal end.

decree nisi A conditional decree of divorce. For most purposes the parties to the marriage are still married until the decree absolute is granted.

deed A written document that must make it clear on its face that it is intended to be a deed and must be validly executed as a deed. It takes effect on delivery. Deeds are often used to transfer land and are enforceable even in the absence of *consideration*.

deemed Treated in law as being something. Many documents rely on this concept, e.g. by stating that a certain thing is to be deemed to fall within a certain expression or description used in them.

default Failure/fail to fulfil an obligation. For example, 'the company has defaulted on its repayment schedule.'

defendant A person against whom court proceedings are brought. See also *prospective defendant*.

defined territory A geographical territory defined in an agreement.

deposit 1) A sum paid by one party to a contract to the other party as a guarantee that the first party will carry out the terms of the contract.
2) The placing of title deeds with a mortgagee of land as security for the debt.

detriment Harm or damage. For example, 'The company has acted to its detriment in agreeing to a variation of the original contract.'

discharge To release from an obligation. For example, 'The parties shall be discharged from all liability once all the terms of the contract have been performed in full.'

disclose Make known, reveal. For example, 'The company disclosed certain information to the distributor.' Hence *disclosure*.

dispose To sell or transfer (property). For example, 'The company had to dispose of some of its assets in order to pay its debts.'

distribution agreement An agreement whereby a distributor is granted the right to offer a company's goods for sale to customers within a *defined territory*.

district judge A low-ranking judge in the English civil court system whose role is to preside over minor claims and interlocutory proceedings in litigation.

dividend The payment made by a company to its shareholders out of its distributable profits.

divorce petition A document presented to the court which states the facts that have led to the breakdown of the marriage. Presentation of a divorce petition to the court represents the first stage in the divorce proceedings.

domestic violence Violence that takes place within the home, either between parties to a marriage or *cohabitants*.

draft A preliminary version of a legal document, e.g. a draft order or a draft contract.

due notice Notice required to be given either as the result of an agreement or by law. See *notice*.

easement A right enjoyed by the owner of one piece of land over an adjacent piece of land.

elect Decide, opt. For example, 'The parties may elect to refer the matter to arbitration if the dispute cannot be resolved by other means.'

employment tribunal employment tribunals are judicial bodies established in the UK to resolve disputes between employers and employees over employment rights.

encumbrance A right or interest in property owned by someone other than the owner of the land itself (e.g. leases and mortgages).

enforce To compel, impose, or put into effect. Hence 'enforceable' (capable of being enforced) and 'enforcement' (the process of enforcing). When a court order is enforced, this means that steps are taken by the court to force the defendant to comply with its terms.

engrossment A *fair copy* of a legal document ready for *execution* (2) by the parties. Hence 'to engross' is to prepare a fair copy.

equitable ownership Ownership in equity, i.e. without formal written legal title.

estate 1) The property of a deceased person. 2) A type of ownership in *real property*; the two estates of real property are *freehold* and *leasehold*.

execution 1) The carrying out or performance of something (e.g. the terms of a contract); or 2) the signature of a contract or other legal document. For example, 'The parties executed the contract.'

executor A person appointed by a will to administer a *testator*'s estate.

exclusive agreement An agreement made between specified parties on terms that neither may conclude agreements for the same purposes on similar terms with other parties. For example, an exclusive distribution agreement arises where a company grants the distributor the right to distribute goods or services in a *defined territory* on terms that no other distributor will be granted similar rights in the same territory by the same company.

fair copy A copy of a legal document made ready for execution by the parties.

fiduciary A person, such as a *trustee*, who holds a position of trust or confidence with respect to someone else, and who is obliged to act solely for that person's benefit. A fiduciary relationship exists, e.g. between company directors and their shareholders.

fitting An item, usually a piece of equipment or furniture, which is not fixed into position.

fixture An item, usually a piece of equipment or furniture, which is fixed into position.

f.o.b. (free on board) contract A type of contract for the international sale of goods in which the seller's duty is fulfilled by placing the goods on board a ship.

force majeure (French): irresistible compulsion or coercion. Often used in commercial contracts to describe events which may affect the contract but are completely outside the parties' control. For example, 'The contract contains the usual provision regarding situations considered by the parties to constitute force majeure.'

forfeiture The termination of a lease in circumstances when the tenant is in breach of the lease agreement.

furnish To provide or send something. For example, 'The distributor agrees to furnish sales information to the Company.'

gaming contract A contract involving the playing of a game of chance by any number of people for money or money's worth. Gaming contracts are generally void and no action can be brought to enforce them.

general damages 1) Damages given for losses which the law presumes are the natural and probable consequences of a wrong (e.g. libel is presumed to have damaged someone's reputation without proof that that person's reputation has actually suffered). 2) Damages given for a loss that cannot be precisely estimated (e.g. for pain and suffering). See also *special damages*.

good faith Honesty. An act carried out in good faith is one carried out with honest intentions.

goodwill The advantage arising from the reputation and trade connections of a business.

grant of letters of administration Authority given by the court to named individuals or to a trust corporation to administer the estate of a deceased person.

grant of probate The procedure by which *probate* is obtained from the court.

harassment Behaviour deliberately intended to torment, bully, or interfere with another person.

hereditament Any *real property* capable of being passed to an heir.

incapacity Lack of legal competence.

incorporated company A company organized and maintained as a legally valid company, and in practice (in the UK) one validly registered at Companies House.

incorporation The process of creating and registering a company.

incorporeal hereditament An intangible right in land capable of being passed to an heir, e.g. *easements* and *profits à prendre*.

Incoterm A term established by the International Chamber of Commerce indicating which price is being quoted to a customer.

indemnity An agreement by one person to pay to another person sums that are owed, or may become owed, by a third person.

infringe To violate or interfere with the rights of another person. For example, 'The company infringed upon another company's intellectual property rights.'

inheritance tax A tax payable on the value of a person's estate on death.

injunction An order of the court directing a person to do or refrain from doing a particular thing.

instructions to counsel A document by which a solicitor briefs a barrister in order to seek the barrister's advice as to whether a case would be likely to succeed in court or not in the event that an application to court was made. See *brief*.

instrument A legal document, usually one which directs that certain actions be taken (e.g. a contract).

intangible assets Assets – i.e. property – that have no physical existence, e.g. *choses in action*.

inter alia (Latin): among other things. For example, 'The contract provides, *inter alia*, that the company will be sold for the sum of...'

intestacy The state in which a person dies without having made a will disposing of his or her property.

issue 1) To print, publish, or distribute. For example, 'the company issued shares.' 2) A person's descendants. 3) To commence civil court proceedings (= to issue proceedings).

joint and several liability If two or more people enter into an obligation that is said to be joint and several, this means that liability for a breach can be enforced against all of them together in a joint action or against any one of them by an individual action.

judicial separation An order made by a court that a husband and wife do not have to cohabit. This does not end the marriage, but it frees the parties of marital obligations and enables either party to make applications to the court for many of the financial and other orders available on divorce.

know-how Practical knowledge or skill.

landlord A person who grants a lease or tenancy.

Land Registry The UK state agency which deals with the registration of ownership and other rights over land. Its website can be accessed at www.landreg.gov.uk.

layperson A person without professional or expert knowledge: in the context of law, a non-lawyer.

lease A contract that creates an *estate* in land for a period of time, involving the right to occupy the land.

lease proforma A document that includes basic details necessary for drawing up a lease, e.g. details of the tenant, property, rent.

legal person A body of persons who together make up a formal entity (such as a company) considered in law to be one legal entity having many of the rights and responsibilities of a natural person, particularly the capacity to sue and be sued.

legal personality The quality of being a *legal person*.

lessee *Tenant*.

lessor *Landlord*.

letter before action A letter sent to a *prospective defendant* before legal proceedings are issued, usually with the intention of giving the prospective defendant a last opportunity to resolve the legal claim without the need for legal proceedings.

liability An obligation or duty imposed by law, or an amount of money owed to another person. For example, 'The company is liable to pay damages to the employee.'

licence 1) Formal authority to do something that would otherwise be unlawful (e.g. driving licence). 2) In land law, a permission to occupy a person's land for a particular purpose.

lien The right of one person to retain possession of goods owned by another until the possessor's claims against the owner have been satisfied.

listed building A building of special architectural or historical interest that is included on a list kept by the state, and may only be demolished or altered with special consent granted by the local planning authority.

litigation 1) The taking of legal proceedings by a litigant or claimant. 2) The field of law concerned with all *contentious* matters.

material Relevant, important, essential. For example, 'Breach of a material term of the contract can give the innocent party the right to rescind the contract.'

memorandum of association This document sets out details of a company's existence and contains basic information such as the company's name, the objects of the company, its address, and a statement of limited liability. See *articles of association*.

minutes Records of company business transacted at general meetings, board meetings, and meetings of managers.

modus operandi (Latin): a way of doing something. For example, 'His *modus operandi* was unusual but effective.'

mortgage An interest in property created as a form of security for a loan or payment of a debt and terminated on payment of the loan or debt. The borrower, who offers the security, is the **mortgagor**; the lender, who provides the money, is the **mortgagee**.

mutual 1) Experienced or done by two or more people equally; 2) (of two or more people) having the same specified relationship to each other; 3) shared by two or more people; 4) joint. For example, 'No assignment may take place without the parties' mutual agreement in writing.'

mutatis mutandis (Latin): 'that having been changed which had to be changed' or 'with the necessary changes'. The phrase is used in contracts to indicate that a stipulation contained in one clause should also be applied in another part of the contract once the necessary changes have been made.

negligence Carelessness amounting to the culpable breach of a duty: failure to do something that a reasonable person would do, or doing something that a reasonable person would not do.

non-contentious The work of a solicitor or other lawyer not involving a contest between the parties.

notice Information or warning addressed to a party that something is going to happen or has happened; a notification. See also *due notice* and *service of notice*. For example, 'Any notice required to be served under this contract must be served in accordance with paragraph 18.'

notice of acting A document notifying the court that a solicitor is acting for a client and that official court documents should therefore be sent to the solicitor.

notice of severance The formal notification that a joint tenancy is to be severed, creating a tenancy in common.

notice to quit The formal notification from a *landlord* to a *tenant* (or vice versa), terminating the tenancy on a specified date.

null Invalid, having no legal force. For example, 'The contract is null [and void].'

omission A failure to do something that one was supposed to do. For example, 'An omission may render the contract void.'

onerous Involving much effort and difficulty. For example, 'The duties laid upon the company are onerous.'

option A right to do or not to do something, usually within a specified time. For example, an option to purchase land generally gives the right for a person to have first refusal on the purchase of a piece of land within a specified time period. Also: the document setting down such a right or rights.

ordinary shares These shares make up the risk capital as they carry no prior rights in relation to dividends or return of nominal capital.

particulars of claim A document filed with the court and served upon the defendant in a court action which sets out the material facts and argument on which a claim is based.

passing off Conducting one's business in such a way as to mislead the public into thinking that one's goods or services are those of another business. It is not necessary to prove an intention to deceive: innocent passing off is actionable.

patentee A person or company that owns patent rights in respect of an invention.

patent agent An expert who prepares applications for patent.

per annum (Latin): for each year. For example, 'The director earned £250,000 *per annum* before tax.'

personal property or **personalty** All property other than *real property* – e.g. *chattels* (physical items of personal property that can be moved, such as jewellery or furniture), *choses in action* (certain kinds of rights, for example, a debt is a right to sue and so a chose in action).

personal representative A person entitled to deal with a deceased person's estate in accordance with a will or under the rules relating to intestacy.

peruse To read or examine something carefully and thoroughly.

petitioner A person who presents a petition to the court (e.g. a divorce petition or a petition for bankruptcy). See also *respondent*.

piracy 1) Any illegal act of violence, imprisonment, or robbery committed on a private ship for personal gain or revenge, against another ship, people, or property on the high seas. 2) (in marine insurance) One of the risks covered by a marine insurance policy, which extends beyond the criminal offence to include a revolt by the crew or passengers and plundering generally. 3) Infringement of copyright.

planning consent / planning permission Permission that must be obtained from a local authority in the UK before building on, developing, or changing the use of a site.

prima facie (Latin): On the face of things; accepted as so until proved otherwise. For example, 'You appear *prima facie* to have a reasonable case, although I will need further information before giving an informed opinion on its merits.'

probate 1) A certificate issued on the application of *executors* appointed by a will, to the effect that the will is valid and the executors are authorized to administer the *estate*. 2) A general term denoting the laws and courts which deal with wills, intestacy, succession, inheritance, administration, and disputes over estates.

professional legal privilege Privilege applies to certain kinds of legal communications. It means that those communications are not disclosable to a third party, even upon request by a state body or official. Professional legal privilege attaches, for example, to communications between a lawyer and his or her client, and to communications that are relevant for litigation. There are detailed rules that clarify the precise circumstances in which such communications are privileged.

profit à prendre The right to enter onto someone else's land to take the produce of the land, be it plants, minerals, wild animals and fish, or oil and gas.

prospective defendant A person against whom a civil claim (e.g. for damages) is contemplated, and who may therefore become the defendant in future proceedings.

provision A term or clause of a contract. For example, 'The contract contains provisions dealing with termination.'

proxy A person (not necessarily a company member) appointed by a company member to attend and vote in his or her place at a company meeting.

quorum From Latin, meaning 'of whom', used to indicate the minimum number of persons required to be present to constitute a formal meeting.

real property, real estate, realty Land and all *corporeal* and *incorporeal hereditaments* (rights over land that can be passed to an heir, such as *easements* and *profits à prendre*. See *personal property*.

reasonable 1) Fair and sensible; 2) appropriate in a particular situation; 3) fairly good; 4) not too expensive.

Registrar of Companies (Companies House) The institution that contains a register of all UK private and public companies, their directors, shareholders, and balance sheets. Its website can be accessed at www.companieshouse.gov.uk

remedy Any method available in law to enforce, protect, or recover rights, usually available by seeking a court order. For example, 'The primary remedy is to claim damages.'

rescission The setting aside of a voidable contract, which is then treated as if it had never existed.

resolution A decision reached by a majority of the members at a company meeting.

resolved amicably This is a well-known lawyers' euphemism which in practice means no more than 'resolved out of court'.

respondent 1) A person named as the defendant in a petition. 2) A person who defends an appeal from a lower court to a higher court made by an *appellant*.

restrictive covenant A clause in a contract that restricts a person's right to carry on his or her trade or profession. For example, a contract covering the sale of a business might include a clause seeking to restrict the seller's freedom to set up in competition with the buyer.

revoke (noun **revocation**) To cancel, annul, or withdraw. For example, 'We revoked the order we had placed.'

rights of audience The right to appear as an advocate representing a client before a court.

royalty A sum payable for the right to use someone else's property for the purpose of gain.

RPI Retail Prices Index.

sealed copies In court proceedings, 'sealed copies' means official legal documents sealed with the official seal of the court. The imprint of the seal indicates that the documents have been authenticated as genuine court documents.

search The examination of the register of an official authority, e.g. the Land Registry. Hence *search fee* – the fee payable for carrying out such an examination.

service The delivery of a document relating to court proceedings in a manner specified by the court. See also *service of notice*.

service of notices The delivery in a manner specified by the court or in a contract of information or a warning addressed to a party that something is going to happen or has happened.

share certificate A document issued by a company which shows that a named person is a company member and stating the number of shares registered in that person's name and the extent to which they are paid up.

share premium The amount by which the price at which a share was issued exceeds its nominal value.

share transfer A document transferring registered shares, i.e. shares for which a share certificate has been issued.

sole practitioner A person who runs an unincorporated professional practice on his or her own.

sole trader An individual who runs an unincorporated business on his or her own.

solicitor A lawyer who works in a law firm or practice, or as a legal adviser in a commercial organization. Solicitors carry out all types of legal work, but have limited *rights of audience*: they are only able to act as court advocates in certain courts, dealing generally with more minor cases.

solicitor-advocate A solicitor who has passed advocacy examinations which entitle him or her to appear as an advocate before the higher courts in England and Wales.

special damages 1) Damages given for losses that are not presumed but have been specifically proved. 2) Damages given for losses that can be quantified (e.g. loss of earnings).

special resolution A decision reached by a majority of not less than 75% of company members voting in person or by proxy at a general meeting.

spouse A wife or husband.

stamp duty A tax payable on certain legal documents specified by statute, e.g. transfers of land and other property.

statement of arrangements for children A statement of proposed arrangements for the children of divorcing parents which must be filed at court with the *divorce petition*.

statement of claim See *particulars of claim*.

statutory rights Rights provided by a statute, i.e. by an Act of Parliament.

strict liability 1) In criminal law, liability for a crime imposed without the need for proving that the accused intended to cause the harm done by the crime (applicable in product liability and road traffic offences). 2) In tort law, liability for a wrong that is imposed without the claimant having to prove that the defendant was at fault (applicable in product liability and defamation claims).

suspended order An order that does not take effect immediately. In civil claims, a suspended order is generally made on certain terms that the defendant must fulfil. If the defendant fulfils these terms, the order will eventually be dismissed.

sworn statement A sworn statement – previously known as an *affidavit* – is a formal and written statement of fact, signed and witnessed (as to the veracity of the signature) by an official authorized to take oaths (e.g. a solicitor). Sworn statements are used in court to allow evidence to be gathered from witnesses or participants who may not be available to testify in person before the court.

tenancy in common *Equitable ownership* by two or more persons in equal or unequal undivided shares.

tenant A person – or a company – granted a lease or tenancy.

tender An offer to supply goods or services. Normally a tender must be accepted to create a contract.

term 1) A substantive part of a contract which creates a contractual obligation. For example, 'One of the terms of the contract deals with delivery of the goods.' 2) The period during which a contract is in force. For example, 'The term of this contract shall be five years from the date of execution.'

termination clause A clause in a contract which specifies the manner in which the contract will or may be terminated.

testator A person who makes a will.

third party A person who is not a party to a contract.

title A person's right of ownership of property.

title deeds The documents that prove a person's ownership of land.

tort A wrongful act or omission for which *damages* can be obtained in a civil court by the person wronged, other than a wrong that is only a *breach* of contract. Tort law embraces different areas of law which have in common the fact that each gives rise to civil causes of action outside the law of contract.

transfer deed A *deed* by which ownership of registered land is conveyed.

tree preservation order An order made by a local planning authority prohibiting the felling of a tree (or trees) without the authority's consent.

trustee 1) A person having a nominal title to property that he holds for the benefit of one or more others, the *beneficiaries*; 2) Personal representative.

undertaking A promise to do or not to do a specified act. In the English legal system, an undertaking given by a solicitor to the court or to another solicitor is binding, and failure to fulfil it may result in professional disciplinary action being taken. Undertakings are routinely used in certain areas of law. For example, in property transactions, solicitors are frequently asked to provide a routine undertaking to lodge certain documents with the relevant authorities or to retain certain documents in a safe place.

vis-à-vis (French): in relation to; compared with.

void Having no legal effect. For example, 'The contract is void due to lack of consideration.'

waiver The act of abandoning or refraining from asserting a legal right, e.g. by agreeing to a variation of the original terms of a contract.

warranty 1) (in contract law) A term or promise in a contract, breach of which will entitle the innocent party to damages but not to treat the contract as discharged by breach.
2) (in insurance law) A promise by the insured, breach of which will entitle the insurer to treat the contract as discharged by breach.

will A document by which a testator (the person making the will) states how their property is to be divided among their beneficiaries (the persons who will inherit under the will) upon their death.

winding-up A procedure by which a company can be dissolved. It may be instigated by members or creditors of the company (voluntary winding-up) or by order of the court (compulsory winding-up).

without prejudice A phrase used to enable parties to negotiate settlement without implying any admission of liability. Letters and other documents headed 'without prejudice' may not be produced as evidence in any court proceedings without the consent of both parties. (However, they may be relevant when costs are discussed in court; hence the phrase sometimes used, 'without prejudice save as to costs'.)

witness statement A statement made by a witness for the purpose of court proceedings which sets out the evidence to which the witness will testify.

written resolution A resolution signed by all company members and treated as effective even though it is not passed at a properly convened company meeting.

Index